GARLAND STUDIES ON

THE FINANCIAL SECTOR OF THE AMERICAN ECONOMY

edited by

STUART BRUCHEY
ALLAN NEVINS PROFESSOR EMERITUS
COLUMBIA UNIVERSITY

A GARLAND SERIES

FINANCIAL INNOVATION IN THE BANKING INDUSTRY

THE CASE OF ASSET SECURITIZATION

LAMIA OBAY

GARLAND PUBLISHING, Inc.
NEW YORK & LONDON / 2000

Published in 2000 by
Garland Publishing Inc.
29 West 35th Street
New York, NY 10001

Published in Great Britain by
Garland Publishing
11 New Fetter Lane
London EC4P 4EE

A Garland is an imprint of the Taylor & Francis Group

10 9 8 7 6 5 4 3 2 1

Library of Congress Cataloging-in Publication Data
Obay, Lamia.
    Financial innovation in the banking industry : the case of asset
securitization / Lamia Obay.
      p. cm. — (Financial sector of theAmerican economy)
    Includes bibliographical references and index.
    ISBN 0–8153–3423–0 (alk. paper)
    1. Asset-backed financing—United States.   2. Banks and banking—
United States. I. Title II. Series.
HG4028.A8402   1999
332.63'2—dc21   99–31494
                                                         CIP

Printed on acid-free, 250-year-life paper
Manufactured in the United States of America

Contents

List of Tables and Figures

CHAPTER 1

Introduction

BACKGROUND

Financial innovation refers to several phenomena. It includes new financial instruments, which are the objects of transactions, new financial markets, which are the fields of transactions, and new media to effect transfers (Yumoto et al. 1986, p.45). While financial innovation is by no means a recent phenomenon, it has become one of the most significant economic phenomena of the last decades. It has exerted considerable influence on the workings of the financial system, the conduct of the monetary policy in a number of countries and on the management of costs and risks by governments, financial institutions, and corporations.

Prominent factors that have been working as common catalysts to financial innovation have been identified as several. First, there was the worldwide trend toward deregulation of capital, currency and money centers which is creating opportunities for corporations, banks, and governments to raise funds and manage risk in new ways. Second, high inflation rates in the United States during the eighties caused not only financial innovation at home but also triggered innovation and deregulation internationally through the indirect impact of high and volatile U.S. dollar interest rates and exchange rates. A third factor that has greatly increased the pace of financial innovation is technical progress particularly in the computer and telecommunication fields.

Other factors have been recognized as contributing to the rise of financial innovation during the last two decades. Among them are 1) the progress in international economic integration; especially growing international capital flows, 2) the persistence of large public deficits and the need for efficient means of financing such deficits, 3) the new trends in corporate organization, 4) the changing dynamics of the international banking system through the redefinition of the role of banks and the evolution of their relationship with the corporate community and the structure of their balance sheet, and 5) the need to improve profitability and/or minimize the cost of regulation.

Despite these common forces, the process of financial innovation and deregulation has differed between countries depending in particular on the maturity of financial markets, the previous regulatory framework, and on the openness of the economy. Indeed, the highest degree of financial innovation has occurred in the United States essentially because all the factors that tend to induce financial innovations were present. Accordingly, in this research, the author will concentrate on the innovative behavior of U.S. commercial banks. One particular innovation that has redefined the process of bank intermediation is asset securitization, that is the repackaging of loans into securitizable assets. In this case, a closer look will be paid to the regulatory framework governing asset securitization and to the adoption and diffusion process of the issuance of asset-backed securities across foreign markets as well.

When analyzing the environment that has greatly conditioned the current pace of financial innovativeness, one question is frequently raised: "To what extent does the dramatic growth of markets in new financial instruments represent long-lasting features of the innovation process and to what extent are the factors behind change temporary and reversible?" (BIS, 1986, p. 184). Commentators agree that, while the pace of change in recent years was to an important extent due to "exceptional dislocations" in the economic and financial conditions, there are powerful, long-lasting forces that support the growth and development of innovations even in a more stable environment (BIS, 1986). Technological advance, both in its hardware aspect—computer and communications systems—and its software aspect—sophisticated financial models and financial product designs—is a major long-term determinant. The global integration of financial markets and the institutionalization of financial innovation are other examples of long lasting determinants.

Global integration of financial markets and financial innovations are closely intertwined and are driven in part by similar deregulatory and technological changes. Financial integration is affecting the development of new products as well as their diffusion in international markets. The increased liberalization of financial markets in Europe and Japan can, in fact, be seen as an aspect greatly favoring the diffusion of innovations generated by the globalization of markets.

Put in a much broader context, financial innovation is, albeit indirectly, very much affected by the overall global integration of overall economic structures. "The integration of national financial markets is related to, and supported by, the broader force of the global integration of overall economic structures. These linkages through increased trade, investment and travel are a long-lasting process, working not only among the industrial nations but among them and the rest of the world as well. So, closer economic integration leads to greater financial integration, which in turn, creates opportunity for new instruments to emerge, and eventually leads to lower cost of intermediation. These connections provide a fundamental, more permanent, support for the process of financial innovation" (BIS, 1986, p.185).

A third important development affecting the character of financial innovations is the institutionalization of the process at the firm level. "[I]n the past few years a number of the major international financial institutions, both investment and commercial banks, have established within their organizational structures "new products" or "product development" groups" (BIS, 1986). If the institutionalization of financial innovations persists, it may change the nature of the economics of future innovations. The pace of financial innovation may become primarily a function of the quantity and quality of resources committed to product development. This may lead to innovations generated by a dynamic that works independently of the kind of developments in the economy that generated innovations in the past.

With respect to the implications of the recent wave of innovations for the stability of the financial system, several points of concern are often mentioned. They include an over-leveraging of the capital, the apparent under-pricing of new instruments, the scope for an undue concentration of risks, and the possibility that the apparent liquidity of marketable instruments could prove illusory under adverse circumstances (European Investment Bank, 1988).

In the specific case of the banking industry, it has been claimed that the adoption and diffusion of financial innovation has allowed banks to operate on much thinner margins of safety. An understanding of why this is possible would require the analysis of the structure of balance sheets, payment commitments and position-making activities of banks. Position making for a bank consists of the transactions undertaken to bring the cash position to the level required by regulation or bank management.

Such transactions involve selling assets off the bank's portfolio and raising cash through money market instruments. Increase in banks' riskiness is due to the interdependence of payment commitments and position-making transactions across institutions.

The shift in position making from trading in liquid assets in the 1960s to transaction in liabilities in the 1970s was accompanied by a decrease in the margins of safety used to cushion fluctuation in the cash flows. As a result, payment commitments have become more closely coordinated with payment receipts so that small changes in conditions can cause a large increase in the need for institutions (and economic units in general) to acquire cash by selling assets that may have thin markets. As asset sales in thin markets become necessary and while the value of liquidity—or marketability—is enhanced, the relative value of assets become subject to change, which change becomes responsible for the institutions' balance sheet instability.

It is these evolved characteristics of asset-liability management that are responsible for deposit institutions' fragility. Indeed, in the position-making view, fragile financial characteristics of debtors, creditors and deposit institutions result from the evolution of asset and liability structure over periods of good economic conditions. The effect of bad economic conditions is to put aspects of balance sheet mismanagement in the open. Weak management can get by during good economic times, but when economic conditions are adverse, problems that existed all along unravel and become significant.

Other ways in which innovation may contribute to systemic vulnerabilities derive from the difficulties in pricing new instruments and the possibility that many new instruments appear to be under-priced, therefore, not allowing for a full compensation for their inherent risk (BIS, 1986, p. 3). Moreover, the general trend toward increased off-balance sheet activities and "unbundling" (which involves separating market risk from credit risk), as well as the complexity of multiple linked transactions, can conceal the interlocking of risks for banks management, regulators, and market participant alike (BIS, 1986). A subsequent point is that the new instruments shift price or market risk from one economic agent to another but do not eliminate that risk.

John G. Heimann, in his address to the 23rd Conference on Bank Structure and Competition held by the Federal reserve Bank of Chicago, expressed his concern as follows: "The bottom line is that *everyone* is now operating in an environment of increased risk. That is because the velocity and volatility of global markets have created the potential for a case of—or recurrent cases of—global jitters. Also, velocity and volatility are the quivering backbone of a new generation of financial instruments which—let's be frank-are not fully understood either by their creators or their users. Today, with so many new, computer-based products on the market, it is evident that some managers may not have a profound grasp of what they are really managing" (1987, p. 29).

An article in the *Washington Post* (April 24, 1994,H1) highlights the risks involved with this 'new generation of financial instruments' when it reported that the private derivatives deals made by corporations, banks, brokerages and others to speculate and hedge now total more than $10 trillion and three-fourths of them are tied to interest rates. "When underlying interest rates change, the value of these deals are affected dramatically. Thus the recent spurt in interest rates set off bombs on the balance sheets of some companies that had tried to play the derivative game[1]." The article further adds that these financial instruments are often so complicated "that even the chief financial officers of Fortune 500 companies confess that they don't fully comprehend them." The facts, however, that financial innovation is neither fully comprehended nor its risks fully assessed does not seem to deter its growth or its pervasiveness.

ORGANIZATION

This book is a study of the diffusion among, and adoption of financial innovations by, U.S. multinational banks and the relationship of such an adoption behavior to their financial characteristics and performances as reported on their financial statements with the proper regulatory agencies. It also is an examination of the characteristics of adopters versus non-adopters of financial innovations. An important aspect of financial innovation has been in the field of asset securitization, an area that despite its well-publicized benefits and potential for growth, has been the subject of little empirical investigation. Accordingly, the author has chosen to use asset-backed securities (ABSs) as an illustration of the adoption and diffusion process of financial innovations. In the remainder of Chapter 1, a statement of the objective, research questions, and scope of the study are presented.

In Chapter 2, the field of financial innovation is briefly surveyed. Securitization being an off-balance sheet activity, special interest is paid to the topic of off-balance sheet activities and the regulatory response to the proliferation to such activities. In Chapter 3, an examination of 1) the process of asset securitization, 2) the accounting and regulatory issues pertaining to ABS activities, and 3) the diffusion of asset securitization to foreign markets are covered.

In Chapter 4, a description of the research design and methodology for the investigation of the relationship between banking performances and financial innovation, proxied by asset securitization, are presented. Findings and conclusions of the research will be presented in Chapter 5 of this study.

Objectives of the Research

The focus of this study is on the securitization of bank assets, a new financial product, which after a decade of its introduction, is still at its growth stage. The study objectives are:

1. to present the field and environment of asset securitization,
2. to identify the differentiating characteristics between securitizing and non-securitizing banks, and
3. to investigate the relationship between the volume of assets securitized during the reporting period and the financial characteristics of the securitizing bank as reported on its financial statements.

Research Hypothesis

The contention of this book is that the inducement and adoption of financial innovation in general, and the securitization of bank assets in this particular case, is to a large degree a response to the new competitive environment. This environment is described by William L. Silber as the changes in the set of internal and external constraints under which firms operate and to which they need to adhere. The banks most likely to engage in financial innovation and asset securitization would appear to share some common characteristics:

- They are likely to be large, therefore able to compete in a number of geographic and product markets.
- They are likely to carry a significant amount of international business.
- They may also carry a larger level of wholesale business as opposed to retail business, wholesale business being the serving of commercial and industrial enterprises and government entities. Wholesale business appears to have been the most affected by the traditional erosion of traditional product and geographic market boundaries.

- These banks are also likely to have capital ratios that are relatively lower than those of other banks. The low capital ratios would be an incentive for them to forego traditional banking activities in favor of activities that are not dependent upon, or that do not affect, the capital ratio[2].

- Banks would not engage in asset securitization unless they expect these activities to be profitable or to have a positive effect on other lines of businesses. Therefore, one might infer that banks involved in the technique of asset securitization are likely to post higher returns than those with little or no involvement in asset securitization.

- Securitizing banks are also likely to exhibit higher loan growth rate. Indeed, the greater a bank's demand for loans and the faster its loan portfolio is growing, the more likely a bank would be to package its loans.

- These banks are also likely to have a lower loan portfolio quality than non-securitizing banks. Asset securitization has been used, among other things, towards achieving a more balanced loan portfolio by financial institutions. If banks use asset securitization to increase diversification, the less diversified a bank is, the more likely that bank is to securitize its loans.

- In a similar vein, banks that securitize their assets are likely to have a higher loan charge-off ratio simply because they have an incentive to securitize their best assets and leave their worst assets on their balance sheets.

- Banks are enticed to use securitization as a funding mechanism rather than deposits. Unlike deposits, funds collected through securitization are free from deposit insurance and reserve requirements. And because of these cost savings, banks that face high loan demand, high funding costs and/or recur often to market mediated deposits are more likely to use securitization to free up capital towards future loan origination or to reduce funding costs.

- Banks may use securitization in order to exploit some comparative advantage they have acquired in the origination of certain types of loans such as credit card installment, auto and mortgage loans. Banks with prior involvement with the technique of securitization are likely to go back to the market to securitize assets.

Therefore, the hypothesis of this research is:
Banks that adopt the technique of asset securitization are likely to differ from non-adopters when compared on the basis of certain

reported financial characteristics (size, level of international banking, wholesale business, capitalization, profitability, level of diversification and net charge-offs, funding costs, liquidity and competitive advantage).

It follows that the null hypothesis is that adopters and non-adopters of the technique of asset securitization exhibit no significant differences when compared on the basis of the aforementioned financial characteristics.

For the purpose of this study, the financial innovation under investigation is US bank asset securitization defined as the repackaging of loans into marketable instruments. Loan repackaging appeared during the seventies with mortgage loans, and later spread to other loan markets such as consumer installment loans. The market for mortgage-backed securities mushroomed to about $1.85 trillion as of December 1995, up from $900 million by the end of 1989, while securitized consumer installment loans reached some $214 billion at the end of 1995, up from $48 billions in 1989. As demonstrated by Figure 1-1 below, securitized consumer installment loans represented 19% of all outstanding consumer loans whereas 40% of outstanding mortgage loans were securitized by the end of 1995.

These figures clearly outline the important change that has affected financial intermediation. In recent years, there has been a pronounced shift of credit flows from bank lending to marketable debt instruments.

Figure 1-1: Pools of Mortgage and Non-Mortgage Securities Outstanding ($Billion)

	1989	1990	1991	1992	1993	1994	1995
Mortgage Debt	3,549.56	3,761.53	3,923.37	4,092.98	4,268.42	4,473.10	4,715.88
Securitized	917.85	1,079.10	1,250.67	1,434.26	1,564.57	1,718.3	1,853.31
Non-Securitized	2,631.71	2,682.43	2,672.70	2,617.38	2,647.15	2,754.8	2,862.27
MBS/Total	25.8%	28.7%	31.9%	35.3%	36.4%	38.4%	39.3%
Consumer Installment Loans	728.88	748.52	749.05	756.94	863.92	990.25	1,131.75
Securitized	48.79	77.90	103.56	120.40	131.07	147.81	214.60
Non-Securitized	680.08	670.62	645.49	636.54	732.85	842.44	917.15
Securitized/Total	6.7%	10.4%	13.8%	15.9%	15.17%	14.9%	18.96%

Source: Federal Reserve Bulletin. Tables I.54 and I.55; October 1996, April 1994, and September 1992.

One specific aspect of this move towards securitization has been the increased marketability of banks' assets. Indeed, in addition to buying and selling securities in the international markets, banks have sought to increase the negotiability of their conventional domestic assets.

Asset-backed securities can be structured in many different ways to fit the individual needs of the participants involved. The accounting and tax treatment desired by the issuer will play an important part on how the securitization will be structured. While ABS issues differ in certain aspects, they all fit into one of the two categories: pass-through and pay-through. Each of these developed out of the secondary mortgage market and each has been applied to securitizing non-mortgage-related assets.

Pass-throughs are single class payment instruments that represent direct ownership in a portfolio of assets that are usually similar in terms to maturity, interest rate, and quality. The portfolio is placed in trust and certificates of ownership are sold to investors. The most common pass-throughs are the mortgage-backed securities (MBS) developed by Fannie Mae and the "participation certificate" developed by the Federal Home Loan Mortgage Association.

Pay-throughs are debt obligations of the issuer collateralized by a pool of assets, thus appear on the balance sheet of the issuer. Cash flows from the underlying assets are dedicated to servicing the bonds in a way similar to that of pass-throughs. The most common pay-throughs are known as the CMO (collateralized mortgage obligation). This type of pay-through directs cash flows in order to support bonds of various maturities, rather than maturities that only match that of the underlying portfolio. Because of certain inefficiencies associated with CMOs, another form of pay-through mortgage derivative (real estate mortgage investment conduits, REMICs) was introduced in the market in 1986.

The securitization of mortgage loans has developed rapidly in the United States, generally by shifting loans to specialized institutions which finance themselves through the issue of long or short-term securities, often with some form of a third party backing. Commercial banks have become major issuers and purchasers of securities as well as arrangers and managers of new issues.

Several reasons for securitization of assets have been suggested. Asset securitization may allow a bank to avoid "regulatory taxes," such as reserve requirements, capital requirements, and deposit insurance premium. Moreover, asset securitization may facilitate gap management and enhance a bank's funding, liquidity, and diversification. This paper attempts to explain which banks are likely to engage in asset securitization based on financial information that are collected on the Call Reports, and especially Schedule RC-L within Call Reports, banks file with the Federal Deposit Insurance Corporation.

The focus of this Research is on whether these aforementioned characteristics differ between securitizing and non-securitizing banks or exert any weight on the repackaging of bank loans into marketable assets. The null hypothesis, therefore, is that banks that adopt the technique of asset securitization do not differ from non-adopters when compared on the basis of certain reported financial characteristics (size, level of international banking, wholesale business, capitalization, profitability, level of diversification and net charge-offs, funding costs, liquidity and competitive advantage). Should the findings, however, lead to the rejection of the null hypothesis of no overall securitization effect, one is led to test for significance at the univariate level, hence leading to the investigation of a number of research questions.

RESEARCH QUESTIONS

The investigation of the study hypotheses entails investigation of a number of subsidiary research questions:

Bank Characteristics

R1   Are banks that engage in asset securitization, measured by the volume of repackaged mortgage and non-mortgage loans sold with and without recourse divided by bank's total assets, likely to have a larger size, measured by assets, than banks with no securitization activities?

R2   Are banks that engage in asset securitization (as defined above) likely to have relatively higher levels of international banking activities, measured by the ratio of international assets divided by total assets, than banks with no securitization activities?

R3   Are banks that engage in asset securitization likely to have higher levels of wholesale business than banks with no securitization activities.

Bank Capitalization/Regulatory Taxes

R4   Are securitizing banks likely to exhibit lower capital ratios than banks with no securitization activities?

Bank Profitability

R5   Are securitizing banks likely to exhibit a higher degree of dependence on fee income, measured by the ratio of fee income divided by interest income, and higher return-on-asset ratios than banks with no securitization activities?

Portfolio Quality

R6   Are securitizing banks likely to exhibit a lower loan portfolio quality, measured by the level of portfolio diversification and the ratio of net charge-offs to total loans, than those with no securitization activities?

Liquidity

R7   Are securitizing banks likely to exhibit higher liquidity needs, measured deposit to asset, and volatile to total deposit ratios, than non-securitizing banks?

Cost of Funds

R8   Are securitizing banks likely to exhibit a higher cost of funds, measured by deposit interest expense to total interest expense and deposit interest expense to interest loan income ratios, than non-securitizing banks?

Loan Origination Competitive Advantage

R9   Are securitizing banks likely to make more use of their loan origination competitive advantage, measured by a higher loan growth rate, a larger securitizable loan portfolio, and their prior experience with securitization) than non-securitizing banks?

SCOPE OF THE STUDY

Today's environment has been characterized by sharp acceleration in the pace of innovation. When combined with deregulation and structural changes in recent years this acceleration has revolutionized the international financial system and the way banks and other financial and non-financial institutions manage their operations. Major new financial instruments have either been created or have dramatically increased their role in the financial structure.

Given the objective of this Research, the primary approach of the research is from a micro-economic point of view of the financial firm. Why do financial institutions embrace financial innovation? W. L. Silber (1975, 1983) gives a straightforward proposition: financial firms, under a set of internal, regulatory and market constraints, engage in financial innovation in order to maximize profits. Banks and financial firms in general are assumed to be profit-maximizers reacting to profit opportunities and/or changes in the constraints of their operating environment by innovating. These profit opportunities and/or internal and external constraints may be in the form of changes in capital requirements, advent of new laws, new forms of competition, new technologies, new markets, new ways of raising funds, changes in savings/borrowing habits of economic agents, etc.

Data used for hypothesis testing are survey data of the largest 200 US commercial banks with domestic and foreign offices from the *"Consolidated Reports of Condition and Income"* for 1994–1995 time period filed with the Federal Deposit Insurance Corporation (FDIC) also known as Call Reports. The principal source of data on asset securitization activities of US commercial multinational banks is *"schedule L"* to the "Call Reports" that banks file quarterly. A valuable source about the market for asset securitization is the *"Asset Sales Report"* published by *American Banker–Bond Buyer* on a weekly basis, and the *Wall Street Journal* in its 'Credit Market' and 'New Issues' daily sections.

The latter two sources report in a timely manner public issues of asset-backed security offerings and the terms relating to each one of them. Securitization of mortgage and non-mortgage assets by institutions other than banks is not included in the empirical analysis, even though alluded to in other sections of the study.

LIMITATIONS OF THE STUDY

As is the case with studies using data from reported financial statements, this study suffers built-in—thus inevitable—drawbacks to its findings. These are the lack of control over the research design as well as over the reporting of the results of the activity under study. Reporting procedures are based mostly upon regulatory requirements. While making the reported data comparable this does not insure its completeness nor its uniformity over time. In the particular case of this study, reporting of securitization was limited to mortgage loans. It wasn't until fairly recently that banks were required to include securitization of consumer loans.

Another problem often encountered with the use of financial data is the absence of normality of financial ratios. This, in turn, places limitations on the ability either to generalize or make predictions based on the research findings. The ability to generalize to other large banks in foreign markets is further constrained by the fact that these banks operate within different regulatory frameworks, financial industry structures, and banking traditions. One unifying feature of large banks worldwide, however, is that they compete in the same global framework, consequently, the same changing and challenging environment when setting up their competitive strategies and tactics. A case at hand is the increased government harmonization of bank regulation and supervision.

Variable definitions, as it shall be seen in later chapters, are based solely on reported financial statements. Qualitative factors such as managerial style, business culture, tradition with innovation and new products, investment in technology, and organizational structures among others, are likely to bear a significant relationship to the decision to adopt the innovation of asset securitization. While the investigation of business culture and its relation to the innovative behavior of institutions is beyond the scope of this research, future investigation of this topic may reveal that the difference between an innovating institution and a non-innovating one may reside more within its business culture then within its financial characteristics.

In this chapter, the field of financial innovation has been briefly surveyed. The field of asset securitization has been succinctly described, the objective and scope of the project have been introduced. The research hypothesis has been stated, and the related research questions listed. In the following chapters the fields of financial innovation and asset securitization will be surveyed and the research methodology will be presented in Chapters 3 and 4, respectively. In Chapter 5, the findings will be discussed followed by a conclusion of the book.

NEED FOR THE RESEARCH

The utility of this research has several dimensions. The research's findings should be useful to the sample's multinational banks, to academia, to bank regulators, and to the general financial community. To bank management, the findings will shed light on the extent of which financial innovation—asset securitization in this case—has provided an added tool towards banks' ability to manage risk, improve returns, meet regulatory requirements, while taking advantage of its most traditional competitive advantage, loan origination.

To academicians, the results of this research will provide further investigation in the topic of financial innovation. The literature abounds with studies of financial innovations that are confined to a general, descriptive treatment of innovative processes with reference to monetary theory or policy. It is in the macro-economic context that financial innovation has received most attention. The author feels there is a great need for more empirical of a micro-economic nature into the field of financial innovation stimuli and processes. The major contribution of this research, therefore, is to add to the existing body of literature focusing on the micro-economic aspects of financial innovation in general and asset securitization in particular.

To bank regulators, a better understanding of banks' motives behind the adoption of new financial techniques and processes should allow a better designed and timely regulatory response. Regulators are overwhelmed by the speed and rate at which financial innovation is occurring, and their response has been a succession of trial-and-error approaches aimed at limiting the risk involved with these new devices. It is believed that regulators should have higher success rate with a better understanding of the banking environment, and subsequently of banks' behavior, than simply trying to find more reasons why the old regulation should work despite the financial revolution that has completely redefined the financial industry dynamic and structure.

As to the general financial community, it is hoped that the findings of this research will yield a better understanding of the adoption process of asset securitization within US banking industry and its diffusion to international markets. To the author's knowledge, diffusion research of financial innovations by financial and non-financial organizations has been rather scarce. This research is an attempt to contribute to both the theoretical and empirical understanding of the adoption/diffusion process of financial innovation by and among US banking organizations. An area of future research would be to test the findings of this research in international markets.

NOTES

1. The following are some of the losses incurred after the recent increase in interest rates. Proctor & Gamble Co. lost $157 million in the quarter on interest rate swap agreements with Bankers Trust of New York. Askin Capital Management, a New York based investment firm, who used mortgage-backed derivatives, was forced to seek protection in bankruptcy court after losing nearly all of the

$600 million at the Granite hedge fund it was managing. Kidder Peaboy & Co., one of the most sophisticated mutual fund player in the derivative market lost $350 million on 'phantom' derivative trades.

2. An area of future research would be to see whether the new risk-weighted capital requirements had any dampening effect on the volume of off-balance-sheet activities in general, and asset securitization in particular, undertaken by banks. Equally important would be to see whether better bank capitalization has had any significant effect on bank safety. It has been noted that the number of failed institutions has declined during the past few years. One may want to dissociate the effect of capitalization from other changes within the banking environment.

CHAPTER 2

Financial Innovation and Regulatory Issues

Financial innovation sometimes involves a quantum leap in the world of international finance. This is the kind of creativity involved in the introduction of revolutionary products such as the first swap, the first mortgage backed security, the first zero coupon bond, or the introduction of the junk bonds to finance leverage buyouts. At other times, it involves a novel twist of an old idea. This is the kind of creativity involved in the extension of futures trading to a commodity or a financial instruments not previously traded in a futures market, the introduction of a swap variant, or the creation of a mutual funds with a new focus (Marshall and Bansall, 1992, p. 3).

SECURITIZATION AND FINANCIAL INNOVATION THEORIES

Several theories attempted to explain the occurrence of financial innovation. While no one framework gives a complete picture of the process of financial innovation, they all agree that not all innovations qualify as significant ones. One of the most significant financial innovation in the nineties has been asset securitization, a technique that revolutionized both the concept of bank intermediation and funding mechanisms. Following is a brief overview of the theories of financial innovation, the proliferation of off-balance sheet activities, and the regulatory response towards a better assessment of the risks involved.

The Constraint-Induced/Adversity-Induced Innovation Hypothesis

Silber (1975) provides the beginning framework for discussing financial innovation as a way of reducing the costs imposed by regulation. While he recognizes regulation as a frequent motivation to innovate, he describes the process in more general terms. He views the financial firm as a utility maximizer which operates in a given environment constrained by some set of internal rules and a set of macroeconomic conditions, a given regulatory environment and set of tax laws, and a given level of technology and knowledge (Silber, 1975, 1983).

Given these initial constraints, firms which behave as wealth maximizers would be expected to gradually exploit the available opportunities to create value for a given set of constraints, which opportunities would be gradually exhausted. He proposes that when the cost of adhering to a constraint increases or when the utility of the firm declines, the firm has an incentive to innovate. If the cost of adhering to an internal constraint increases, the firm may reevaluate the policy, relaxing or removing that constraint. However, if the costs are imposed by a binding external constraint, there is an incentive for the firm to innovate to reduce these costs. Silber refers to this type of innovation as constraint-induced innovation. In the second type, adversity-induced innovation, the firm's utility declines and the firm has an incentive to innovate to return to the previous utility level. Silber acknowledges that these motivations to innovate are not mutually exclusive. In fact, if the cost of adhering to a constraint increases, the utility of the firm would be expected to decline.

Innovative financial instruments and processes are, therefore, characterized as an attempt by corporations to lessen the financial effect of the constraints they face. Firms are viewed as utility maximizers subject to a number of constraints, some of which are imposed by government regulation, and the rest being dictated by the marketplace or by the firm itself. Innovative activity is spurred by economic impulses that increase the cost of adhering to a particular constraint, which innovative activity should lead to a relaxation of the constraint and thereby a reduction in the cost of adherence (William Silber, 1975, 1981, 1983).

Van Horne's description of the innovation process, unlike Silber's, does not rely on some adverse event (tightening of a constraint) to stimulate innovation, but only a change in the environment or constraints under which firms operate. It is the fact that the change in the constraint alters the opportunity facing the firms that motivates innovation. In some cases, the constraints are tightened, in some cases relaxed. Tighter capital adequacy constraints encouraged the implementation of new sources of financing and the development of off-balance sheet items, while the removal of regulation Q as a constraint motivated the implementation of bank money-market accounts (Van Horne, 1985). Financial innovation is therefore stimulated when changes in the environment occur. He identifies the following changes as stimuli to financial innovation :"(1) volatile inflation rates and interest rates ; (2) regulatory changes and circumvention of regulation ; (3) tax changes ; (4) technological advances ; (5) the level of economic activity ; and (6) academic work on market efficiency and inefficiencies" (p.622). Please refer to Figure 2-1 below regarding Finnerty's compilation of certain financial innovations and their respective stimulating factors.

With volatile inflation and fluctuating nominal interest rates, new products are devised to reduce such risk. New deposit and investment accounts as well as floating rate loans are examples of responses to these stimuli. In part, the trend towards increased negotiability and marketability of financial instruments is the result of interest rate volatility.

Van Horne (1985) and Finnerty (1988) have also identified academic work as an important stimulus to innovation. To take it a step further, one may add that financial innovation is greatly aided by the level of sophistication of the profession of finance in the fields of valuation theory, portfolio theory, hedging theory, accounting profession, and tax treatment of different forms of instruments in the market. One may expect innovation to arise in countries where the profession of finance is highly regarded and well advanced. The United States falls well into this category.

Finnerty reckons that securitization occurred because of risk reallocation, liquidity enhancement, and transaction cost motives. It is a known fact that the mortgage-backed sector was initiated by the U.S. government in order to enhance the liquidity to the housing sector. It has often been advanced that banks use securitization as a cheaper funding mechanism than deposits.

The third motive behind asset securitization is risk reallocation. The mechanics of asset securitization requires that the securitized assets be sold to a separate entity, referred to as a bankruptcy remote vehicle that is legally independent of the originator. This technique insures the insulation of these two entities and the reallocation of both credit and interest rate risk from the originator to the bankruptcy remote vehicle[3]. Securitization, however, was stimulated by more then risk allocation and liquidity enhancement concerns. As we shall see later, regulatory constraints,

Figure 2-1: Factors Primarily Responsible for Financial Innovation, Finnerty's Compilation

Innovation	Factors	Innovation	Factors
Consumer-Type Financial Instruments			
Broker Cash Management Accounts	7	Money Market Accounts	6,7
Debit Cards	2,7,11	Now Accounts	6,7
Variable Rate Mortgages	7	IRA/Keogh Accounts	1,6
Money Market Mutual Funds	6,7	Convertible mortgages/reduction option loans	2,7
Financial Processes			
Shelf registration	2,6,7	Direct public securities	2,6
Discount brokerage	2,6	Automated teller machines	2,11
Point-of-sale terminals	11	Electronic security trading	2,11
EFTs/Automated clearing houses	7,11	CHIPS (same day settlements)	7,11
Cash management/sweep accounts	7,11		
Financial Strategies/Solutions			
More efficient bond call strategies	7,9	Debt-for-debt exchanges	1,7,10
Stock-for-debt swaps	1,7,10	In-substance defeasance	1,7,10
Preferred dividend rolls	1	Hedged dividend capture	1
Leveraged buyouts structuring	1,9,11	Corporate restructuring	1,9,11
Project/lease/asset-based financial structuring	4		

Innovation	Factors	Innovation	Factors
Securities			
Stripped Debt Securities	1,4,7	Stripped Debt Securities	1,4,7
Floating Rate Notes	4,5,7	Floating Rate, Rating Sensitive Notes	3,4,5,7
Floating Rate Tax-Exempt Notes	4,5,7	Auction Rate Notes/Debentures	2,3,4,7
Real Yield Securities	2,4,5,8	Dollar BILS	4,7
Puttable-Extendible Notes	2,3,4	Increasing Rate Notes	3
Extendible Notes	2,4	Variable Coupon/Rate Renewable Notes	2,4,6
Puttable/Adjustable Tender Bonds	2,4,7	Variable Duration Notes	4,7
Euronotes/Euro-Cps	2,4	Universal Commercial Papers	4
Medium Term Notes	2	Negotiable CDs	2,5
+Mortgage-Backed Bonds	4	+Mortgage Pass-Throughs	2,4,5
+Collateralized Mortgage Obligations	2,4,5	+Stripped Mortgage-Backed Securities	4
LOC/surety bond credit support	4,11	Yield curve/maximum rate notes	4,6,7
Interest rate swaps	4,6,7	Currency swaps	4,6
Interest rate caps/floors/collars	4,7	Re-marketed reset notes	2,3,4
Foreign-currency-denominated bonds	4,7	Eurocurrency bonds	7
Dual currency bonds	4,6	Indexed currency option notes/ Principal exchange rate linked securities	4,6,7

Figure 2-1 *(Cont.)*

Innovation	Factors	Innovation	Factors
Commodity linked bonds	4,6,8	High-yield (Junk) bonds	2,5,7,9
Puttable common stocks	3,4,10	Foreign currency futures	4,9,11
Exchange-traded options	4,9	Stock index futures	4,8,9
Interest rate futures	4,7,9	Forward rate agreement	4,7
Options on futures contracts	4,7,9	Adjustable rate preferred stock	1,4,5,6,7
Warrants to purchase bonds	4,7	Auction rate preferred stocks	1,4,5,7
Convertible adjustable preferred stock	1,4,5,7	Indexed floating rate preferred stock	1,4,5,7
Remarketed preferred stock	1,4,5,7,11	Stated rate auction preferred stock	1,3,4,5,7
Single point adjustable rate stock	1,2,4,5,7	Convertible exchangeable preferred	1,3,10
Variable cumulative preferred stock	1,2,3,4,5,7	Zero coupon convertible debt	1,11
Puttable convertible bonds	3,4,7	Mandatory convertible/equity contract notes	1,6
Synthetic convertible debt	1,10	Exchangeable auction preferred	1,2,4,5,7
Convertible reset debentures	3	Participating bonds	34
Master limited partnership	1	Additional class(es) of common stocks	11,
Adjustable rate convertible debt	1,10		

Source: Finnerty, 1988. *Note:* 1, tax advantages; 2, reduced transaction costs; 3, reduced agency costs; 4, risk reallocation; 5, increased liquidity; 6, regulatory/legislative factors; 7, level and volatility of interests; 8 level and volatility of prices; 9, academic work; 10, accounting benefits; 11, technological and other factors; +, mortgage- and asset-backed innovation.

competition, cost and return considerations, accounting benefits, and portfolio management, all have been cited as motivating factors.

The Regulatory-Dialectic Hypothesis

The second environment factor of the constraint-induced hypothesis to financial innovation, (that is, changes in regulation and circumvention) was chosen as the basis for Edward Kane's framework of the regulatory dialectic hypothesis (Kanes, 1986, 1984, 1981, 1975). Financial innovation occurs as a result of conflicts between the goals of the regulators and the wealth-maximization behavior of the firm. A regulatory action that creates a binding regulatory constraint or increases the cost of an existing constraint reduces shareholders wealth and alters the constraint set of the firm. If the firm can identify one or more ways to reduce the costs imposed by regulation which defeats the intent of regulators, regulators have an incentive to re-regulate, and then firms have the incentive to re-innovate.

The regulation-innovation process is very dynamic and cumulative. The successful introduction of one instrument encourages the introduction of another in the same country or in a different country. Financial futures contracts encouraged financial options in the United States and a large set of strategies culminating in a fertile set of portfolio insurance schemes, which ebbed and flowed as portfolio managers learned more about them and as financial market conditions changed. The fundamental proposition here is that regulation begets circumvention. Once proved successful, it produces an information set which expands nationally and then internationally (often vice-versa), culminating in a general acceptance of the product, process, and/or strategy. This can lead to the expansion into derivative areas or to re-regulation of the market or to development of new regulations to establish boundaries on the market, allowing for necessary comfort zones for regulators (Khoury, 1990, p.185). The cycle can then be established as follows:

The Regulatory Dialectic:

Regulation ⇨ Circumvention ⇨ Deregulation ⇨
Innovation ⇨ Market Acceptance through Information ⇨
Internationalism ⇨ More Deregulation ⇨
Innovations of Different Types ⇨
Possible new forms of re-regulation or new forms of regulation

---

Edward Kane (1984) in his Microeconomic and Macroeconomic Origins of Financial Innovations, argues that innovations represent a deliberate, albeit unintended, economic responses to macroeconomic and regulatory policies. Viewing the burdens imposed on financial firms by policy as implicit taxes, he suggests that innovation is the outcome of a regulatory dialectic process: firms respond to the regulatory-imposed burdens by innovating to minimize the burdens, and regulators respond to the induced innovations by changing the regulations to regain control over the firms.

Kane (1977, 1981) treats political processes of 'regulation' and economic processes of 'regulatee avoidance' as opposing forces that, like a seesaw, continually adapt to each other (Please refer to Figure 2-2 for an illustration of the process). This type of adaptation is labeled " structural arbitrage", whereby firms seek to provide services in a form that draws the least amount of regulatory interference.

While Kane recognizes that financial changes have been governed to a great degree by technological change and volatility of inflation and interest rates, it is the preexisting patterns of financial regulation that predominantly affect the adaptative efficiency of different institutions. Such efficiency is featured by two lags : the 'avoidance lag' between regulation and avoidance, and the 're-regulating' lag between avoidance and re-regulation, with the second being the longest due to the non-profit making motivation of regulators and asymmetric information between regulators and regulatees. Indeed, the regulators are woefully short of data on what is happening in many markets. " How can you predict the knock-on effect of a crisis in one financial market when you do not know the scale of trading or its relationship with other markets?" (*Financial Times,* 1992a).

Information asymmetry is also attributed to the fact that banks have gotten far more sophisticated and knowledgeable than their regulators. In the case of derivative products, for instance, Richard Waters reports that " [i]t is now commonplace to witness bank regulators all but admitting to ignorance on how derivative markets work" and that " the division of responsibility . . . has left the impression that no one is in the position to assess the full risks accruing in the financial system" (*Financial Times,* 1992a).

Miller (1986, 1991), although very much in agreement with Kanes, chose to emphasize tax changes as an initiating force in financial innovation. "For a variety of reasons, including especially the desire to blunt the force of previous successful innovations by taxpayers, governments, or more properly, the shifting coalition of interest groups, that vehicle for protection and advantage, prefer to keep changing the structure, thereby

Figure 2-2: An Illustration of the Regulatory Dialectic:
The Evolution of the US Banking Regulatory Framework

Old Regulation	Circumvention or Elimination	New Regulation
• Ban on interstate banking (McFadden Act 1927)	Circumvented through: (a) Bank holding companies (BHCs) which owned subsidiaries in several states	(a) 1966 Douglas Amendment to BHCA (1956) applies nearly the same restrictions to BHCs as to banks.
	(b) One bank holding company loophole, which allowed BHCs only to use "non-banks" across state lines.	(b) A 1970 amendment of BHCA closed this loophole. The one bank amendment also set standards for the approval of closely related non-banking activities.
	(c) ATM networks are used for interstate expansion. Many states either relaxed or eliminated restrictions on out-of-state banking.	
• Companies operating in non-banking industries are prohibited from owning banks.	Circumvented through the use of non-bank banks (which accepted demand deposits or made commercial loans, but not both).	A 1970 amendment to BHCA closed this loophole.
• Capital adequacy requirements	Off-balance sheet financing	Risk adjusted capital ban (proposed).
• Ban on insurance activities of banks	BHCs own insurance companies.	Title VI of the Garn–St. Germain Act explicitly bans BHCs from insurance activities.
• Interest rate ceiling (reg. Q)	Circumvented through: (a) Certificates of Deposit (first offered by Citibank in 1961). (b) money market mutual funds.	DIDMCA provided for gradual elimination of Reg. Q between June 1981–March 1986 (deregulation).

Figure 2-2: An Illustration of the Regulatory Dialectic:
The Evolution of the US Banking Regulatory Framework

Old Regulation	Circumvention or Elimination	New Regulations
• Prohibition of interest on demand deposit (GSA 1933).	DIDMCA provided for gradual elimination of in rate ceilings between June 1981–March 1986.	Prohibition is eliminated by DIDMCA of 1980.
	NOW accounts are initiated by mutual savings banks in the early 1970s in Massachusetts and spread throughout New England.	
	The prohibition is eliminated by DIDMC (1980).	
• Separation between investment and commercial banking (GSA 1993)	Partially eliminated by a court ruling 1975 (banks can offer brokerage and automatic investment services) and by a host of other court rulings, deregulatory changes, and manuevers by banks.	
• State usury laws limit interest rates charged on certain types of loans.	Banks established credit card subsidiaries in South Dakota and Delaware (these two states passed special legislation to attract capital).	
• Fixed security commission rates.	Circumvented to some extent through non-price competition. Completely eliminated on May 1, 1975.	No change
• Margin requirements on securities loans (1934 Act)		
• Real estate loan restrictions (on size and interest rates)	Most eliminated by 1983 (Comptroller of the Currency).	
• Selective credit controls	Were used only during brief periods during the 1960s and 1970s	

**Figure 2-2: An Illustration of the Regulatory Dialectic:
The Evolution of the US Banking Regulatory Framework**

Old Regulation	Circumvention or Elimination	New Regulation
• Controls on credit quality		No change
• Limits on loans to single borrower		No change
• Loans to insiders		No change
• Restrictions on types and maturity distribution of securities held as investments		No change
• Restrictions on credit transactions with nonbanking affiliates		No change
• Reserve requirements (apply to members of FRB)		DIDMCA (1980) extends requirements to all depository institutions on an equal basis
• CAMEL rating system (p. 79)		No change
• Reporting requirements (on quarterly basis)		No change
• Entry regulations (charters) administered by Comptroller of the Currency on state authorities		No change
• Restrictions on bank ownership		New restrictions imposed on bank ownership by individuals by the changes in Bank Control Act (1978).
• Regulation of management interlocks (only FRB members)		The Depository Institution Management Interlocks Act (1978) extends restrictions to all depository institutions.

**Figure 2-2: An Illustration of the Regulatory Dialectic:
The Evolution of the US Banking Regulatory Framework**

Old Regulation	Circumvention or Elimination	New Regulation
• Restrictions on bank mergers (Bank Merger Act of 1966). The opinion of the Department of Justice on any competitive factors regarding bank mergers in required.		No change
• Regulation of international expansion of U.S. banks.		
• Truth in Lending Act (1968) (Regulation Z) requires accurate disclosure of lending terms.	Ten years after enactment, 80% of banks were not in compliance.	The regulations are simplified in the Truth in Lending Simplificatin and Reform Act (1980).
• Consumer Leasing Act (1976) (Regulation M) requires accurate disclosure of the terms of personal property lease.		No change
• Real Estate Settlement Procedures Act (1974) requires lenders to inform potential home buyers in writing of settlement charges (Regulation X of HUD).		No change
• Electronic Fund Transfers Act (1978) (Regulation E) applies to personal accounts.		In 1984, the regulations were extended to debit card transactions.

Source: Sarkis, 1990, p. 87–91.2

altering the internal rate differentials and creating new opportunities for financial innovation." (Miller, 1991, p.8) This results in a sequence of endless action and reaction aptly dubbed the "regulatory dialectic" by Edward Kane.

Miller (1986) further states that changes in the tax structure both motivates and defines a 'successful' innovation. "Each innovation that does its job successfully earns an immediate reward for its adopters in the form of tax money saved" (p. 461). In this case, the government is practically "subsidizing the process of financial innovation just as it subsidizes the development of new seeds and fertilizers but with the important differences that in financial innovation the government's contribution is typically inadvertent."[4]

Finnerty (1988, 1992), refers to tax asymmetries instead as one of the major incentives behind financial innovation (or what he refers to as financial engineering). Tax asymmetries exist for a number of reasons. Some industries are granted special tax exemptions and preferences in order to encourage the their development and growth or to redirect their energies in particular directions. Another reason is that different countries impose different tax burdens. This is further complicated by the fact that some countries have different tax provisions for domestic and foreign firms operating within their boundaries. Such asymmetries in the effective tax rates can be exploitable through the introduction of new financial instruments, tax arbitrage, swaps, etc. . . . A new financial instrument should generate a reduction of differential taxes, among other things, if it were to enable markets to operate more efficiently and be more complete (Van Horne, 1985 : 621).

Innovation, Market Completeness, and Efficiency

Finnerty (1988, p. 18), in agreement with Van Horne, defines a truly "innovative" security one that " (i) enables an investor to realize a higher after-tax risk-adjusted rate of return without affecting the issuer's after-tax cost of funds, and/or (ii) enables an issuer to realize a lower after-tax cost of funds without adversely affecting investors, than had been possible prior to the introduction of the new security." Only innovations that make the market more complete or efficient can accomplish these goals. If the financial markets were perfect and complete, there would be no opportunities for (nontrivial) financial innovation.

Financial intermediation entails substantial costs in conveying financial instruments from sellers to buyers—explicit costs in the process of intermediation itself paid to brokers, dealers and investment bankers, for example, and the implicit costs in terms of the time required to accomplish financial transactions to buyers or sellers. Financial innovation will be cost effective in this case when the cost of developing and implementing an innovation is less that the value of the savings provided by the innovation.

The second foundation for financial innovation is the movement toward market completeness. A market is complete "when every contingency in the world corresponds to a marketable security" (Van Horne, 1985, p.622). In contrast, markets are incomplete " when the number and types of securities available do not span these contingencies" (Van Horne, 1985, p.622). Copeland and Weston (1983) describe the capital market as complete when "the number of unique linearly independent securities is equal to the total number of alternative future states of nature" (1983, p.112). This implies that an investor may purchase securities with any desired set of payoffs in any possible state. However, such an academic construct is not useful in a practical sense because of the existence of an unaccountably infinite number of futures states, and securities cannot be offered costlessly (Ingram, 1990, p.33.)

Financial innovations, which offer a set of payoffs previously unavailable in the market will only be made when it is cost effective to do so, i.e., when the marginal cost of developing and offering the security is less than the marginal benefit it provides. Asset securitization, it is believed, lagged behind mortgage securitization partially because of cost concerns. The economies of scale reached through securitization of high volumes of government agencies mortgages were not readily available to the non-mortgage sector until standardization was achieved on consumer and other types of loans.

A state of completeness, if ever reached, can only be temporary. Macroeconomic shocks, such as unanticipated shifts in inflation rates, interest rates, stock prices, and exchange rate exposure, usually lead intermediaries to rebalance their portfolios. In the process, the existence of marketing costs may render the bundling and unbundling of claims to form new securities a more efficient avenue than holding old ones (Ross, 1988).

Financial Innovation: A Classification Framework

A classification scheme offered by the Bank for International Settlements is based on the type of financial intermediation function performed. The reference system employed highlights three broad functions of a financial system, those are of risk transference, provision of liquidity, and the provision of claims on economic agent revenues. These functional distinctions led to the following classifications:

i   *risk-transferring innovations* : new instruments or techniques that allow economic agents to transfer among themselves the price or credit risks inherent in financial positions;

ii   *liquidity-enhancing innovations* : new instruments or techniques that increase the moneyness or the negotiability or transferability of existing financial instruments with enhanced liquidity properties;

iii   *credit-generating (or debt-generating) innovations* : those which broaden the access to credit supplies. These may result in an general increase in the volume of all credit or they may result in a shift from traditional credit channels for some agents—say bank borrowings—to non-traditional channels—say, the capital markets.

iv   *equity-generating innovations* : may broaden the access of economic agents to equity finance. Some innovations may result in an observed greater leverage in the economy, i.e., a greater reliance on debt relative to equity, that has as a consequence an actual contraction of equity positions (BIS, 1986, p. 171–2).

This framework, like any other framework for the classification of financial novelties, does not capture the full richness of the process of financial innovation. But "it does provide a workable reference system for recent innovations that focuses on the macro-financial consequences of financial innovations" (BIS, 1986, p.172).

Some innovations fall into more than one category, which is probably indicative of the degree of their significance, as defined by Miller. Securitization covers all but the last category, equity enhancement. It allows for risk transfer, liquidity enhancement, and credit generation. A yardstick towards evaluating the significance of an innovation is its ability to spur other innovations, and thus, bring the markets closer towards completeness and farther from inefficiencies. Figure 3-6 in the following chapter is a testament that credit securitization has offered new investment instruments for mutual funds, insurers, pension funds and foreign investors, among others.

Financial Innovation and Financial Instability

An important issue that has been often raised in the case of financial innovation is its induced financial fragility and instability. Such instability arises from the changing characteristics of financial structure of institutions. Because of innovative products, payment commitments have become more closely coordinated with payment receipts so that small changes in conditions can cause a large increase in the need for institutions to acquire cash by selling assets that may have thin markets. As asset sales in thin markets become necessary, while the value of liquidity—or marketability—is enhanced, the relative value of assets become subject to change, which change becomes responsible for the institutions' balance sheet instability.

Minsky (1984) explains that when people think of instability, the concern is usually about downward instability. "However, before the threat of downward instability can be serious, the liability structure has to be complex, so that a systematic failure to validate a set of liability structures because profits fall or other costs rise will lead to an attempt to unwind liability structures." He warns that efforts to "unwind have serious implications for asset prices, financing possibilities, and, therefore, investment. Before downward instability is a threat, it is necessary to have a period of financial innovation during which the complexity of liability structures increases. These prior development imply an upward instability to the economy".

Another important way in which innovation may contribute to systemic vulnerabilities derive from the difficulties in pricing and forecasting price changes of new instruments and the possibility that many new instruments appear to be under-priced, therefore, not allowing for a full compensation for their inherent risk (BIS, 1986, p.3). Moreover, the general trend toward increased off-balance sheet activities and "unbundling" (which involves separating market risk from credit risk), as well as the complexity of multiple linked transactions, can conceal the interlocking of risks, for banks management, regulators, and market participant alike (BIS, 1986). A subsequent point is that the new instruments shift price or market risk from one economic agent to another, but do not eliminate that risk.

Most of new financial instruments has been in the form of derivative products. This market for highly technical, tailor-made instruments created through stand-alone or embedded interest rate and currency swaps, options and the complex combinations thereof has mushroomed to $10 trillion in notional value as of 1995 year-end, up from less then a trillion dollars in 1988. What terrifies regulators is that a panic involving derivatives, because they crisscross borders and financial markets, could consist of an interbank payment crisis, a stock market crash and a huge interest rate leap combined. Furthermore, the peculiar nature of derivatives is such that dealers generally don't unwind positions, they simply hedge them with other positions. Hence their market risk can be swept from their books only by piling on credit risk. (Hansel and Muerring, 1992).

The links derivatives form between markets are subtle and outside the regulators regular purview. "We do not know the web of interconnections between banks that has been established through derivatives," concedes a BIS official in a interview with Institutional Investor. "The market is losing transparency, and we do not know who is dependent on whom anymore. Now we will only know after the fact, and by then it could be too late" (Institutional Investor, 1992, p.57). And since most governments explicitly or implicitly commit themselves to bailing out commercial banks that get into trouble, supervisors seem to have a legitimate right to insist in the strongest way that these risks be understood and handled prudently.

FINANCIAL INNOVATION AND OFF-BALANCE-SHEET ACTIVITIES

As part of the financial innovation process, there has been an increasing tendency for banks to engage in off-balance sheet activities. The growth of these activities can generally be attributed to the same factors affecting the trend toward financial innovation and securitization[5], with two main influences. Firstly, bankers have been drawn to off-balance sheet activities due to constraints imposed on their balance sheets, particularly regulatory pressure to improve capital ratios. Concerns over the latter has led to the "rapid extension of off-balance sheet exposures in order to reduce prices of credit and minimize the requirements for additional, expensive equity capital" (Channon, 1988, p. 55).

Moreover, OBS activities offer a way to improve the rate of return earned on assets. Heightened competition for traditional banking products along with increased reliance on market intermediated finance (broadly referred to as securitization) has led to margin reductions for banks. This in turn has led banks to seek non-traditional, mainly off the balance sheet, products in order to improve the return on their assets.

Secondly, for similar reasons, banks have sought ways to hedge interest rate risk without inflating their balance sheets, as would occur with the use of the interbank market (BIS, 1986).

Classification of OBS Activities

In most schemes offered, credit risk has been used as the differentiating criteria between different OBS items (Hempel et al. 1990; Khambata, 1989; and BIS, 1986b). Their approach is to differentiate between contingent claims and financial services. Contingent claims generate income, involve the commitment of the bank to some future action should a contingency materialize, and, hence, entail credit risk (Goldberg, Altman, and Furash, 1984). Hempel et al. (1990) and Khambata (1989) further break down bank's commitments and contingent claims into three subcategories. The first category includes financial guarantees such as standby letters of credit, lines of credit, revolving loan commitments, note issuance facilities, and securitization with recourse. The second category encompasses trade finance such as commercial letters of credit and acceptance participation. The last one looks at investment activities such as interest rate and currency swaps, forward and futures contracts, and options.

All of these activities have the same characteristics: a bank usually receives a fee or changes a risk position immediately for an activity that does not immediately appear on the balance-sheet but for which the bank may have to take future action.

Financial services also generate income and/or expenses without the creation or holding of an underlying asset or liability. However, they do not produce contingent assets or liabilities. Moreover, "the credit risk they produce is not as large or apparent as that produced by contingent claims" (Holland, 1988). These financial services, of which a number of items have long been offered by banks, include investment advisory services, insurance and securities underwriting, payment services, and fiduciary services such as trust and portfolio management (khambata, 1989, and Goldberg et al., 1984). In Table 3-1, the volume of OBS items as reported on Schedule RC-L by US commercial banks is presented.

Off-Balance-Sheet Risk and Regulatory Response

The proliferation of OBS transactions has raised concerns over their impact (reckoned to be significant and not fully understood) on enterprise risk and valuation, and subsequently questions about the appropriate regulatory response to and adequacy of accounting standards for these activities. "Off-

Figure 2-3: Total OBS vs. Total Assets:
Top 20 US Commercial Banks Activities, 1986–1995

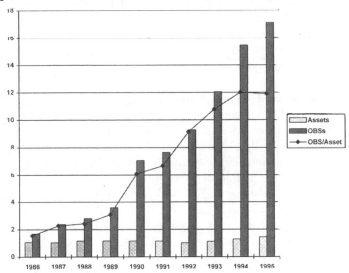

Source: FDIC tapes 1992–1995.

balance sheet (OBS) activities are invariably economic transactions and events with real current or future cash flow consequences" admit Ronen and Sondhi in their discussion of *Financial Reporting and Off-Balance Sheet Transactions* (1990).

They further recognize that problems arise because "the resulting economic assets and/or liabilities do not meet existing accounting definitions and/or measurement standards and are not currently recognized as accounting assets or liabilities. Since all OBS activities involve, to some degree, transfers of interest rate risk, credit risk, or liquidity risk, their non-recognition in financial statements makes it difficult to assess their impact on risk and return" (Ronen and Sondhi, 1990). While early attempts to monitor the growth of OBS activities focused on the commercial banking industry, new accounting rules and disclosure requirements increasingly brought other financial and non-financial firms under more scrutiny.

Disclosure Requirements

In the particular case of the banking industry, disclosure is partially achieved through Schedule RC-L that banks file quarterly with the Federal Reserve System (see Appendix II). Disclosure for the rest of the financial and non-financial sectors is being implemented through SFAS 105 , SFAS 107, and SFAS 119. These standards are part of FASB's ambitious project to provide better understanding, evaluation, and disclosure of the different risks involved with OBS activities and financial instruments in general.

Schedule RC-L Traditionally, bank regulators have responded to higher levels of risk among banks by increasing capital requirements. Ironically, this action gave an added impetus to the increased involvement on OBS activities. By increasing disclosure requirements, regulators hope to impose market constraints on off-balance sheet (OBS) activities and avoid additional government regulation. "Regulators believe that banks are more likely to exercise care in the management of OBS activities if investors are adequately informed of the potential risks associated with such activities" (Apostolou et al., 1991).

Schedule RC-L: Commitments and Contingencies, was the outcome of banking regulatory agencies concern over two issues. The first concern was the enormous growth of OBS product complexity and volume. The second one was the alarming expansion the "invisible" bank to the detriment of visible balance sheet, mostly at the large money center banks (Please refer to Figure 2-3 below). Starting September 30, 1983 all commercial banks were required to supply data regarding their off-balance sheet commitments[6]. Several refinements were brought to the requirements since its inception, greatly improving the disclosure usefulness.

The disclosure was not intended to quantify off-balance-sheet risk in a comprehensive way. It was intended to be used as an indicator of each bank's volume of activities. The Schedule, however, was criticized as being superficial, and even misleading (Cates and Davis, 1987), for the Schedule "does not fully embrace all OBS products and volumes, nor does it adequately measure the risk of these products it does track" (Cates and Davis, 1987). The Schedule has constantly been revised since then, as the focus of the Federal Reserve has shifted towards a better understanding of the market risk embedded within these activities and a better valuation of the instruments involved. The outcome is Schedule RC-L as it appears in Appendix I at the end of this document. Table 2-1 below provides the composition and volume of OBS activities for the largest 20 U.S. banks and a detailed description of items reported in Schedule L, respectively.

The Financial Instruments Project Off-balance sheet disclosure is not a new issue in accounting, but it is far from being fully resolved. The FASB first addressed the topic when it was faced with some lease issues by issuing FASB 13. In a later standard (FASB 47), the FASB dealt with disclosure of off-balance sheet long-term obligations, such as unconditional purchase obligations. In another standard (FASB 49), the Board looked into off-balance sheet product financing transactions in which a company sells inventory and agrees to repurchase it at a specified price.

The FASB continues to be concerned with off-balance sheet financing because of the explosion in the number and variety of financial instruments offered in the marketplace. Accounting for many of these instruments is not yet specified under generally accepted accounting principles. Recognizing this problem, the Board designed three stages to the financial instruments' projects:

a. Disclosure;
b. Recognition and measurement;
c. Distinguishing liabilities and equities

SFAS 105 addresses the first phase of the project by requiring new disclosure standards for financial instruments. However, "[i]t does not alter any current requirements for recognizing, measuring or classifying these instruments." (Lavin, 1992).

The Standard defines a financial instrument with off-balance-sheet risk if the risk of accounting loss[8] exceeds the amount recognized as an asset, if any, or if the ultimate obligation may exceed the amount that is recognized as a liability in the statement of financial position. "The risk of accounting loss from a financial instrument includes (a) the possibility that a loss may occur from the failure of another party to perform according to the terms of a contract (credit risk), (b) the possibility that future changes in market prices may make the instrument less valuable or more onerous (market risk), and (c) the risk of theft or physical loss" (FASB, 1990, para. 7)[9].

FASB Statement No. 105 requires the following information to be disclosed for financial instruments with off-balance-sheet risk:

- The face or contract amount (or notional principal if there is no face or contract amount)
- The nature and terms, including as a minimum the credit and the market risk and the cash requirements
- the accounting policy

Table 2-1: OBS Activities for Top 20 U.S. Banks[7] (Dollars in 000,000)

Year	1983	1984	1985	1986	1987
Unused Commitments	278,954.35	311,711.38	342,342.85	361,515.01	361,741.33
Total Standby L/C Conveyed	2,383.29	125,766.18	148,489.79	141,073.43	136,554.16
Commercial Letters of Credit	21,496.60	21,286.44	19,754.48	19,094.32	20,741.40
Participation in Acceptances Conveyed	4,634.39	6,338.93	6,514.32	4,889.97	3,597.49
Participation in Acceptances Acquired	1,592.97	166.44	133.49	99.27	120.68
Securities Borrowed	NA	2,034.25	2,224.66	3,308.58	3,084.15
Securities Lent	NA	1,080.12	995.17	1,618.46	1,349.45
Residential Mortgage Pools (MBS)	377.79	392.97	380.10	NA	NA
Private Residential Mortgage Pools	431.68	238.91	135.29	NA	NA
Farmer Mac Agriculture Loan Pools	262.40	140.68	101.67	NA	NA
Securities Issued (Purchased & Sold)	NA	6,275.47	6,770.05	12,911.16	1,961.67
Interest Rate Swaps	50,239.49	59,107.34	77,785.07	155,805.92	231,739.06
Futures and Forward Contracts	NA	NA	NA	NA	NA
Option Contracts (Written & Purchased)	1,447.56	3,974.57	11,910.41	35,021.31	60,266.93
Foreign Exchange Rate Contracts	446,852.48	563,578.81	712,835.03	869,724.14	1,474,514.79
Contracts on Other Commodities	NA	NA	NA	NA	NA
All Other OBS Liabilities	14,219.97	20,456.22	54,192.15	66,109.49	79,087.41
TOTAL OBS ACTIVITIES	**822,946.98**	**1,122,604.73**	**1,384,564.54**	**1,671,189.35**	**2,370,758.52**
TOTAL ASSETS	**854,512.38**	**890,172.56**	**979,264.60**	**1,072,657.72**	**1,044,433,7.51**
TOTAL OBS/TOTAL ASSETS	**96.31%**	**126.11%**	**141.39%**	**155.80%**	**226.99%**

Table 2-1 (*Continued*): OBS Activities for Top 20 U.S. Banks[7] (Dollars in 000,000)

Year	1988	1989	1990	1991
Unused Commitments	398,804.13	406,865.22	482,742.20	438,873.84
Total Standby L/C Conveyed	140,716.14	142,860.58	148,393.02	139,470.40
Commercial Letters of Credit	21,107.46	21,380.48	21,601.30	20,555.51
Participation in Acceptances Conveyed	3,453.83	2,513.45	981.03	597.36
Participation in Acceptances Acquired	105.77	114.69	87.79	54.09
Securities Borrowed	3,812.88	2,802.61	3,408.74	2,957.69
Securities Lent	1,468.22	791.89	32,557.75	50,618.98
Residential Mortgage Pools (MBS)	NA	10,240.09	10,513.84	9,661.34
Private Residential Mortgage Pools	NA	1,776.76	3,713.13	7,787.25
Farmer Mac Agriculture Loans	NA	NA	NA	NA
Securities Issued (Purchased & Sold)	7,094.33	13,833.27	3,065.14	2,268.49
Interest Rate Swaps	370,924.93	470,512.02	1,607,165.08	1,601,375.15
Futures and Forwards Contracts	NA	NA	833,318.60	1,150,369.97
Options Contracts (Written & Purchased)	91,176.64	167,896.91	648,867.14	800,947.60
Foreign Exchange Rate Contracts	1,647,909.71	2,200,558.36	2,887,860.19	3,275,332.15
Contracts on Other Commodities	0	0	82,124.45	136,045.52
All Other OBS Liabilities	118,881.52	149,270.88	56,976.73	6,880.87
TOTAL OBS ACTIVITIES	**2,805,455.63**	**3,591,426.24**	**7,051,616.67**	**7,643,696.22**
TOTAL ASSETS	**1,158,525.31**	**1,165,967.79**	**1,158,953.88**	**1,148,104.50**
TOTAL OBS/TOTAL ASSETS	**242.16%**	**308.02%**	**608.45%**	**665.77%**

Table 2-1 (Continued): OBS Activities for Top 20 U.S. Banks[7] (Dollars in 000,000)

Year	1992	1993	1994	1995
Unused Commitments	380,140.10	429,546.49	497,440.23	550,719.08
Total Standby L/C Conveyed	105,839.14	105,121.28	148,393.02	120,473.82
Commercial Letters of Credit	18,030.13	17,287.90	21,601.30	21,467.12
Participation in Acceptances Conveyed	360,883	440,176	981.03	680.28
Participation in Acceptances Acquired	49.11	37,167	87.79	130.23
Securities Borrowed	4,938.00	11,420.66	3,408.74	8672.69
Securities Lent	68,524.70	89,834.40	32,557.75	94,254.99
Residential Mortgage Pools (MBS)	5,443.36	4,395.11	10,513.84	3,532.06
Private Residential Mortgage Pools	920.07	694.32	3,713.13	821.97
Farmer Mac Agriculture Loans	0	0.70	0	0
Securities Issued (Purchased & Sold)	4,899.23	12,810.70	3,065.14	7,875.89
Interest Rate Swaps	1,889,757.48	2,625,510.58	1,607,165.08	5,183,383.00
Futures and Forwards Contracts	1,639,420.05	2,415,020.13	833,318.60	2,944,037.80
Options Contracts (Written & Purchased)	921,680.47	1,627,719.81	648,867.14	2,323,295.28
Foreign Exchange Rate Contracts	4,125,376.42	4,525,376.42	5,269,851.84	5,868,461.51
Contracts on Other Commodities	100,784.06	177,641.79	82,124.45	0
All Other OBS Liabilities	6,942.54	5,727.00	56,976.73	2,329.00
TOTAL OBS ACTIVITIES	**9,273,105.76**	**12,048,584.61**	**15,443,585.63**	**17,130,134.72**
TOTAL ASSETS	**1,015,248.13**	**1,117,267.19**	**1,286,886.24**	**1,439,332.14**
TOTAL OBS/TOTAL ASSETS	**913.38%**	**1078.40%**	**1200.07%**	**1190.1%**

Source: American Bankers Association, Economic Research Department, 1992, FDIC Tapes, 1992–1995.

However, it must be acknowledged that disclosure of information about financial instruments with off-balance-sheet risk "in accordance with FASB 105 requires considerable judgment" (AICPA, 1992). Furthermore, the ambiguities associated with many OBS items make it difficult to attach a realistic weight to them for the purpose of computing capital requirements. A certain degree of arbitrariness will be inevitable, and supervisors will, if any thing have to err on the side of caution.

SFAS 105, although dealing with only one type of risk— credit risk, reports that the accounting risk associated with financial instruments has three components: 1) credit risk, 2) market risk, and 3) liquidity or control risk. Late in 1991, the FASB issued two documents toward further progress of the project: SFAS 107, *Disclosures About Fair Value of Financial Instruments*, and a Discussion Memorandum (DM) entitled, *Recognition and Measurement of Financial Instruments*.

SFAS 107 completes the first phase of the financial instrument project—establishing disclosure applicable to financial instruments, and extends the requirements to include market risk factors as well. The discussion memorandum deals with the second phase of the project, that is, recognition and measurement of financial instruments in financial statements (Munter, 1992).

In managing the disclosure of market value of financial instruments, SFAS 107 states in paragraph 10 that:

> An entity shall disclose, either in the body of the financial statements or in the accompanying notes, the *fair value of the financial instrument* for which it is practicable to estimate that value[10]. An entity also shall disclose the method(s) and significant assumptions used to estimate the fair value of financial instruments [emphasis added].

Highly publicized stories about derivative losses have caused Congress, the SEC, business and other groups to become concerned about derivatives products. These groups have called on the FASB to improve its disclosure requirements regarding derivative financial products. The FASB has intended to help financial statement readers understand more about derivatives through the release of FASB 119, '*Disclosure about Derivative Financial Instruments and Fair Value of Financial Instruments*', which builds upon the disclosure requirements of FASB 105. For the purpose of FASB 119, the board considers a derivative financial instrument as a future, forward, swap or option contract or other financial instrument with similar characteristics of options. FASB 119 can be broken down into three parts (Woodward, Steven, Joel G. Siegel, and Anique A.Qureshi, 1996, p. 18–21):

- It requires the disclosure of the amounts, nature and terms of all derivative financial instruments.
- It differentiates between financial instruments held or issued for trading versus other purposes.
- It further amends Statement Nos.105 and 107 to require that a greater distinction be made regarding specific disclosures

As FASB continues its deliberation on the topic of financial instruments, the project, once completed, may create sweeping changes in accounting, particularly for financial institutions. The FASB decided to undertake this project to its agenda "primarily for five reasons: prolifera tion of financial instruments, lack of guidance in the existing accounting standard, inconsistent guidance in the existing accounting standards, SEC concerns, and Emerging Issues Task Force concerns" (Stewart, 1989). The FASB decided early on that they could not possibly deal with this issue on an instrument-by-instrument basis. The number of existing instruments is far too great for that to be feasible. Indeed, the task "[t]o develop a standard for every instrument would mean tremendous duplication as many of the instruments could be broken down into understandable parts. Once these understandable parts are dissected, sorting them into similar categories would be necessary in order to develop a standard for recognition and measurement." (Lavin, 1992).

Capital Requirements

Underlying the subject of off-balance sheet activities of banks is the subject of bank capital. Presumably, bank capital serves useful purposes, and the level of a bank's capital is inadequate to the extent that it does not serve these purposes[11]. According to *Management Policies of Commercial Banks*, the primary function of bank capital is:

> to keep the bank open and operating so that time and earnings can absorb losses—in other words to inspire confidence in the bank on the part of depositors and the supervisors so that it will not be forced into costly liquidation (Cross and Hempel, 1980).

George Vojta (1973) stated that bank capital should "provide protection against unanticipated adversity leading to loss in excess of normal expectations. The capital provisions against loss permits the bank to continue operations in periods of difficulty until a normal level of earnings is restored."

The primary concern about soundness and confidence as the primary function of bank capital lies in proper measurement. "Any measure of how much capital is necessary for depositors, borrowers, regulators, shareholders, and other interested parties to remain confident is at best imprecise and may vary widely with economic and regulatory conditions" (Hempel et al., 1990). Understandably enough, over the years, bank regulators have adopted several measures in an attempt to devise an adequate measure of capital. The latest risk-based capital standards represent a significant change from past capital guidelines, for risk-based capital replaces capital guidelines that have required US banks to hold a flat minimum percentage of capital against all assets since 1981.

In late 1981, the three federal regulatory agencies announced new minimum capital/asset ratios for all banks, irrespective of risk. These agencies however had slightly different definition of the new capital adequacy measures[12], which differences disappeared by 1985. Banks and bank holding companies of all sizes were supposed to have primary capital of at least 5.5% of adjusted total assets (that is, total assets plus reserves for loan and lease losses minus intangible assets and assets classified as loss but not charged off). Primary and secondary capitals need to be at least 6% of total assets.

It was soon realized, however, that uniform capital adequacy did not mean the desired objectives were being accomplished. First, the capital-to-asset ratio used did not penalize banks for having high-risk assets (Hempel et al., 1990). Indeed, capital requirements were the same for Treasury bills and high-risk consumer loans. Second, US banks appeared to be at a competitive disadvantage to foreign banks because of lower capital requirements elsewhere. Third, some banks, mainly the large money-center banks, began to use off-balance sheet items extensively because, as explained above, they improved both their return-on-assets and capital-to-asset ratios.

In light of these concerns, new risk-based capital adequacy measures were adopted and international convergence, under the auspices of the Cooke Committee (on international regulation and supervision practices) was expanded to include at least a dozen countries[13]. The final version was approved in December 1988, and was expected to be fully phased in by January (March for Japanese banks) 1993[14] (Boot and Thakor, 1991).

The Risk-based capital standards require that different minimum capital percentages be held against different categories of assets according to their perceived risks[15]. The new standards also require for the first time that capital be held against off-balance sheet activities. Figures 2-5 and 2-6 below list some of the key elements of the capital convergence framework and a summary of the new risk-based capital standards.

The Basle committee is continuing work on the capital adequacy framework by monitoring national implementation and taking account of the effect of accounting standards and fiscal policy on this implementation (Price Waterhouse, 1991). In February 1991, the Basle Committee published proposals aimed at achieving a more uniform definition of the treatment of provisions in the definition of capital. The committee is also continuing work on the scope of the framework. "The existing capital convergence framework essentially addresses only credit risk" reported Price Waterhouse (1991). Banks are exposed to a range of other forms of risks such as interest rate risk, foreign exchange risk, and settlement and operational risk. Both the Basle committee and the European Commission have been pursuing intensively the ways in which these other risks may be most appropriately incorporated within the regulatory arrangements (Price Waterhouse, 1991).

On April of last year, the Basle Committee on Banking Supervision has announced amended market risk proposals for banks. The committee has proposed a number of important changes to the way in which it thinks market risk capital should be calculated (*The Economist,* 1995a, p. 70–71; Financial Regulation Report, 1995, p. 2–9).

On January of 1996, the Committee published its final capital standards for market risk. The rules came into effect for all internationally active banks of the G10 countries in 1998. The Basle rules are designed to prescribe capital cover for the market risk incurred from trading activity and therefore supplement the existing international standards for credit risk. Banks are allowed two approaches to calculate new capital requirements. A standardized methodology may be used that, for most instruments, splits capital requirements into specific risks and general market risk. Also, banks may at the discretion of their supervisors also employ internal value-at-risk (VAR) models to calculate capital charges. The ability to use VAR models to calculate capital requirements for the first time is a major innovation in supervisory practice. It is expected to

Figure 2-4: THE KEY ELEMENTS OF THE CAPITAL CONVERGENCE FRAMEWORK

- *Capital Definition*
  - Capital is split between Tier 1 or core elements (equity and disclosed reserves) and Tier 2 or supplementary elements (undisclosed reserves, asset revaluation reserves, general provisions, hybrid debt/equity instruments and subordinated debt). Some practitioners choose to distinguish between Upper Tier 2 (perpetual debt) and Lower Tier 2 (dated debt). The inclusion of the individual Tier 2 elements is at national discretion.
  - Deductions from capital cover goodwill; investment in unconsolidated financial subsidiaries and, at national discretion, holdings of other bank's capital.
  - Tier 2 elements are only eligible up to 100% of Tier 1; subordinated debt must not exceed 50% of Tier 1; and general provisions are limited to 1.25% of risk assets.

- *Risk Asset Weightings*
  - For on-balance sheet assets five basic scales of risk weightings are applied (0%, 10%, 20%, 50%, and 100%). Certain distinctions are made between OECD and non-OECD counterparties (see Figure 2-6 below).
  - For off-balance sheet items a system of credit conversion factors is used. These include such categories as commitments and contingencies.
  - The conversion factors are applied to the nominal principle amount of exposure to produce credit equivalent amount which in turn is weighted according to the category of the counterparty. Interest rate and foreign exchange rate contracts are treated similarly but with adjustments to take into account their particular nature.

- *Target Ratios and Timetables*
  - The Basle guidelines envisage that banks should build up gradually to the 8% minimum standard by the end of 1992 (of which at least 50% must be in Tier1 capital). An interim standard of 7.25% was set to be reached by end 1990.
  - In building up from the interim to the full target ratio the balance between Tier 1 and Tier 2 and the amounts of subordinated debt and general provisions allowed in Tier 2 are gradually reduced.

Source: Adapted from "Capital Adequacy Guidelines," Board of Governors of the Federal Reserve Board (May 1994), and "A User's Guide for the Uniform Bank Performance Report," Federal Financial Institutions Examinations Council (March 1995).

Figure 2-5: Summary of the New Risk-Based Capital Standards

Risk Categories

On-Balance Sheet Items
- Category A1 (0% weight)
    Cash, Federal Reserve Bank balances
    Securities of the US Treasury, OECD government and some US agencies
- Category A2 (20% weight)
    Cash items in process of collection
    US and OECD interbank deposit and guaranteed claims
    Some non-OECD bank and governments deposits and securities
    General obligation municipal bonds
    Some mortgage-backed securities
    Claims collateralized by the US treasury and some other government securities
- Category A3 (50% weight)
    Loans fully secured by first liens on 1–4 family residential properties
    Other (revenue) municipal bonds
- Category A4 (100% weight)
    All other on-balance sheet assets not listed above, including:
    Loans to private entities and individuals, some claims on non-OECD governments
    banks , real assets and investment in subsidiaries

Off-Balance Sheet Items
- Category B1 (counterparty guarantees)
    Direct-credit substitute standby letters of credit (mainly 100%)
    Performance-related standby letters of credit (mainly 50%)
    Unused portions of loan commitments with original maturity > 1 year (mainly 50%)
    Other loan commitments (0%)
    Commercial letters of credit (20%)
    Bankers acceptance conveyed (20%)
- Category B2 (market risk contracts)
    Interest rate swaps, forward commitments to purchase foreign exchange and
    other items (between 0 and 5% of the notional value, plus the mark-to-market
    value of the contract, capped at 50%)

Capital Requirements
- Tier 1
    Common equity, some preferred stocks, minority interests in consolidated sub-
    sidiaries less goodwill
    Tier 1 capital must be at least 4% of risk-weighted assets
- Tier 2
    Loan loss reserve (limited to 1.25% of risk weighted assets), subordinated debt
    (limited to 50% of Tier 1) and other preferred and convertible stocks
    Tier 2 capital can not be larger than Tier 1 capital
    Tier 1 plus Tier 2 capital must be at least 8% of risk-weighted assets
- Leverage requirements
    Tier 1 capital must be at least 3% if total on-balance sheet assets (will be higher for
    banks with poor examination ratings and for those not meeting certain conditions)

Source: Based on "Capital Adequacy Guidelines, Board of Governors of the FRB" (May 1996), and
"A User's Guide for the UBPR," Federal Financial Institutions Examinations Council (March 1995).

move internal risk management and regulatory standards into close alignment (Elderfield, 1996, p. 7–10).

Value at risk (VAR) is a new concept in portfolio risk management. It gives the maximum loss that an institution can expect to incur with a certain frequency over a specific horizon, and it can be calculated by using a constant volatility or time-varying volatility method (Hopper, 1996, p. 19–31).

Capital Guidelines in the Banking Literature The regulatory intent behind the risk-based capital requirement is "to reduce the incentive for insured depository institutions to hold riskier portfolios than socially optimal" (Bradley, Wambeke, and Whibdee, 1991). Given the newness of the topic, little empirical work exists to support the risk weights included in the regulation. An exception to that is the work of Avery and Berger (1990) and Boot and Thakor (1991). The literature abounds, however, with empirical research trying to shed light on whether an increase in flat-capital requirements has any effect on bank riskiness.

Virtually all authors who probed into this topic agree that a mandatory increase in capital has the *direct* effect of reducing insolvency risk. Higher capital requirements seem to provide an increased 'buffer stock' of reserve funds to absorb losses (e.g., Koehn and Santamero, 1980; Kim and Santamero, 1988; Keeton, 1988; Keeley and Furlong, 1990; and Boot and Thakor, 1991). However, "portfolio changes may also be induced, creating *indirect* effects on insolvency risk" (Avery and Berger, 1991)[16]. It is in the area of these indirect effects that most of the disagreements occur[17].

Koehn and Santamero (1980) and Kim and Santamero (1988) showed that an increase in flat-rate capital requirements somewhat restricts the risk-return tradeoffs, but that banks may still choose higher-risk portfolios as a result of the capital increase. Keeton (1988) found that it is quite possible to have an increase in portfolio risk as a result to higher capital requirements. This is in sharp contrast with Keeley and Furlong's findings (1990) which stipulate that banks will never increase portfolio risk as a result of higher capital requirements.

An investigation of the implications of the effectiveness of the new capital guidelines in controlling bank risk is still at an infant stage. Boot and Thakor (1991) concluded that higher capital requirements induce banks to choose lower risk on their on-balance sheet assets. They also assert that loan commitments reduce the bank's incentive to take risk, an assertion that is supported by Avery and Berger's (1990) findings[18].

"Thus, if the purpose of capital requirements is to depress risk taking by banks, it is not worthwhile imposing a capital requirement at all on loan commitments" reported Boot and Thakor (1991). They further add that this prescription "does not necessarily extend to other off-balance sheet liabilities. For example, many financial guarantees and standby letters of credit transfer additional credit risk to the bank because of its role as a third party guarantor". It is believed in this case that for "these contracts, capital requirements serve the same risk-curtailing purpose as they do for on-balance sheet claims, and thus should be imposed." Future research in the area of off-balance sheet activities may bring clearer answers to the issue of bank capital and risk-taking behavior of banks.

CONCLUSION

It should be reiterated that the phenomena of financial innovation is not new or unique to the eighties and nineties nor is it likely to subside. Interest in financial innovation on a micro-economic base has been rather limited. Although the literature abounds with cases of causal relationships between financial innovation and the macro—and micro-economic environment, the extent to which financial innovation increases the allocative efficiency of the economy, induces market completeness, generates higher profits, and causes financial instability is rather difficult to assess and has rarely been attempted. The purpose of this research is to present an investigation of the relationship between financial innovation and financial performances in the case of US multinational banks.

NOTES

3. The reallocation of risk is contingent on wheter a 'true sale' has occurred. Please refer to Section 3–5 for a detailed explanation of the mechanics of securitization.

4. One should acknowledge the fact that there are cases where the government has been the major pioneer of new financial instruments and/or new processes. An example is debt-equity swap programme first introduced by the government of Chile in 1985 in attempt to manage its loan portfolio (Askari, 1991, p.23). Asset-securitization, as we shall see later, was also initiated by the US government in order to enhance the liquidity of the mortgage market. For the most part, however, "the role of government in producing the pearls of financial innovation over the past twenty years has been essentially that of the grain sand in the oyster." (Miller, 1990, p.6)

5. Please refer to Section 3 of the following Chapter regarding factors affecting securitization.

6. Beginning June 30, 1986, all bank holding companies with assets over $150mn were required to file a parallel "Schedule H" on a fully consolidated basis.

7. Data is for top 20 U.S. existing banks at the end of each year. Due to deregulation regarding interstate banking, a lot of mergers and acquisitions have occurred between large banks.

8. Accounting loss refers to the loss that may have to be recognized due to credit and market risk as a direct result of the rights and obligations of a financial instrument.

9. FASB 105 addresses credit risk and market risk only.

10. Market value can be determined, depending on the financial instrument, based on exchange (or auction) market, dealer market, brokered market, and principal-to-principal market values.

11. Four functions of bank capital have been stressed in the literature: 1) to protect the uninsured depositor in the event of insolvency and liquidation, 2) to absorb unanticipated losses with enough margin to inspire continuing confidence to enable a bank, when under stress, to continue as a continuing concern, 3) to acquire the physical plant and basic necessities needed to render banking services, and 4) to serve as a regulatory constraint on unjustified asset expansion (Hempel, Coleman and Simonson, 1990).

12. The FDIC stated that equity capital of 6% or more of total assets is acceptable for all sizes of FDIC member banks (equity capital consists of all common stocks and capital reserves, allowance for loan losses, noncallable preferred stocks, and debt that must be converted into common stock less doubtful loans). The Comptroller and the Federal Reserve jointly announced that most banks' total capital (that is, primary and secondary capital) must be at least between 6 and 7% of total assets, depending on size and financial strength.

13. Risk-based capital proposals were first issued in 1986 for public comment. Because of concerns over placing US banks at a competitive disadvantage vis-a-vis foreign banks, the US agencies began working with the Bank of England on the development of a common approach. In January 1987, a joint US-UK Risk-Based Capital proposal was published. The Cooke committee gave the proposal an international framework when all countries represented on the committee adopted similar agreements in December of 1987.

14. The Financial Institutions Reform, Recovery, and Enforcement Act of 1989 required the Office of Thrift Supervision to establish similar risk-based capital guidelines for savings and loan associations (Bradley, Wambeke, and Whidbee, 1991).

15. These guidelines stipulate minimum capital levels. Individual countries are free to adopt higher levels.

16. emphasis added.

17. There is agreement that when capital is below some sufficiently low level, this indirect effect of increased capital will reduce insolvency risk, for "mandatory capital increase induces a reduction in portfolio risk by mitigating the moral hazard incentives to undertake excessive risk (Avery and Berger, 1991).

18. Notice that the most prominent off-balance sheet activity has been in the field of loan commitments which amounts to over half a trillion dollars in the U.S.; approximately 80% of all commercial bank lending is done under commitments (Boot and Thakor, 1991, p. 826).

CHAPTER 3

Financial Innovation in the Case of Asset Securitization

> *"In its simplest form, securitization is nothing
> more than the selling of assets. In this respect,
> banks have been selling assets, which they origi-
> nated for some time—more particularly, via
> participations or outright sales with or without
> recourse. While the former are associated with
> the sale of a single, large credit, banks have also,
> for some time been "packaging loans for resale."*
> —FEDERAL RESERVE BOARD, 1989

BACKGROUND

One of the most prominent recent features of the financial sector has
been the very strong growth in securities markets transactions. Transactions in the securities markets take a wide variety of forms. Investors
may hold security market claims on borrowers directly or buy shares in
mutual funds that acquire most, if not all, of their assets in the financial
markets. Alternatively, they may own securities representing an undivided interest in a pool of loans, or, investors may hold either securities
issued by banks or deposit claims on banks that own securities rather
than loans.

All of these transactions are types of securitization. In its broadest
sense, securitization is financial intermediation that involves at some
stage the buying and selling of financial claims. Indeed, "perhaps the
best definition of securitization is the matching up of borrowers and
savers wholly or partly by way of the financial markets…. Such a definition covers issuance of securities such as bonds and commercial papers—a practice that entirely replaces traditional financial
intermediation—and also sales of mortgage-backed and other asset-
backed securities—transactions that rely on financial intermediaries to

originate loans but use the financial markets to seek the final holders"
(Cumming, 1987, p.11, 12.) This definition is broad enough to include
the sale of loan participations among banks or packages of commercial
mortgages among thrifts, and yet excludes not only traditional bank
lending but also similar activities at finance and insurance companies.

A narrower definition refers to the pooling and repackaging of loans
or generally illiquid assets of banks, thrifts, and other intermediaries for
sale in securities forms in the financial market (BIS, 1986; Cumming,
1987; Pavel, 1989; Federal Reserve Board, 1989; Bryan, 1989;
Borkowski, 1991; and Kavanagh, 1992). As such, asset (or credit) securitization is simply a "subset of a broader trend seen throughout the capital
markets for many years, 'securitization', that is, the general phenomenon
whereby more and more fund raising is occurring through the agency of
securities." (Rosenthal and Ocampo, 1988, p.3)

While the selling of whole loans dates back to the 1880 (Pavel,
1989), securitization is a recent innovations in loan sales. Like whole
loan sales and participations, securitization provides an additional funding source and may eliminate the assets form the originator's balance
sheet. Unlike whole loan sales and participations, securitization is often
used to market loans that would be difficult to sell on a stand-alone basis.

The US government can be credited with the creation of securitized
assets and the initiation of a process that was unknown prior to 1970 and
that was relatively unused prior to 1985. Through the creation of three
quasi-government agencies: The Government National Mortgage Association (Ginnie Mae), the Federal Home Loan Mortgage Corporation
(Freddie Mac), and the Federal National Mortgage Association (Fannie
Mae), the government achieved its goal of establishing a secondary
mortgage market[19]. The existence of these agencies helped standardize
mortgage underwriting and documentation, eventually leading to Ginnie
Mae's development of the first "securitized" assets.

GNMA[20] issued the first pass-through mortgage-backed securities
in 1970. This issue was collateralized by single family Federal Housing
Administration and Veteran Administration mortgage loans[21] (Hempel et
al., 1990). Since its inception in 1970, the volume of outstanding US
government agency-related, mortgage-backed securities has increased to
$1.8 trillion (see Figure 3-1), representing 40% of all mortgage debt out-
standing as of 1995 year-end (Federal Reserve Bulletin, 1996).

The success realized by these agencies generated interest and participation by other financial institutions. Commercial banks, savings and loan
associations, and various non-deposit taking firms started to securitize

multi-family and commercial mortgage loans, automobile loans, credit card receivables, computer and truck leases, loans for mobile homes, various trade receivables, and other types of assets, as demonstrated by Figure 3-2 below. In the mortgage sector, the majority of asset-backed securities are collateralized by single-family, residential mortgage loans. Credit card installment loans have dominated the non-mortgage sector.

From the very beginning, banking organizations have been involved in the securitization process as originators and securitizors of residential mortgages. Over the last decade commercial banks, little by little, have steered away from the mortgage-backed securities market and focused on the securitization of consumer installment debt. According to the Federal Reserve, around 38% of all outstanding credit in the United States is in the form of installment loans, of which 20% have been securitized at 1995 year-end.

Also, many banking organizations have increased their reliance on securitization for funding, and have acted as servicers or trustees for securitized assets, and have increased their holdings of asset-backed securities. More recently, banking organization have begun to purchase asset-backed securities and their derivative instruments for investment,

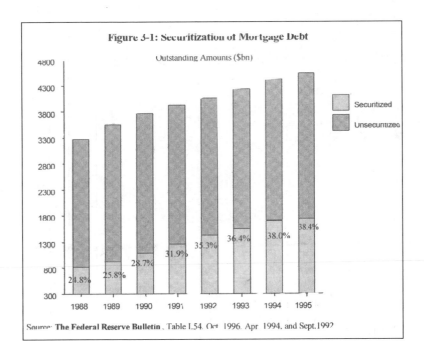

Figure 3-1: Securitization of Mortgage Debt

Figure 3-2: Types of Public Issues of Non-Mortgage Related Assets Securitized

1985	1986	1987	1988	1989	1990	1991	1992	1995
Auto Loans	Auto Loans	Auto Loans	Auto Loans	Auto Loans	Auto Loans	Auto Loans	Auto Loans	Auto Loans
Computer Leases	Computer Leases	Credit Card Receivables	Credit Card Receivables	Credit Card Receivables	Credit Card Receivables	Credit Card Receivables	Credit Card Receivables	Credit Card Receivables
		Mack Truck Loans	Mack Truck Loans	Mack Truck Loans	Mack Truck Loans	Mack Truck Loans	Mack Truck Loans	Mack Truck Loans
		Manufactured Home Loans	Manufactured Home Loans	Manufactured Home Loans	Manufactured Home Loans	Manufactured Home Loans	Manufactured Home Loans	Manufactured Home Loans
		Trade Receivables	Trade Receivables	Trade Receivables	Trade Receivables	Trade Receivables	Trade Receivables	Trade Receivables
		Auto Leases	Auto Leases	Auto Leases	Auto Leases	Auto Leases	Auto Leases	Auto Leases
		Unsecured Consumer Loans	Unsecured Consumer Loans	Unsecured Consumer Loans	Computer Leases	Student Loans	LDC Debt	LDC Debt
		Equipment Notes	Equipment Notes	Equipment Notes	HTL Loans	HTL Loans	HTL Loans	Non-Performing Notes
		Junk Bonds	High Yield Notes	High Yield Notes	High Yield Notes	High Yield Notes	Health Care Receivables	Health Care Receivables
			RV Loans	RV Loans	RV Loans	RV Loans	RV Loans	Trade Factoring
			Boat Loans	Boat Loans	Boat Loans	Boat Loans	Boat Loans	Boat Loans
				Insurance Premium Loans	Insurance Premium Loans	Insurance Premium Loans	Insurance Premium Loans	Insurance Premium Loans
				Other Leases	Other Leases	Other Leases	Other Leases	Franchise Loans
								Small Business Loans
								Equipment Loans

Source: Various Issues of *Asset Sales Report*, 1985–1995

hedging purposes, and asset-liability management purposes (United States Congress, 1991).

The achievement of the secondary mortgage market makes it hard to understand why the securitization of mortgage and non-mortgage assets by institutions other than government agencies has taken so long to develop. The annual volume of ABS securities issued by other than government agencies increased from slightly over $1 billion in 1985 to $108 billion by the end of 1995 (see Figure 3-3), nearly 5% of the total amount of mortgage-backed securities. And despite the growth rate of the market, only 17% of all consumer installment loans have been securitized, as opposed to around 40% in the mortgage segment (see Figure 3-4 below).

Tax law changes have reduced the benefits of traditional bank investments such as municipal securities[22] (Hempel et al., 1990). In addition, interest rate volatility has forced banks to become much more active in the management, not only of both sides of the balance sheet, but its off-side as well. The newly adopted risk-based capital guidelines has put increased pressure on institutions to raise capital, book quality assets, unload their balance sheets and/or control asset growth. This, coupled with both national and international debt problems, has emphasized the

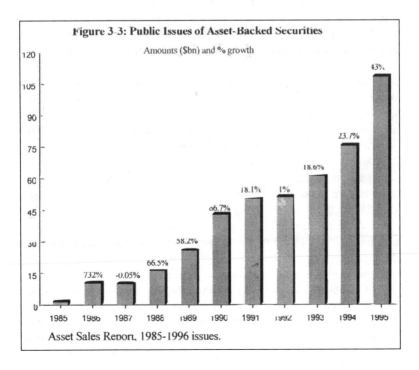

Figure 3-3: Public Issues of Asset-Backed Securities

Amounts ($bn) and % growth

Asset Sales Report, 1985-1996 issues.

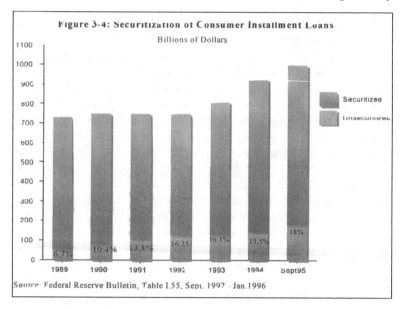

Figure 3-4: Securitization of Consumer Installment Loans

Source: Federal Reserve Bulletin, Table I.55, Sept. 1992 - Jan.1996

desirability of liquidity and marketability of bank assets while generating acceptable returns on equity to the shareholders.

With all these changes in the world of commercial banking, bankers have moved towards full utilization of banks' existing resources and expertise, seeking to achieve better economies of scale. Through new products and services and enhancement of existing ones, value is added for which banks can assess a fee. Commercial banks are more and more looking for ways to increase fee income while moving assets off the balance sheet. One course of action in the pursuit of such goal is through the securitization of bank assets (Zweig, 1989).

A probable reason for this is that previously there was no incentive for banks to develop the technology necessary to create other types of asset-backed securities; however, deregulation has necessitated major changes in the way commercial banks do business (Moss, 1989). Increased competition from thrifts, investment banks, and nonbank companies has narrowed net interest margins and made funding asset growth through core deposits hard to achieve (Cumming, 1987; Moss, 1989), and thus, asset securitization more attractive as a funding source.

In addition to the difficulty in raising funds, deregulation has resulted in an increased cost for all deposit liabilities for commercial banks. This expense, when passed on to borrowers, has resulted in banks' prime customers deciding to directly access capital markets at a cheaper cost. The entry of finance companies owned by manufacturers into the consumer market has practically eliminated indirect automobile financing in some financial institutions because the net interest spreads are not sufficient to remain in that line of business (Moss, 1989).

ASSET SECURITIZATION VERSUS BANK INTERMEDIATION

> *"Financial futurologists—mostly resident at universities, consulting firms and think-tanks—believe almost unanimously that securitization will defeat intermediation as surely as capitalism triumphed over communism. . . . If securitization goes far enough, banks will become little more than managers of mutual funds holding portfolios of liquid securities. Like mutual funds they would mark their assets to their market values"*
> *—THE ECONOMIST*, 1992

Throughout most of history, lending money has been a straight-forward business and the fundamentals of lending have remained essentially the same. Banks have provided depositors with safe, liquid instruments in which to invest their funds and have taken those funds and lent them to borrowers under the agreement that they would be repaid with interest. In the process, banks absorbed the credit risk inherent in lending. Safety to depositors was provided by the bank's capital or by government backing in the form of deposit insurance or other type of support.

Different Forms of Intermediation

Almost all financial transactions involve some kind of intermediation at some point. The most significant exception is the direct issuance of commercial paper, although even in this case the holders are often financial intermediaries. Indeed, as was reported by *The Economist* (1992, p. 10) commercial paper "looks like the most extreme form of 'Disintermediation'." The term intermediation covers several functions. In its simplest form, it is brokerage where borrowers are matched with lenders for a fee. A second form of intermediation is underwriting. Once again, borrowers and lenders are matched together. This time, however, the underwriter bears and absorbs uncertainties about the demand for the securities in return for a certain spread (Cumming, 1987).

A third type of intermediation is carried out by money market mutual funds. It involves selling shares in a pool of assets, where returns to the investor are based on the return of the portfolio of assets the fund holds[23]. Besides matching lenders with borrowers, the principal benefit of a mutual fund is that it can offer an investor a liquid and diversified investment with a low minimum denomination.

A fourth kind of intermediation, known as traditional intermediation, is the one performed by depository institutions, insurance companies, and finance companies. Such financial firms make loans and issue liabilities against the intermediary as a whole. They absorb the interest rate and the funding risks over the life of their loans. They will generally also transform maturities and absorb credit losses, and in the case of banks, thrifts, and finance companies, issue fairly liquid liabilities against rather illiquid assets.

The new technology for lending—asset securitization is beginning to render the classic bank intermediation process obsolete. Under the traditional system, the same institution would originate the loan, structure the terms, absorb the credit risk, fund the asset, and service the collection of principal payments and interest. Under the new system, several different institutions might be involved, each of which might play different roles (Bryan, 1989).

The process of transferring saving and borrowing activities from banks to non-banks is known as disintermediation. Historically, bank disintermediation has occurred whenever bank borrowers or savers could get a better deal from non-bank alternatives. In the United States, disintermediation took place when market interest rates rose above the ceilings set by Regulation Q. Today, bank disintermediation is being driven by increasing deposit insurance premiums, the high cost of raising bank capital, and, in some instances, the inability to raise capital (Napoli and Bacr, 1991). As a response to these pressures, banks are *initiating* disintermediation, shrinking both to control risk and to remain in compliance with regulatory requirements.

Securitization is different in kind from disintermediation. Broadly, while securitization breaks with traditional financial intermediation, disintermediation tries to emulate it. Unlike securitization, disintermediation does not change the form of financial claims to any extent. Rather, it shifts the holding of particular kinds of claims when the traditional holder is constrained by institutional features such as deposit interest rate ceilings, capital requirements, and the like. Securitization, by contrast, changes the form of claims—from loans to securities—and through that change also alters the distribution of holdings among types of investors.

Still, securitization and dsintermediation are not entirely distinct, since both involve a shift of intermediation away from banks and thrifts.

Aspects of Bank Disintermediation

Since their introduction in 1972, money market mutual funds (MMMFs) have facilitated disintermediation by making it possible for savers to indirectly purchase small portions of a large pool of high denomination money market instruments—such as commercial paper. In 1980, MMMFs held $77 billion in assets, 3.5% of total bank and thrift deposits. In September 1993, MMMFs held $409 billion in assets, roughly 15% of total bank deposits (Federal Reserve Bulletin, 1994).

In the past decade the number of mutual funds more than trebled, to around 4,500. Their assets have grown more than sixfold to around $2 trillion, not far short of the $2.7 trillion held in deposits within the American banking system (Federal Reserve Bulletin, 1994). And the composition of mutual funds has changed. In 1982, money market funds (which buy mainly treasury bills and commercial paper) accounted for more than 70% of all mutual fund assets. Today they make up only about 30% (*The Economist,* 1993a, p.11). Mutual funds have become a well-established part of household finances: it has been estimated that up to 28% of American households own a mutual fund, up from 6% in 1980. Between 1980 and 1990 the proportion of American household assets held in bank deposits fell from 46% to 38% (*The Economist,* 1994, p. 11). American households have clearly been finding bank intermediated finance increasingly unattractive relative to other investment alternatives (see Figure 3-5 below). Indeed, in the 1988–1992 period, while stock and bond funds and money market funds grew by 108% and 51%, respectively, Savings accounts grew by a meager 27%. Small denomination CDs have even registered a negative growth during the same period (Washington Post, April 24, 1994, H1)[24].

It is, meanwhile, not only savers who are fleeing the banks. Borrowers have shown equal shift in their financial habits. It used to be that companies in need of capital would turn automatically to banks. Nowadays, more companies take their borrowing needs directly to the capital markets by issuing short-term promissory notes, known as commercial paper. According to *The Economist* (1992, p. 10) "[c]ommercial paper seems to be a crueler form of securitisation. Indeed, it is not really securitisation at all, since it spends no time at all on banks' balance sheets. Instead its issuance supplants short-term bank loans to investment-grade companies."

In 1970 commercial lending by large banks made up 65% of the

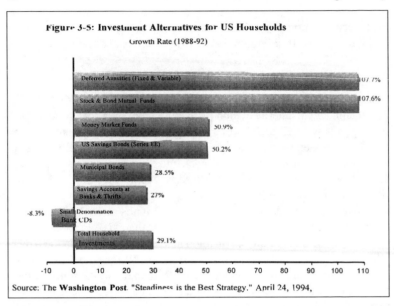

Figure 5-5: Investment Alternatives for US Households
Growth Rate (1988-92)

Source: The **Washington Post**. "Steadiness is the Best Strategy." April 24, 1994,

total short-term borrowing of non-financial companies. By the end of 1992 the banks' share had plunged to 36% (*The Economist,* 1994, p.11). At first, only blue-chip companies could raise capital by issuing commercial paper, but the practice has inexorably moved down the credit spectrum. The amount of outstanding commercial paper totaled $530 billion by the end of 1991, up from $325 billion in 1986 (*The Economist,* 1992, p. 10). Non-financial commercial paper issuance has increased by more than 80% during the same period (Napoli and Baer, 1991).

In order to offer customers lower funding costs, banks have increasingly sold C&I loans to investors outside the banking system thereby avoiding mandatory capital and reserve requirements, and deposit insurance premiums. Although an interbank loan sales market has been in existence for many decades, the sale of banks loans to nonbanks is a relatively new phenomena. Nonbank C&I loan purchases from commercial banks rose to $19 billion in 1990 as compared to $9 billion in 1987 and only $.7 billion in 1985. The 1990 nonbank loan purchases represents almost 6% of commercial loans held by large U.S. banks and almost 25% of total secondary market commercial loan sales (Napoli and Baer, 1991). A substantial portion of these loans was used to fund mergers, acquisitions, leveraged buyouts, and recapitalization, the so-called highly leveraged transactions (HLTs)[25.]

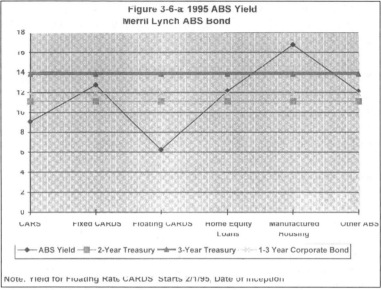

Figure 3-6-a 1995 ABS Yield
Merril Lynch ABS Bond

Note. Yield for Floating Rate CARDS Starts 2/1/95, Date of inception

Source: Based on data from Asset Sales Report, January 8, 1996.

WHY SECURITIZE?

Technological advances and innovations bring benefits, and asset securitization is no exception. Borrowers, originators (that is, banks, thrifts, finance companies, or other intermediaries making loans to ultimate borrowers), and investors all may reap the advantages from this innovation. Asset Securitization can lead to more efficient financial markets (reduced costs of intermediation for both loan originators and borrowers, a more complete market for investors[26] and a better satisfaction of regulatory objectives of safety and soundness (Rosenthal and Ocampo, 1988).

Benefits to Borrowers

Asset-Backed securitization can provide borrowers with cheaper sources of funds. This benefit is already evident in residential mortgages. Home buyers are now paying approximately 100 basis points less in interest (versus U.S. Treasury yields) on fixed-rate mortgages than they used to a decade ago when the securitization of mortgage was much less pervasive. GMAC, for instance, was able to raise funds at 130 basis points below the cost of traditional lending (Euromoney, 1989). In more recently securitized loans, such as automobile and credit card receivables, savings achieved through securitization have not yet been passed on to borrowers, but some believe that it should not be long in coming (Rosenthal and Ocampo, 1988).

Benefits to Investors

Credit securitization has offered new investment instruments for mutual funds, insurers, pension funds, and other investors (Please refer to Figure 3-6 Below). In addition, these securities offer a greater level of protection from rating downgrades than traditional debt securities. Unlike a normal corporation, a special purpose vehicle cannot be restructured by management through increased leverage or other means. Investors in these assets are, therefore, protected from the event risk that the originator's credit quality may deteriorate.

Institutional and other investors have been increasingly turning to ABS securities as investment channels. One reason may be that ABS securities, on average, offer higher yields than comparable government and corporate securities. Figure 3-6a above indicates that for the year 1995, yields on Manufactured Housing were at least 500 basis points higher than 2-year treasury notes, 450 basis points over 1–3 year corporate bonds, and 300 basis points over 3-year treasury notes.

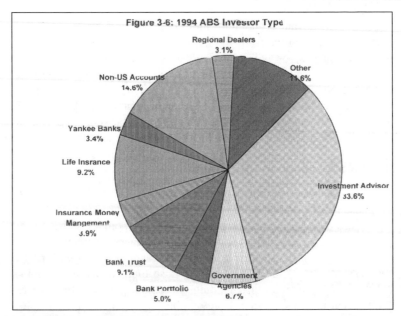

Figure 3-6: 1994 ABS Investor Type

Source: Author's compilations, Asset Sales Report 1994–1995.

Benefits to Loan Originators

Traditionally, the functions of lending and funding were bundled into an integrated process and asset size and growth were simply proxies for greater competitive advantage. The combination of new technology, deregulation, and nonbank competition, however, has weakened the correlation between asset size and competitive advantage.

Credit securitization provides banks with the technology to break this once vertically integrated process of lending and funding into a discrete series of steps. "Many banks are now reevaluating each function of their value-added chain—origination, servicing, and funding—to determine where they possess a competitive advantage." (Kopff and Lent, 1988, p. 14) Such reevaluation has led them to focus on a limited number of roles (or a single role) in the process and to build a competitive advantage through specialization and distinctive economies of scale and scope (See Figure 3-7).

Initially, the bulk of securitized assets have been collateralized by assets originated and serviced by the same banks. Increasingly, however, these banks (money center and super-regional banks) have been looking beyond their own portfolios to provide securitization services to other financial institutions for a fee.

Bypassing Regulatory Costs/Generating of Fee Income Stricter government capital-adequacy requirements have made it increasingly expensive for banks to keep loans on their balance sheets. Although banks can still earn a fee by originating and sometimes by servicing the loans, they are understandably reluctant to hold them.

For many banks, the holding of loans is no longer seen as an attractive business in its own right, and forms a rapidly diminishing proportion of banking profits. Taking the case of Chase Manhattan, for instance, fifteen years ago, nearly 80% of its revenues would have been net interest income (a fair proxy for such loan activity). By 1993 this share had dwindled to about 56%, and Chase expects to drop further. The bank expects to earn more in the future from fee income and less from the holding of loans. A decade ago, says Art Ryan, the bank's new president, Chase would have originated *$2 billion-3 billion in mortgage loans*. "Today we originate about *$17 billion* in mortgage loans, but we keep very few of them on the balance sheet. We originate them, we put them in the form of securities, selling them to investors who do want to put them on the balance sheet, retain the servicing right and get paid for them." (The Economist 1994, p.20)

332

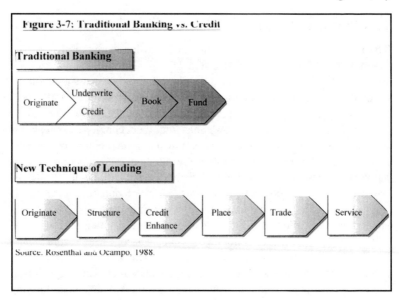

Figure 3-7: Traditional Banking vs. Credit

Source: Rosenthal and Ocampo, 1988.

Lowell Bryan of McKinsey, a management consultancy, estimates that the total cost of intermediating a security over the lifetime of an asset is well under 50 basis points. In contrast, the cost of bank intermediation is well over 200 basis points. Lowell has been arguing for many years that securtization is much more than a new financial technology. It is, he says, an alternative system to banking, and an intrinsically efficient one, not only because of the cost savings, but because of the inherent liquidity embedded in securities and the ability to fix their value in a marketplace (*The Economist,* 1994, p. 11).

Therefore, in the case of banks and thrift institutions, the selling of assets in such a fashion in order to meet the regulatory requirements for removal from the balance sheet might mean substantial cost savings by having avoided capital maintenance requirements. If an asset that is originated meets the legal and regulatory accounting requirements for sale (addressed in section 7 of this chapter) and, thereby, be removed from its books, the cost associated with capital and reserve requirements may have been eliminated, or greatly reduced, by securitization (Rosenthal and Ocampo, 1988).

In process-intensive businesses (e.g., the origination and servicing of credit card, auto loan, and residential mortgage portfolios), financial institutions have an economic interest in growing the customer base from which they earn origination and servicing fees in order to reach economies of scale and competitive advantage. Funding this growing asset base, however, would strain the balance sheets that are already over-leveraged and often would lead to over-concentration in a single asset type (Albert, 1991; Federal Reserve System, 1990a). Securitization has allowed institutions to grow the source of *fee income* without straining the balance sheet. "By securitizing loans, banks can remove assets from their books and either invest the proceeds in a more lucrative venture or begin the loan origination again and utilize *turnover and volume* to generate profits[27]" (Morrison, 1988, p.156). As a result, banks may achieve a higher return on equity and a higher quality of earnings, that is, having *predictable sources of noninterest* income as *opposed to highly volatile earnings pegged to interest rate fluctuations* (Kopff and Lent, 1988).

Funding and Liquidity Securitization provides originators with an additional source of funds, and is sometimes referred to as furthering "asset-based" liquidity (Federal Reserve System, 1990a). It allows securitizors to free up funds tied to already outstanding loans and meet fund the demand for new loans. Furthermore, proceeds from asset securitization are not subject to regulatory taxes such as reserve requirements and insurance costs, thus making securitization a more attractive source of funding/liquidity compared to traditional deposits.

In most cases, securitized issues carry a higher credit rating than the debt obligations of the originator. This is generally achieved by use of what is termed a bankruptcy-remote vehicle such as a trust that acts as a repository for the assets and issuer, or obligor, of the securities funding those assets. This improved rating (triple A in most cases) affords the originator savings on funding costs and also substantially broadens the investor base available to the originator.

One key element to the success of securitization is the ability to arbitrage credit ratings of assets. The credit rating of the asset-backed security is generally greater than that which would be assigned to securities directly issued by the bank and collateralized by those same assets. While there are costs associated with the mechanical process of obtaining higher rating, in most cases these costs are less than those associated with direct funding, thereby making securitization a more effective means of funding.

It is argued that the ABS market (excluding the one for MBS) has yet to become deep if banks are to use it as a lower cost of funding source. While this may be the case, the ABS market is certainly deeper than the market for the loans themselves.

Whereas the funding/liquidity benefits are perhaps most fully enjoyed by banks—because of the inherent comparative advantage banks have to generate credit—other corporations have been able to enjoy cost savings through the securitization of their assets. The use of a separate entity or a trust to hold the assets, and in turn funds its purchase of those assets by selling its own securities under an AAA rating allows corporations to realize cost savings similar to those enjoyed by credit generating entities (Federal Reserve System, 1990a).

Asset-Liability Management Asset securitization can be used to significantly reduce any interest rate risk associated with an asset-liability mismatch on the part of the originator (Albert, 1991; Ocampo, 1989; Pavel, 1989, and Kopff and Lent, 1988). In his 1989 article, Juan Ocampo, reporting the results of a survey conducted by Boston University's School of Management, states that "while securitization may not yet have been embraced wholeheartedly by senior bank officers, there appears to be widespread recognition of its potential. The promise of better managing interest rate risk seems to be perceived as the principle benefit although there is also some belief that the use of securitized credit can reduce funding costs."

Many thrifts started selling off their thirty-year fixed rate mortgages which were funded with expensive short-term deposits in order to achieve a better maturity match between their assets and their liabilities (Pavel, 1989). The same holds true for the captive finance subsidiaries of major auto makers, thus moving away from funding through the short-term commercial papers towards funding via asset-backed securities with a closer maturity to the asset being funded (Federal Reserve System, 1990a). In fact, securitization may be needed solely for this purpose, even though the cost of securitization might exceed the savings on funding attributable to improved ratings.

ACCOUNTING AND RISK BASED CAPITAL PROVISIONS AFFECTING ABSs

"Securitization transactions cover a wide spectrum of activities. At one extreme are outright, irrevocable, sales of assets or interest in assets. At the other end are borrowings collateralized by assets. In between are sales of assets with recourse to the seller and non-recourse borrowings collateralized by assets" (Stewart, 1989). While the transactions at the end of the spectrum are easy to account for, those in the middle create the accounting issues. That is, transactions in the middle have characteristics of both sales and borrowing. As a result, the design of particular structures and the related retention framework have given rise to important accounting ramifications and supervisory concerns. For asset securitization transactions are frequently structured to obtain certain accounting treatment, which, in turn, affect profitability and capital adequacy measures.

Accounting Treatment: GAAP vs. Call Reports

A key issue for management when asset-backed securities are issued is to determine whether the transfer should be treated as a sale of the pool or as collateralized borrowing. When sale treatment is permitted, the asset pool and the related liabilities are removed from the sponsor's balance sheet, thus resulting in higher performance and capital ratios. Accordingly, banks have generally sought to structure these transactions as sales.

Treatment of these transactions as financing, on the other hand, retains the pool of assets and related liabilities on the balance sheet. Except for few cases, asset securitization that involve risk retention by the transferring bank will generally result in financing treatment for regulatory reporting requirements.

Since its issuance in December 1983, FASB No. 77, *Reporting by Transferors for Transfers of Receivables with Recourse*, has become the main source of guidance relevant to the determination of "sale vs. financing" treatment of asset securitization for both public and private US corporations (Stewart, 1989, p.250). Treatment of securitized assets for purposes of the commercial bank Call Reports, however, was adopted long before the issuance of FASB 77 and has since been reaffirmed by the federal banking agencies. Prior to the adoption of FASB No. 77, the treatment of sales of assets with recourse under GAAP was the same as that specified in the Call Report instructions. While GAAP and the federal banking agencies generally follow the same guidelines in their treatment of securitization transactions, few differences do arise.

Assets Sold with Recourse Under GAAP FASB No. 77 defines recourse as the right of a transferee of receivables to receive payment for the transferor for the "failure of the debtors to pay when due, effects of prepayments, or adjustments resulting from defects in the eligibility of the transferred receivables." In addition, the Statement establishes three criteria that, if satisfied, permit a transfer with recourse to be recognized as a sale rather than a financing transaction:

- The transferor surrenders control of the future economic benefits relating to the receivables;

- The transferor can reasonably estimate its obligation under the recourse provisions, and
- The transferee cannot return the receivables to the transferor except pursuant to the recourse provision.

Call Report Instructions for Asset Sales with Recourse The Call Reports currently contain a general rule applicable to "sales of assets" other than participation in pools of residential mortgages. It stipulates that a transfer of loans or other assets is reported as a sale "only if the transferring institutions: (1) retains no risk of loss from the assets transferred resulting from any cause and (2) has no obligation to any party for the payment of principal or interests on the assets transferred resulting from any cause". Hence, a transfer involving any retention of risk of obligation for payment, even if limited under the terms of the transfer agreement, is considered a borrowing transaction and the entire amount of the assets transferred must remain on the books of the transferring institution.

Contrast between GAAP and Call Report Instructions The main difference between GAAP and Call Reports instructions lies in the criteria used for recognizing a transfer of receivables as a sale. FASB 77 uses the criteria of the transfer of benefits of ownership rather than of the transfer of both the benefits and the risks of ownership. For reporting purposes by banks, primacy has been given to the retention-of-risk standard, that is, where does the risk reside after the transfer of assets. "Transfers of assets are treated as sales if, in substance, they involve transfers of all the risks and rewards of ownership of the assets" (Federal Reserve System, 1990b). The three banking supervisory authorities, under the auspices of the Federal Financial Institutions Examination Council (FFIEC), after lengthy considerations, opted for the retention-of-risk standard in October 1985 (Federal Reserve System, 1990b, p.14)[28]. Accordingly, insured commercial banks must report the securitization of assets in concurrence with regulatory reporting requirements as set forth in the instructions to the Reports of Conditions and Income (Call Reports)[29]. Bank holding companies and their nonbank affiliates, on the other hand, need to follow GAAP standards in their accounting treatment of securitized assets[30].

The banking agencies cited a number of reasons for their decisions not to adopt FASB 77 for reporting purposes. FASB 77 establishes as a necessary condition for 'sale' that "future economic benefits are forfeited" and "the transferor's obligation under the recourse provisions can be reasonably estimated." The banking agencies acknowledge that it may be possible to make estimates for pools of consumer loans or residential mortgages, but may be very difficult, if not impossible, to achieve when it comes to commercial loans, construction loans, and loans to less developed countries. Furthermore, what is a 'reasonable' estimate at the time of the transfer may no longer be so at a later date (Federal System, 1990b). Hence, it was deemed that the existence of risk to the transferor a more relevant criteria for supervisory purposes than the transferor's ability to estimate this risk.

Other Accounting Matters Another principal accounting matter involved in asset securitization pertain to the consolidation of the issuing entity by the sponsor or other entity. The rules that deal with consolidation of subsidiaries with their parent companies for financial reporting purposes are contained in (1) FASB Statement No. 94, *Consolidation of All Majority-Owned Subsidiaries* of October 1987 and (2) FASB Technical Bulletin 85–2.

FASB 94 requires that all finance subsidiaries be consolidated for financial reporting purposes beginning of 1988. As a result this frequently used vehicle for off-balance sheet treatment of receivables and related debt by commercial companies was eliminated (Randall, 1990, p.66)[31]. The most common application of this provision was the nonconsolidation of finance subsidiaries of commercial/industrial parent companies. This practice is no longer acceptable under FASB 94. Finance subsidiaries of financial institution parents have been always consolidated by their parents and thus are not generally affected.

Technical Bulletin 85–2, which addresses collateralized mortgage obligations (CMOs), rules that a majority owned entity formed to issue CMOs is merely a conduit for the sponsor, and the financial statements of the entity should be consolidated with those of its sponsor. These special-purpose subsidiaries are therefore not affected by Statement 94[32].

Asset-Backed-Securities and the New Capital Requirements

The risk-based capital framework has three main features that affect the asset securitization activities of banking firms. First, certain asset-backed securities categories are often assigned risk categories that are lower than those assigned to direct holdings of the underlying pool of assets. This creates incentives for banking organizations to 1) securitize certain assets in order to lower their capital requirements and 2) hold US government agency or US-government—sponsored agency asset-backed securities because of lower capital requirements associated with these assets.

Second, bank holding companies that transfer assets with recourse as part of the securitization process now have to hold capital against their off-balance sheet credit exposures. Third, banking organizations that provide credit enhancement to assets securitization issues through standby letters of credit or by any other means will generally have to hold capital against the related off-balance sheet credit exposure. These two features can be expected to have raised the cost of securitization activities.

The risk weights assigned to an ABS depend on the issuer and whether the assets are mortgage-related assets. ABSs issued by a trust or single-purpose corporation and backed by non-mortgage assets are to be assigned a risk weight of 100%. Alternatively, if a bank issues an ABS, then the security is accorded a 20% risk weight regardless of the nature of the underlying pool of assets.

Securities guaranteed by US government agencies and those issued by US government-sponsored agencies are assigned risk weights of zero and 20%, respectively, due to the low degree of credit risk.

BASICS AND MECHANICS OF ASSET SECURITIZATION

The first step in securitization is to identify a pool of similar loans targeted for sale. The pool must be relatively homogenous with respect to credit, maturity, and interest rate risks to facilitate actuarial analysis of payment patterns as well as risks associated with these assets. This explains why the majority of assets banks have securitized have been mortgages, auto loans, and credit card loans. Most commercial and industrial loans have not been targeted so far largely because they lack elements of homogeneity and communality.

While the credit originator may choose to simply issue directly a bond collateralized by the pool of the identified assets, banks rarely recur to this approach. Direct issuance of the so-collateralized bonds means that the bond proceeds are subject to reserve requirements, the capital ratio will be affected, and the bank's credit rating is assigned to the securities (Federal Reserve, 1990a). Instead, a separate entity, commonly referred to as a bankruptcy remote vehicle, is generally established. The originator sells the pool of assets to that entity, and the entity uses the proceeds from securities it has issued backed by those assets to pay for the purchase of those assets from the originator (see Figure 3-8 below).

The second step then is to convey—or sell—the pooled assets to a trust or other remote vehicle. "Of paramount concern here is that a *true sale* has taken place", primarily for purposes of regulatory accounting

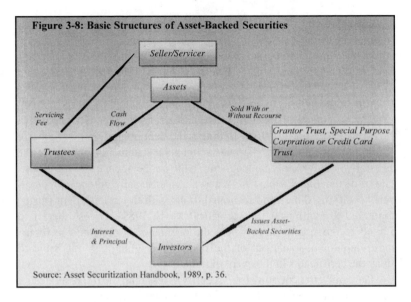

Figure 3-8: Basic Structures of Asset-Backed Securities

Source: Asset Securitization Handbook, 1989, p. 36.

practices (RAP), . . . and secondarily, for purposes of generally accepted accounting practices (GAAP) and matters of law—i.e., to insure "insulation between the originator and the issuer" (Federal Reserve, 1990a).

Basic Structures

Asset securitization involves different kinds of capital market instruments. These instruments may be structured as pass-throughs and pay-throughs. Each of these developed out of the secondary mortgage market and has been applied to non-mortgage assets. The legal structures underlying ABS are:

1. the grantor trust, ownership of which is evidenced by pass-through certificates; and
2. the bankruptcy-proof, special purpose financing corporation, which issues single—or multi-tranche bonds such as owner trust vehicles.

These structures isolate the assets in such a way that the limited rights and obligations of all parties are clearly defined (Asset Finance Group—The First Boston Corporation, 1989).

Pass-Through Securities Pass-through securities are single class payment instruments created when the loan originator pools a portfolio of like term and interest rate loans and sells them into a trust and certificates of ownership are sold to investors (Pavel, 1989; Moss, 1989; and Bryan, 1989). The originator is ordinarily the servicer of the portfolio. The role of the latter is to collects interest and principal and pass them on to the trust, generally a grantor trust, less a servicing fee. Ownership of the assets in the portfolio are no longer the debt obligation of originator and do not appear on the originator's financial statements, but that of the investor who buys a direct ownership in the pool evidenced by the certificate of ownership (Pavel, 1989). The servicer usually enters into a contract specifying duties and responsibilities with the independent trustee appointed to administer the securities (Moss, 1989). Unless there is a limited recourse provision, where the originator is obligated to repurchase delinquent loans out of the pool, the originator is not liable to repay the certificates in the event of default.

Generally, the coupon of the security is less than the interest rates on the underlying collateral (Moss, 1989). This generates an excess flow of cash that is retained by the originator/servicer with a portion going to pay other fees and the third party guarantor. In this structure, all payments of principal and interest received are "passed through" to investors as payment of the underlying assets is received. As a consequence, *"any pre-payment on the underlying asset must be passed on to security holders,* necessarily affecting the principal balance and therefore the yield to certificate holders" (Federal Reserve System, 1990a), thus the risk of loss of yield in the event of large prepayment.

Pass-through asset-backed securities are generally structured so as to qualify as participations in grantor trusts. Grantor trusts are non-taxable entities as long as the trust is passive in nature, i.e., the trustee is not allowed to purchase additional assets or the alter cash flows. IRS restrictions also requires that the trusts issues only a single class of security (Federal Reserve System, 1990a)[33]. Therefore, by their very nature, pass-through securities involve high prepayment risks. This is especially true in the case of pass-through mortgage-backed securities, which prepayment risk increases with falling interest rates[34]

The first and most common pass-throughs were Ginnie Mae issues collateralized by government-insured bonds (Pavel, 1989). This structure has two major drawbacks. First, it is limited to the issuance of only one class of securities, thereby limiting the number of interested investors. Secondly, the pass-through of all payments as received by the trust can result in irregular and/or rapid prepayment of the issue[35] (Moss, 1989).

Pay-Through Securities Pay-through bonds are collateralized debt obligations of the issuer and are usually set up through the creation of a financial subsidiary or a conduit into which a pool of assets is sold. Like pass-through, the originator usually continues to service these loans. Notes are then issued against this pool with the cash flows from the underlying dedicated to servicing payments on the bonds with any excess being retained by the issuer/servicer. Pay-throughs have a fixed interest rate and a set schedule of payments. The pool must always generate cash flows in excess of what is needed to retire the interest and principal in full of the outstanding obligation, usually resulting in over-collateralization of the issue.

The pay-through structure, with multiple classes, combines the cash flows from the underlying pool of assets and reallocates them to two or more issues of securities that have different cash flow characteristics and maturities. An example is the collateralized mortgage obligation (CMO), which has a series of bond classes, each with its own specified coupon and stated maturity. Pay-through certificates and the special purpose vehicle structures associated with them (owner trust) were developed to circumvent the cash flow restrictions associated with grantor trusts. Pay-through certificates also provide protection for investors against prepayment risks and allow for a broadening of the marketability of these securities to investors interested in maturities other than those generally associated with pass-through securities (Federal Reserve System, 1990a, 1990b; Moss, 1989).

Because ownership of their underlying collateral is retained by the issuer, pay-throughs are taxable entities under the Internal Revenue Code. Due to this classification, the issuer is free to structure the security into several classes, with different coupons and maturities. The interest income received is taxable and the interest paid on the debt is tax deductible. The issuer must be careful to structure the transaction as a debt rather than equity investment. To qualify, there must be equity present in the special purpose vehicle and cash flow from the underlying collateral cannot be closely matched to the cash flows to the bondholders. This is why payments are usually made on a quarterly or semiannual basis rather than monthly basis as might be expected from the most collateral payment characteristics.

The type of accounting and tax treatment desired by the issuing institution will determine the structure used to create the asset-backed security and the special purpose vehicle associated with it. The primary reason for favoring a pass-through over a pay-through structure would appear to be the issuing entity's desire to qualify the transaction as a sale for accounting and regulatory purposes. The primary advantages of a pay-through structure, on the other hand, are that the securities can be issued in multiple classes and there is limited prepayment risk to the buyers, thus making them very attractive to investors.

Since Freddie Mac developed the first CMO in June 1983, multi-class pay-throughs have become the most popular. According to the *Wall Street Journal* (April, 20, 1994, C1) CMOs constitute about half of the $1.5 trillion of the mortgage-backed securities outstanding. Growth in the MBS market has also induced the development of a wide array of different MBS derivatives (see Figure 3-9 below for a partial listing of ABS and MBS market instruments)[36]

These instruments, however, when tested with changing interest rate environment proved to be poor investment alternatives. Indeed, the latest increase in interest rates by the Fed "have caused the mortgage-backed securities market to unravel unpredictably across the board. Even under the best of circumstances, these bonds are difficult to manage, because their values depend on assumptions on how fast homeowners will prepay the mortgages that back these securities" and "[t]he problems are most evident in risky mortgage derivatives, such as 'principal only' strips and 'inverse floaters'" (WSJ, April 20, 1994, C1). Following is a more detailed description of the instruments offered in the structured finance market.

ABS Instruments: CARS and CARDS

Since the majority of non-mortgage-related issues have been backed by either automobile loans or credit card loans (73% of public issues in 1993), these two types of securitized credit will be discussed in detail[37]. There are some features that are common to both types of transactions. The issuer generally establishes some type of separate legal company or trust, a "bankruptcy-remote" entity, to which it can sell the assets. This is necessary to prevent the consolidation of the issue and its assets with the seller in the event of the seller's insolvency. In this way, the investors in the issue can continue to receive payments as scheduled.

Both types of securities are created through the selection of a discrete set of accounts. Funds received from these assets can not be commingled with other cash for any length of time on the seller's books or the security interest of the issuer might become unperfected.

CARD (Solomon Brothers' acronym for Certificates for Amortizing Revolving Debts) and CAR (Solomon's acronym for Certificates for Automobile Receivables) issues are collateralized by numerous, small dollar accounts with short maturities. Therefore, changes in interest rates would not have a major effect on the pay-down of the pools. In addition, due to this volume of small accounts, prepayment in general would not have a great effect on the yield, unless some economic stimuli generated prepayments greatly in excess of historical rates.

For both a CAR and a CARD, the issuer generally retains the right to call the security when the amount outstanding declines below a predetermined percentage of the original balance (usually between 5% and 10% of the original balance). This is a necessary feature to avoid having the cost of servicing a relatively small outstanding balance.

CAR Instruments Two basic structures have been used in the market of CAR issues. The first is a pass-through structure analogous to mortgage pass-through securities. The second type of structure is a "pay through" format analogous to cash flow bonds or CMOs. Pay-through structures can be used to create collateralized borrowings or multi-class structures.

The pass-through, utilizing a grantor trust format, is the most common format for CAR securities, since it achieves sales treatment for GAAP, tax, and legal purposes (Asset Sales Reports, 1990–94). In a typical pass-through, auto receivables are sold to a grantor trust, which issues certificates representing undivided interests in the trust. Principal and interest are passed through monthly as received. All principal received, together with interest at the pass-through rate, is paid to certificate holders. The spread between the loan rates and the CAR coupon is used to pay servicing fees, guarantee fees, and other expenses. In addition, the spread is often used to support the credit enhancement mechanism known as the spread account. As explained later, a spread account is a common mechanism for protecting third party credit enhancers from loss. Part or all of the interest earned on the auto receivables, in excess of the CARS coupon and monthly servicing fee, is placed in escrow to protect the credit enhancer's position.

Pay-through structures allow for active management of the cash flows. In this case, it is possible to add enhancements that afford a greater certainty to the cash flows. One such device is the GIC, or guaranteed investment contract, which guarantees a reinvestment rate on all cash flows received prior to its scheduled payment date. In effect, the GIC eliminates prepayment uncertainties and produces an investment opportunity similar in performance to a sinking-fund obligation[38]. Since greater cash flow certainty is attractive to investors, the pay-through structures usually result in tighter spreads to Treasuries than conventional pass-through securities. This would make this structure a more attractive alternative if it were not for the high setup and other costs involved with it[39].

CARD Instruments In spite of the enormous volume of these assets, the development of credit card asset-backed securities had been constrained by the complexity of credit card receivables, relative to installment receivables such as automobile loans, and the fact that even a sold portfolio of credit card receivables is affected by ongoing condition of the issuer and the industry. Indeed, credit card receivables have some unique characteristics. They generally pay down rapidly, having an average life of six to nine months (compared with 48 to 72 months for auto receivables). Balances fluctuate daily, as some accounts pay down and others increase, but historically, the balances of the overall portfolio of accounts increases—charges on accounts tend to exceed repayments. Yields are customarily high relative to the coupon rate on the securities issued, making a spread account a viable mean of enhancement (Federal Reserve Board, 1990a). It is worth noting, however, that one-third of all credit card users are "convenience" users, that is, people who repay charges on their accounts immediately and incur no finance charges (Federal Reserve Bulletin, 1992a. p. 663). This reduces the average yield on the protfolio from that being charged by banks; for example, if its rate on credit cards is 18%, the yield on the portfolio will be lower, perhaps 14%, because of the volume of convenience users and the volume of charge-offs experienced, making spread accounts less profitable than actually anticipated.

Despite these hurdles, in 1986, Saloman Brothers applied the emerging securitizing technology to credit card loans in a manner that allowed these loans to be restructured, credit enhanced, and sold to the broader investor community. Nowadays, CARDS represent 49% of the non-government agencies asset-backed securities (Asset Sales Report, Jan 22, 1996, p. 5).

MBS Instruments: CMOs, REMICs and IO/POs

The appeal of the MBS both as an investment vehicle for individual and institutional investors was soon to be recognized after the introduction of the first MBS in the early 1970s. Consequently, the demand for these types of securities, and their derivatives, witnessed an exponential increase during the last decade. The appeal of traditional fixed-rate MBS that were introduced in the 1970s, however, had serious drawbacks for some classes of investors. This was primarily attributed to the fact that prepayments on these securities were passed through to the MBS bonds.

Figure 3-9: Most Popular Instruments in the ABS Market.

Mortgage Derivatives

MBS: a pass-through securities representing an undivided ownership interest in the underlying mortgage loan.

CMO: a multi-class pay-through security representing a debt-obligation of the issuer supported by either whole loans or, more typically, pass-through securities.

REMICs: an extension of the basic CMO. They were created by 1986 tax reform legislation to avoid taxation and other tax—related restrictions of multi-class issues.

ARMs: Adjustable-, or Floating-Rate MBS. While most of MBSs (and ABSs) are fixed rate securities, a growing volume is issued with adjustable-rate and variable-rate coupons. The volume of ARMs is highly cyclical and tends to increase most when mortgage rates are falling. An important variant of ARMs are Floater/inverse floater combinations.

Floater/Inverse Floaters:

Inverse floaters are mortgage-backed security instruments (mostly REMICs) with a short average life and whose interest rate moves in opposite direction from short-term rates change. Generally, the coupon on the inverse floater is determined as [Cap − (Multiplier *Index)]. These are one of the growing sector in the securities market. Inverse Floaters are always combined with a floater in order to work as a fixed-rate security.

Stripped Mortgage-Backed Securities:

Two main types: IOs and POs. They have highly volatile price characteristics based, in part, on the prepayment of the underlying mortgage.

POs: Principle-only strip. POs will increase in value when interest rates decline (since prepayment shorten the maturity of mortgages.

IOs: Interest-only strip. IOs will increase in value when interest rates rise.

Non-Mortgage ABSs:

CARS: ABSs collateralized by car loans

CARDS: ABSs collateralized by credit card loans

Other types of ABSs have recreational vehicle (RV) loans, home equity loans, boat loans, and different types of equipment and machinery leases as collateral.

Since prepayments usually occur in a declining interest rate environment, MBS investors were faced with the reinvestment risk associated with their securities maturing at a time when comparable new instruments have lower yield. In addition, changes in prepayment rates cause balance sheet interest-rate risk to institutional investors, especially when the maturities of assets and liabilities become significantly different.

The possibility of prepayment affects mortgages in two ways. First, it reduces the potential capital gains to the investor when interest rates fall. Most fixed income investments' prices increase as interest rates fall, making it possible for them to trade above par. That is not true with MBSs. In case of a prepayment, the investor receives only the mortgages' outstanding principle, not any market premium. "This is equivalent to a borrower calling a bond away from an investor at its par value even though the bond's market value is selling above par." (Guttery and McCarthy, 1995, p. 19) Since falling interest rates increase the probability of prepayment, hence the redemption at par value, MBSs have limited potential appreciation relative to other bonds that do not have prepayment risk[40].

The second risk faced by MBS investors when rates fall is that of reinvestment. Because prepayments increase as rates fall, mortgage investors find themselves forced to reinvest at lower returns. This can cause a serious problem in forecasting investment cash flows and total returns[41].

In an attempt to minimize interest-rate and reinvestment risks associated with traditional, fixed-rate MBS, mortgage-backed derivatives, such as CMOs, REMICs and interest only/principal only securities (IOs/POs), were introduced in the market and emerged as important investment vehicles for the 1990s.

CMO and REMIC Instruments Freddie Mac introduced collateralized Mortgage Obligations in 1983. The main feature of the CMOs was to divide the cash flows from the traditional MBS into various maturity classes, often called 'tranches', thus making them appeal to a wider range of investors.

CMOs are made up of bond classes created by redirecting the cash flows of mortgage-related products in order to moderate prepayment risk. CMOs offer the same credit quality and yield advantages of mortgage pass-through securities. In most cases, the assets that make up the CMO collateral pools are pass-through securities (Federal Reserve System, 1990b). As mentioned above, CMOs, because of their debt rather than asset sales structure[42], had certain 'inefficiencies', such as a minimum capital requirement, built in their structure. This led to limited CMO issues.

The Tax Reform Act of 1986, however eliminated many of the structural inefficiencies of CMOs by authorizing REMICs—real estate investment conduits (Pavel, 1989). "Congress enacted the REMIC legislation largely in order to enable issuers to issue multi-class and multiple maturity securities without tax-related, structural constraints" (Rosenthal and Ocampo, 1988, p. 60). That is, mortgage issuers are not taxed at the REMIC level, irrespective of the legal from of the issuer or of the security. REMICs need not maintain the equity layer required to obtain the tax deduction status for debt. Since equity is much more expensive than debt, REMICs are more economic vehicles for mortgage issuers. All of these features broadened the customer base for MBS by "offering near U.S. Treasury credit quality, customized performance characteristics, attractive yields across a range of maturities, and a variety of risk/return profiles that fit investors' needs" (Ames, 1993, p.5). The success of REMICs is reflected in the fact that almost all multiple class-securities are issued as REMICs.

Types of REMICs Structures. According to the Internal Revenue Code, a REMIC may include any number of classes of "regular interest" and a single class of "residual interest". The Regular interest classes, or tranches, are often labeled by letters (A class, B class, etc). These classes are assigned a fixed, floating or zero interest rate; a fixed principal amount; and a variety of payment conditions. Often, one or more Z classes, similar to a zero coupon or accrual bond, are included as regular interest classes (Parks, 1993).

Starting from the basic structure described above, several innovations were introduced, making REMICs (or CMO structures) in general fall under one of two broad categories: 1) one that provides for the redirection of principle payments only. This is the case of sequential pay, PAC/Companion, and TAC/Companion structures, and 2) one that provides for the redirection of both principle and interest as is the case of floating rate CMOs and accrual Z bonds.

Sequential Pay Tranche. In the case of *sequential pay tranches*, principal on regular classes is usually returned sequentially in alphabetical order, i.e., to the shortest maturity class. All investors in a regular class (except principal only and accrual or Z classes) are paid interest currently on their pro rata share of remaining principal. Principal payments to individual tranches do not start until previous tranches are retired. For instance, in the case of a four-tranche REMIC: A, B, C and Z, while tranche A receives payment on both principal and interest, tranches B and C receive interest payments only. After the tranche A is repaid in full, investors in the B tranche begin receiving payment on principal as well.

The final tranche, usually the accrual tranche Z, receives no interest payment until other classes have paid down. Instead, interest accrues and the balance of the Z tranche grows at the coupon rate of interest, compounded monthly, until all other priority classes have been retired. At that time, the Z tranche converts to an ordinary interest-paying mortgage security that pays principal monthly until it is fully amortized (Parks, 1993). In some REMICs, the Z tranche receives principle, but no interest from the underlying MBS, similar to a zero coupon bond.

Planned-Amortization Class (PAC) bonds. PACs are similar to a sinking fund bond and offers the greatest degree of cash flow certainty to the investor. A REMIC structure can contain a number of PAC tranches. The PAC investor is set to receive fixed payment over a predetermined period of time under different prepayment scenarios. The right to cash flows are arranged to give PAC holders first right to certain cash flows over all other class holders. Faster-than-expected prepayments will pay down other "support tranches" first, thus insulating the PAC investor from increased prepayments and providing call protection. The other classes within the REMIC structure, often referred to as *companion* or *support* tranches, absorb excess cash flows and make up for shortfalls. Their average lives may be extremely variable for they bear substantial prepayment risk (Parks, 1993; Hyre and Pendergast, 1993). PACs have become so popular that, by the end of 1993, they were estimated to account for up to 70% of all tranche issues.

Recently, PACs have been structured with varying protection levels and yield trade-offs. The most common variant types are primary and secondary PAC classes. Secondary PAC bonds offer less protection than Primary ones and are compensated for that through higher yields (Parks, 1993).

Targeted-Amortization Class (TAC) bonds. Like the PAC, a targeted amortization class is designed to pay a specific or "targeted" amount of principal to the class holder each month. A TAC structure, however, typically provides protection only against increasing prepayments and early retirement (Parks, 1993). If prepayment increases, excess cash flow will be paid to non-TAC tranches, or companion bonds, rather than speeding up the retirement of the TAC. This bond offers more protection than sequential pay bonds, but less than PAC bonds. Like PACs, TACs structures offer variants such as primary and secondary TACs.

Floating Rate CMOs: Floaters and Inverse Floaters. The first floating-rate CMO (FRCMO) was issued on September 22, 1986. The interest rate on a floating-rate tranche, or *floater*, adjusts periodically relative
to a spread over a specific benchmark, usually the LIBOR. Floaters are
always paired with an *inverse floater*[43] having an interest rate that moves
in reverse of the benchmark index. Structurally, the floater/inverse floater
works in tandem as a fixed-rate security (Epstein, 1993, p. 33).

The floater/inverse floater combination can be created from any security or CMO class which collateral is stripped into two parallel classes: a
floating rate and a second one, which will float inversely to it. The coupon
on both is reset regularly, using the same base index. Inverse floaters have
caps and floors. Together, floaters and inverse floaters are matched so that
the impact of a higher coupon on one tranche is exactly offset by a lower
coupon on the other. There is frequently a *leverage factor* (or multiplier),
since the two cash flows must offset perfectly, not the face amounts of the
floaters and inverse floaters.

If, for example, the formula that determines the coupon change for
the inverse floater is as follows: [40% – 4.6 * LIBOR][44]. The multiplier,
4.6 in this case, determines the impact of the index movement on the inverse floater coupon. The coupon will change inversely by 4.6 times the
movement of LIBOR. In a floater/inverse floater structure, the multiplier
on the inverse floater is generally equal to the ratio of floaters to inverse
floaters[45]. And if, according to our example, there are 4.6 times as many
floaters as inverse floaters, a 10 basis point decline in one-month LIBOR
will create a 10 basis point decline in the floater's coupon while the 4.6
multiplier will create an exact dollar offset with a 46 basis point increase
in the inverse floater's coupon. In the same vein, should the LIBOR increase by 100 basis points, the inverse floater's coupon will decrease by
460 basis points[46].

Investing in Floaters/Inverse Floaters. The appeal of inverse floaters
is the ability to profit from a steep yield curve through leverage and a
significant interest margin. The greater the leverage available to the investor, the higher the potential returns on investment and, consequently,
the greater the risk. The Inability to accurately predict prepayment rates
makes investing in MBS inverse floaters exceptionally risky.

The purchaser of the inverse receives the interest differential between the coupon of the fixed-rate bond and the coupon of the floater
tranche. The price of the inverse will be determined primarily by the
value of the underlying fixed-rate bond and any embedded caps. It is,

therefore, conceivable that the price of an index floater could decline even if the index on which it is based falls (Borg, Lancaster, and Tang, 1992, p. 486). The common misconception about inverse floater is that "[m]any investors mistakenly expect the price of an inverse floater to increase with a decline in short-term rates. In fact, major impact on the price of inverse floaters comes from changes in long-term rates, since so many inverse floaters are created out of long average life, fixed rate cash flows." (Winchell and Levine, 1992, p. 519) In the particular case of mortgage-backed securities, "[b]ecause the investor, in effect, has purchased a long position in the underlying fixed-rate bond, the yield of the entire investment position will be affected if prepayment speeds change." (Borg et al., 1992, p. 486) Furthermore, the "yield of inverse floaters that have greater leverage or are backed by more volatile classes of bonds . . . will be affected more by changing prepayments[47]." (ibid)

Prepayments are affected by movements in interest rates. When rates fall, it is possible that prepayments increase, causing a shortening in the average life of the security just when it is least desired since the coupon of the inverse would have increased. Similarly, when rates rise and the inverse coupon declines, the average life of the underlying asset will increase if prepayments slow, again when it is least desired. "In general, the less negatively convex the collateral, the better the inverse floater." (Borg et al., p.487) Thus, inverse floaters backed by longer term, lower coupon mortgages will tend to have better average life stability and convexity characteristics.

Stripped MBSs, IOs/POs. Stripped mortgage-backed securities (referred to as IOs/POs) separate mortgage-backed securities into principal payments and interest payments. Interest-only (IO) segments perform better in sustained rising-rate environments because their cash flow pattern is heavily loaded toward the early years and the cash flows become available for reinvestment at higher and higher interest rates. The principal-only (PO) segments perform well in falling-rate environments because of increase in prepayments. Prepayment of principal, however, causes a lesser accumulation of interest payment, thus, depressing the value of the IO instruments. With IOs, neither the timing of receipt, nor the total amount of cash flow is guaranteed. Both IOs and POs have greater price volatility than that of the mortgage itself (Hempel et al., 1990, p. 632). An investor, therefore, would choose between IOs and POs based on the forecast of future interest rate movements. A bullish investor who expects rates to decline would buy a PO to benefit from the faster return of principle resulting from increased prepayments. A bearish investor looking for higher rates would select an IO. An IO's interest is based on the pool's outstanding principle, and slower prepayments generate a longer-lived cash flow, therefore, higher interest accrued.

Credit Enhancement

Since the purchaser of the securities generally does not get to examine the underlying assets, the foremost risk associated with investing in ABSs, as opposed to MBSs, is credit risk, or default on the underlying asset[48]. Minimization of this risk is achieved through credit enhancement mechanisms, the types and amounts of which are dictated by the quality of the underlying assets and nature of the security issued (Moss, 1989). Figure 3-10 below is a summary of the various credit enhancement and collateral types for non-government issues of asset-backed securities during 1993.

As can be seen, there was a noted preference for 'subordination /overcollateralization' as a credit enhancement mechanism. According to *Asset Sales Report*, "[t]he types of credit enhancement were driven largely by the types of issuance" (July, 1993). With auto issuance constituting more than 40% of total issues, the senior/subordinate structure was the most common form of credit enhancement. Enhancement through cash collateral has been less popular due to declining credit-card issuance[49].

Based on the historical profile of the underlying asset, the rating agency will dictate the amount of enhancement, or protection, necessary for any given security to be issued at the desired rating (Moss, 1989). The highest rated ABSs have generally enhancements at levels several times the highest historical default rates associated with the underlying assets (Federal Reserve System, 1989). For example, a credit card portfolio may have a historical loss rate of 3% and the enhancement would cover a 12% loss rate, four times the historical rate.

Credit enhancement may be provided by a third party or the originator, and in many instances, more than one type of enhancement is associated with a given security (Federal Reserve System, 1989). In the beginning of the non-government mortgage-backed market, credit enhancement was achieved by providing a pool of underlying collateral that was greater than the amount of the bond issue. But having to overcollateralize can reveal to be expensive as the tied up collateral can not be used for other purposes (Moss, 1989).

Senior/Subordinated Structure Due to the involvement of a third party as credit enhancer, there is always the risk of a downgrade in the security's rating in the event of a lowering of the credit enhancer's rating. The development of a senior/subordinated enhancement structure has helped alleviate this risk. In this type of structure, the subordinated portion is retained by the seller. The investors hold the senior debt and have first rights to all cash flows in the event of shortfalls, including cash flows to the subordinated interest (Federal Reserve System, 1990a).

Financial Guarantee Insurance Companies Due to the uncertainties of the corporate debt market, general insurance companies were not eager to expand into this business. Monoline financial guarantee companies were developed instead to provide this form of credit enhancement. Capital Markets Assurance Corporation, for instance, was specifically established by Citicorp to insure ABSs and other structured corporate financing (Milligan, 1988). Guarantees by insurance companies can be written the same way as LOCs, based on a percentage of the original issue or on the remaining pool balance.

Limited Guarantee and Spread accounts In some cases the transaction is structured as a general obligation of the issuer, or it is being guaranteed on a limited basis by the issuer or the parent company. This will work only if these corporations already enjoy a high credit rating. These types of guarantees and limited recourse have generally been provided by non-financial corporations (Moss, 1989, Asset Sales Reports, various issues). But for accounting and regulatory purposes, financial institutions have generally avoided providing recourse for their ABSs, for direct recourse is inconsistent with a regulatory sale of assets. This led to the development of a reserve fund, referred to as a spread account.

Spread, or incremental reserve account, have been mostly associated with auto loans and credit cards securities, as it "requires a sufficiently large difference, or spread, between the interest rates attached to the security and the rate of return on the underlying asset " (Federal Reserve System, 1990a). A spread account is, in essence, a reserve to cover losses and a mechanism whereby the originator absorbs initial credit risk without having a recourse provision built into the issue which would prohibit sale treatment (Zigas, 1987). The spread's account balance accrues over a period of time as cash flows come in from the underlying assets. The originator/servicer passes on all funds collected, and the spread account is then accrued from the difference between interest earned on the assets and that paid out to investors minus fees paid to the servicer and any other credit enhancers.

Letter of Credit Up to 1988, the most commonly used type of credit enhancement was the letter of credit (LOC), used either with another type of credit support or on a stand alone basis[50]. LOCs can be structured in two ways. They can provide coverage based on the remaining outstanding in the pool, which would be constantly decreasing as the pool is paid off. LOCs can also be based on the original amount issued, which would provide an increasing percentage of coverage as the balance of the pool decreased. The amount of LOC is usually equal to a multiple of the historical loan loss experience of the originator on that particular type of loans (generally three to four times that rate). The fee is also based on the loss experience of the issuer, usually 0.5% of the LOC balance (Ellspermann, 1988). An issue can not be rated higher than the rating of the provider of the credit provider, that is the main reason why the primary providers of LOCs are foreign financial institutions[51]

In many cases, a combination of two or more credit enhancement mechanisms is used. However, regardless of the enhancement(s) associated with the issue, initial credit losses are commonly borne by the originator. For example, credit-card-backed securities commonly have both a spread account and LOC to enhance them, with the spread account being the first line of defense against losses. The LOC issuer will only begin ab-

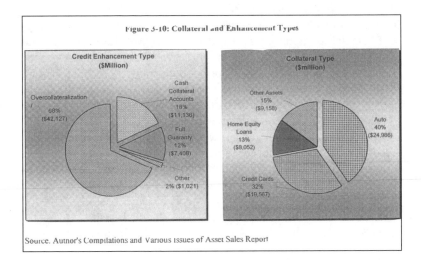

Figure 5-10: Collateral and Enhancement Types

Source. Autnor's Compilations and Various issues of *Asset Sales Report*

sorbing losses after the originator have absorbed losses via the spread account (Federal Reserve System, 1990a).

DIFFUSION OF ASSET SECURITIZATION TO INTERNATIONAL MARKETS

The European markets are, compared with the US, small and diverse and
in each country there are specific legal, tax, regulatory and accounting
problems that surmount before an issue can be brought to market. In
France, legislation to enable securitization specifically excludes the inclusion of receivables of less than two years' maturity. This rules out credit
card backed issues, presumably based on Bank of France concern about
the monetary control implications of allowing credit card securitization. It
is true, that as a group, European banks are better capitalized than their
US counterparts, reducing the incentive for securitization. Many also prefer to leave the relatively high-yielding credit card portfolios on their balance sheets. However, for some institutions, the capital pressures to
lighten balance sheets do exist and the attraction of securitization is there
if the obstacles are surmounted, and these obstacles are many.

Even in the UK, probably the most favorable regime in Europe for
securitization, the securitization of credit cards is an expensive option
unless a company plans to use the product over and over again. It has
been reported that in 1990, the legal bill alone for a ground-breaking
issue by Goldman Sachs of a car loan package of £328 million run well
into seven figures (*Financial Times,* 1991). Still, since 1992 there has
been a worldwide growing interest in asset securitization schemes, as
several countries in Europe, Asia and Australia have relaxed the rules and
laws governing asset securitization in their markets. The figures below
(Figures 3-11 and Figure 3-12) indicate both countries' market share in
MBS issuance and the evolution of the international residential MBS
market between 1992 and the first quarter of 1996).

A growing number of countries have embraced the technology. In
1995, German and Irish mortgages were securitized for the first time. The
Australian market has been active for some time. Hong Kong had its first
residential MBS issue in 1994 and more countries are expected to join in
once the technology standardized (Mortgage Banking, 1996, p. 78). As
indicated by Figure 3-11, non-US residential MBS has seen a steady
stream of issuance over the last four years. The total, however, was still
under $18 billion, representing issuance from eight different countries.

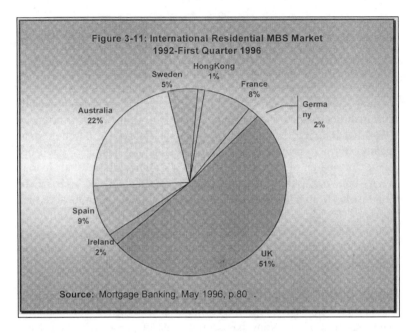

Figure 3-11: International Residential MBS Market
1992-First Quarter 1996

HongKong 1%
Sweden 5%
France 8%
Germany 2%
Australia 22%
Spain 9%
Ireland 2%
UK 51%

Source: Mortgage Banking, May 1996, p.80 .

Each of these countries, even those within the European market, has developed its market more or less independently from the others. To a large extent, however, the securitization technology was borrowed from

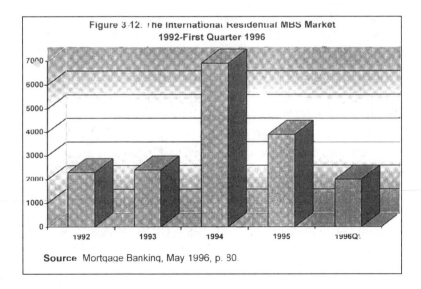

Figure 3-12: The International Residential MBS Market
1992-First Quarter 1996

Source Mortgage Banking, May 1996, p. 30.

the United States, even though the motivations to securitize and the legal and regulatory securitization frameworks remain unique to each country (Mortgage Banking, 1996, p. 0).

Latin American and Asian emerging market issuers are turning to securitization as an alternative and cheaper funding source when other sources are scarce. Asset securitization can enable borrowers, especially during difficult times, to tap foreign markets for valuable hard currencies (World of Banking, 1996). The International Finance Corporation, in an effort to further promote securitization in emerging markets, established in the first quarter of 1996 a new financial institution, the Global Guarantee Association. Its mission is to provide financial guarantee insurance on bond issues from emerging markets. The issues could be in local or hard currency (Project & Trade Finance, 1996, p. 26). Before that, the International Finance Corporation broke ground in the summer of 1995 with a pioneering securitization of loans from Latin and Asian companies, the first time a pool of loans to companies in developing countries has been securitized and sold through a public offering (Khan, 1995, p. 22–23).

Of special interest is the Asian market. Asset-backed bankers view the fast growing Asian region as a major source of new corporate and bank business. Hong Kong has seen a spate of property-backed deals, while securitization is also on the way in Thailand, Indonesia, Malaysia, and the Philippines. The region, however, holds considerable pitfalls, for many of the structural elements necessary for the creation of flourishing structured finance markets are not yet in place. According to Euroweek (1995a, p.26), three problems need to be addressed: 1. How to develop a triple-A debt sector in countries with lesser ratings, 2. How best to structure and sell deals to provide the best cost to issuers and reach the largest pool of investors, and 3. How to assess and control the various commercial and political risks in these new markets.

The German Market

Industrial and trading companies have for quite some time converted receivables and other financial assets into cash through factoring. There have also been several repackaging transactions involving the transformation of loans into tradable securities through the intermediation of special purpose vehicle or a bank (Asset Sales Report, 1992). However, when compared with the dramatic developments in America and, to a lesser extent, in European countries such as UK and France, asset securitization has been slow to develop in Germany—at least as it relates to assets other than home mortgages.

Ironically, development outside the mortgage sector may have been slowed to some degree by the fact that a form of mortgage-backed financing has been in existence in Germany for almost 200 years. Since 1769, private mortgage banks and their predecessors have funded their mortgage loans through the issuance of mortgage collateralized loans known as *Pfandbriefe*. The intent was solely to provide these banks with a funding instrument that took into account the long-term nature of their assets. Yet, the Pfandbriefe cannot meet the extended objectives that have caused the securitization boom in the US, where the financial technology involved in securitizing mortgages was readily transferred to other assets (Fugal, 1992). With a volume of Dm1.26 trillion, the German market for Pfandbriefe, or mortgage bonds, is the 7th-largest fixed-income market in the world and yet with limited appeal to foreign investors. Efforts to globalize the Pfandbriefe market encountered limited success. The Pfandbriefe are safe, but not that liquid. This is why bankers are finding it difficult to sell German asset-backed bonds to foreign investors (Bass, 1996, p.119–123).

In addition, some of the key forces driving the growth of the asset-backed market—most notably the need to meet international capital requirements—have not been a major concern for most German banks. It is believed, however, that political events such as German reunification and the development of a single market in Europe are expected to have a profound effects on the German economy and are likely to induce interest in asset-backed securitization as an important capital market instrument. More over, some German banks have been large purchasers of receivables and other financial assets from industrial and trading companies. The tougher capital ratios may discourage banks from buying such assets, thus opening up additional opportunities (Asset Sales Report, 1992).

Unlike France, there is no special legal framework for the securitization of assets in Germany. Nonetheless, from a purely legal prospective, asset securitization is feasible. The fundamental question is whether the benefits are worth the efforts and costs that the development of a viable structure involves.

A milestone was reached in German and European securitization in April of 1995 when JP Morgan structured and sold the first public German mortgage-backed bonds (Euroweek, 1995a, p. 24). The transaction combined residential, multifamily and commercial properties (Mortgage Banking, 1996, p.82). Although Germany's large Pfandbriefe (mortgage) market provides the bulk of the financing required by the country's mortgage lenders, it is estimated that the mortgage-backed bonds could appeal to investors seeking rated securities and originators liking to diversity their funding.

The first German non-mortgage-backed deal was issued by Volkswagen in February of 1996. The deal, issued in the United States, was sold out within hours of pricing largely to German investors that had already developed a taste for asset-backed securities (Asset Sales Report, Nov 4, 1996, p. 1,11). Other Deutsche Mark-denominated deals followed during the year, mostly encouraged by the new attitude espoused by the German financial authorities in their recently published proposed guidelines regarding securitization.

The British Market for Asset-Backed Securities

The UK asset-backed market, Europe's first and largest securitization sector, is suffering from a chronic lack of supply. The relentless erosion of the traditional issuer base—through the takeover and disappearance of several home loan specialists—has brought the mortgage-backed bond issuance to record low levels. Another problem has been the continued low level of residential mortgages despite relaxation in underwriting criteria. This low turnover has dominated the U.K. housing market since its last cyclical peak in 1988.

The mortgage-backed securities market started in 1987 and has suffered numerous setbacks. In May 1991 the market passed a milestone with the total amount of securities in issue reaching £10 billion (roughly $15 bn.). The market, however, had to struggle to survive as it underwent a crisis of investors confidence. Although new issues have continued to trickle on to the market, interest margins (that is, the spread over LIBOR) on securitized bonds have widened significantly and investors have shown interest in only shorter-term paper.

One reason for the fragility of the market during late 1991 was simply that investors were not willing buyers of sterling floating-rate securities. Following the entry of the UK currency into the European exchange rate mechanism in October 1990, sterling interest rates were widely expected to fall—as they have done[52]. In that environment fixed rate securities were the most attractive investment vehicle.

A second problem is the precarious state of the UK housing market, which knocked investor's confidence in securities backed by residential mortgages. Indeed 44,000 homes were repossessed in 1990 alone, three times the level of the previous year. As mortgage defaults were rising fast, it looked as if the UK mortgage market was heading for a crisis. Mortgage-backed securities were not a popular form of investment despite the different credit enhancement schemes attached to the securities and their triple-A rating.

Another blow came in January 1991, when the Accounting Standard Board and the Bank of England proposed new rules and accounting procedures when securitizing assets. The Accounting Standard Board proposed that all securitized assets should remain on the originator's balance sheet, thus removing a significant attraction of such arrangements. The Bank of England, on the other hand, said that UK banks would probably have to set aside more capital against holdings of mortgage backed securities than previously to comply with European legislation.

In 1991, the Bank of England ruled that the securities would have to carry a 100 percent risk weighting under its capital adequacy guidelines from January 1993, rather than 50% weighting—effectively doubling the amount of capital that banks are required to hold from that date (*Financial Times*, 1991). There were mounting pressure and concerns, however, that the liquidity of the market would dry up as many banks, a mainstay of the market's investor base, were driven away of the market. Accordingly, the Bank of England rescinded its plans to increase the risk weighting on mortgage backed securities from 50% to 100% late November of 1992 (*Financial Times*, 1992b). In mid-1996, the European Union itself has introduced rules that reduce the risk-based capital charges from 100% to 20%. (Asset Sales Report, Sept 16, 1996, p. 8)

An impetus to ABS market, however, came in March of 1992 when the Bank of England has given banks the go-ahead to securitize revolving credit, provided that the amount taken off the balance sheet does not exceed 10% of the bank's capital base. The Bank of England has come to consider securitization schemes involving the transfer of a pool of receivables to a special purpose vehicle as qualifying for off-balance sheet treatment (Asset Sales Report, 1992).

Another boost to the securitization market came in late November of 1992 when the Accounting Standard Board gave in to pressure to change proposed rules. While still requiring companies to record assets, the new system allows them to express a net asset figure reflecting only the residual risk left with the company from securitizing (*Financial Times*, 1992b).

The non-mortgage sector was very slow to take off. The first credit card deal sold in the UK market was issued by MBNA International in July of 1995. The issue encountered heavy over-subscription resulting in investor allocations being cut back. (Euroweek, 1995c, p.38) Although these asset classes are growing, including credit cards and commercial mortgages, they have yet to fill the gap left by the steady decline of the residential mortgage backed sector. Commercial mortgage pools generally require more exhaustive analysis by structurers, rating agencies, and investors than do residential mortgage pools (Euroweek, 1995a, p. 10–12).

The French Market

The French experience with asset securitization has been rather unique. Since the 1988 law, which authorized for the first time the securitization of loans in France, the market, has been slow to take off. Only a handful of the *Fonds Communs de Créance* (FCC) or mutual credit funds—the legal formula adopted by the French—launched so far have adopted the formula familiar in the US of repackaging a large quantity of mortgages or consumer loans into securities. Most funds have securitized a small quantity of loans, or even a single loan (*Financial Times*, 1991). Because of the small number of credit included in such funds, initial cost of the vehicles could not be spread over a broad pool of assets, and investors could not gauge the likely yield on the securities in the same way in the US. "In this type of montage, statistical evaluation of the risk of default is impossible; so qualitative methods for determining the risk are generally used by the managers and the rating agencies," reports the *Commission des Opérations de Bourse*, the regulator of the French financial market, in its annual report. The probability of default, however, is reckoned to be small at least in the short run. Indeed, most of the assets used to back these funds have been top quality public sector or banking assets (Asset Sales Report, 1992).

A number of constraints have greatly reduced the range of loans, which can be candidate for securitization. Loans with less than two years to run are excluded by law. The French authorities were expected to lift this restriction by the end of 1992. However, objections by the Bank of France, which is worried about the huge stimulus to the money supply that might result, have resulted in banning the securitization of credit card debt. That leaves short term car loans and other consumer debt free to be securitized, but excludes what banks had hoped would be a key market (Asset Sales Report, 1992).

Also under debate in the rules governing the market is the one that determines which institutions are allowed to issue asset-backed securities. Currently, only banks can securitize bank assets. Non-bank institutions are not allowed to securitize their own assets. Banks, however, securitize assets originated by non-banks.

Home loans, which represent the bulk of the US asset-backed securities market, have remained largely untapped. Between December 1988, date of enactment of the French securitization law, and the end of 1993, only one mortgage-backed issue has been marketed, backed by assets originated by the government-controlled *Crédit Foncier de France* (Asset Sales Report, 1992, 1993; Mortgage Banking, 1996, p.82). But in 1994, the market woke up and French housing loans-backed securities issuance jumped to FF8 billion, around $1.6 billion. The market dropped to FF4.5 billion in 1995 (Euroweek, 1995b, p. 63), and has been rather slow to pick up in 1996 (Mortgage Banking, 1996, p. 82).

The French market for housing loans to individuals is among the most complex in Europe because of the growing diversity of institutions involved, the diversity of mortgage products, and the coexistence of regulated market (with government subsidies) and a free sector (Mortgage Banking, 1996, *Financial Times,* 1991). In addition, banks have been slow in coming to grip with the problems of reorganizing their lending operations to make packaging feasible and profitable.

Over the longer term, market conditions appear likely to evolve in favor of securitization. Until recently, most French banks were busy improving their capital base by issuing Tier 2 instruments such as perpetual subordinated debt rather than taking assets off their balance sheets. But as capital becomes more expensive, asset securitization may reveal to be a cheaper means of complying with the BIS capital requirements. In addition, regulatory developments may encourage other key players (non-bank institutions) and key markets (credit card debt) to be involved.

Despite these regulatory impediments and structural banking quirks that are sometimes at odds with other jurisdictions, the French asset-backed market has recently shown an impressive degree of innovation. Bankers say that the investor and issuer bases are enlarging, the range of assets being sold is widening, and the market is showing signs of reaching maturity (Euroweek, 1995a, p.14–16).

The Japanese ABS Market

Bankers have often expressed disappointment that the Asian market in general and the Japanese market in particular have not taken off as originally predicted (Asset Sales Report, Sept. 16. 1996. P.8). Whereas over one-third of residential mortgages were securitized in the US, only 0.6% of outstanding total housing loans were securitized in Japan in 1991 (*Financial Times,* 1991). Housing loans were the first assets to be securitized in 1988 and have not become popular in spite of their potential to cut the size of the balance sheet. Ban on corporate loan securitization was lifted in March 1990 to reach a size of almost Y400bn (around $3bn) within less than three months of the market inception (*Financial Times,* 1991). However, the development of a secondary market for securitized corporate loans did not follow due to corporate borrowers' reluctance and to financial disclosure requirements in case of loan sales of corporate debt.

There are several reasons for the slow development of the housing loan instrument. The system restricted securitized loans to fixed rate instruments, making it impossible to securitize the majority of new housing loans which carried floating rates. Further, since the instruments took the form of a trust, operations were consigned to the trust bank. The fees charged by the trust banks and other operational costs lowered profitability of securitization for the city banks (*Financial Times,* 1991).

Until late 1994, under the then prevailing Securities and Exchange Law, only two activities of trust banks were classified as securities, and therefore, available for trading. Mortgages were not included in this definition, preventing them from trading in the secondary market.

Another main obstacle to securitization in Japan was the regulatory restraints imposed by article 65 of the Securities and Exchange Act, the Japanese version of the Glass-Steagall Act, which defines what qualifies as a security and what does not.

Article 65 permits banks to repackage debts and sell them to investors in the form of certificates. But these are not classified as securities and there are severe limits on trading them, which means there is virtually no secondary market (*Financial Times,* 1991). Moreover, the costs are high because the rules stipulate that an instrument has to take the complex form of a trust or a partnership. This is expected to change, however, with the introduction of a new definition of what constitutes a security, which definition is expected to be similar to that in the US law (*Financial Times,* 1991).

In an effort to give a boost the ABS market, the Diet, the Japanese parliament, has introduced wide-ranging reform and liberalization proposals from the Ministry of International Trade and Industry and from the Ministry of Finance. They had both been considered until then to be a bar to the progress of the market till now.

In April of 1993, Japan enacted its Financial System Reform Act, providing a significant shift in the Japanese banking regulation. It allows banks and securities firms to participate in other business segments such as banking, securities, and trusts through subsidiaries in which they have a majority equity stake. In a typically cautious fashion, though, the Ministry of Finance has adopted a step by step approach to the issuing of licenses to subsidiaries (The Banker, 1994, p. 52–5). This relaxation of Article 65 of the Securities and Exchange Act allowed for broader banks involvement in the securitization process.

On July 11 of 1994 a Japanese newspaper reported that consumer-finance company Nippon Shinpan would issue between Y20 billion ($200 million) and Y30 billion worth of asset-backed securities in the Euromarket and that the deal would be lead-managed by Goldman Sachs. Up till then, these transactions were thought to be illegal in Japan. Foreign bankers, as well as the U.S. government, had long lobbied for a general easing of Japan's restrictions on securitization. However, rather than inviting all comers to bid for business, the finance ministry singled out Goldman for a specific deal[53] (*The Economist,* July 1994, p. 71). This move signaled the de facto debut of the asset-backed market in Japan.

The official beginning, however, didn't come until August of 1995 when the Japanese MoF announced its plans to create a market for asset-backed securities, much to the relief of U.S. securities houses and bad-debt—ridden Japanese banks. A special advisory panel was appointed to deliberate on securitization of non-performing assets (*Wall Street Journal,* 1995, p. A5F).

Since then, Japan's banks and non-bank financial institutions, which face severe constraints on their balance sheets because of the collapse of property and share prices and the introduction of tougher bank capital requirements, have become aggressive in securitizing nonperforming loans and real estate collateral. The moves are designed to recover funds tied up in the bad loans and lift sagging land prices (Nikkei English News, 1996).

On November 10th of 1996, the Japanese government committed itself to even more far-reaching reforms of its financial markets by 2001, in its latest attempt to reverse the decline in Tokyo capital markets. The main points of the ambitious package, described as "Tokyo's equivalent of London's Big Bang", are deregulation of stock-brokering commissions and abolition of the barriers between banking and securities business (*Financial Times,* 1996). The slow growth of the market so far, with the perceived Japanese lack of commitment towards financial reforms is keeping bankers pessimistic as to the future of securitization in Japan.

THE ARGUMENT AGAINST SECURITIZATION

The "unbundlings" of risks made possible through the new technology of asset securitization and the ensuing off-balance sheet financing have obvious benefits. It is feared, however, that this may facilitate acceptance of greater risk not by the financial entity able to do so most efficiently, but by those most desperate to increase their rate of return or those with access to federally insured funds.

An example of this is the use of commercial bank standby letters of credit to enhance the negotiability and market price of debt instruments issued by non-banks. The commercial banks in effect assumes the risk of default on the issuer's debt offering and receives a fee for this service. Its recorded assets, and hence, its required capital, do not increase. Yet the bank's letter of credit has a market value in large part because of the privileged access to loan market conferred on it by federal deposit insurance protection (Carter, 1989, p. 789). The capital adequacy requirements are part of the regulatory mechanism designed to prevent excessive risk taking with insured funds.

There have been no major defaults in these markets. Indeed, the securities offered typically receive AAA or AA credit ratings based on the credit enhancement structure adopted. However, there is fear that an economic downturn may prompt widespread defaults on the underlying assets collateralizing the ABS securities. From a structural point of view, the economic incentive for a thorough credit analysis of each and every loan by the originating institution is clearly diluted by the knowledge that the loan will only be booked for a few weeks or months. Once a loan has been packaged along with hundreds or thousands of other loans into a security such a REMIC, a CMO, a CARD, or a CAR, its individual characteristics, including default risk, becomes completely unclear. The purchaser of the security is relying entirely on guarantees by federal and other agencies and on the pooling of risks to maintain the flow of revenue from the securities purchased. Moreover, there is fear that banks are merely unloading their balance sheets of their least risky assets, leaving it with a portfolio of risky assets, thus increasing the fragility of banks.

CONCLUSION: FUTURE PROSPECTS OF THE ABS MARKET

Following a 43% jump in public issues of asset-backed securities to a record $108 billion in 1995, supply is expected to increase modestly in 1996, but at a slower pace. Demand is expected to keep pace as the investor base for ABS will continue to broaden. New types of assets such as computer leases, agricultural equipment loans and trade receivables will post the largest gains. More conventional assets like auto and credit cards are likely to remain stable (Asset Sales Report, 1994; Oster and Wood, 1992). More innovative structures will be used. Increased tranching of transactions and more issuance of subordinated securities are expected.

The most problematic asset to date to be securitized has been corporate loans. While syndicated HLT loans and loan participation have been securitized to a limited degree, the corporate loan market still lies largely untouched and may continue to be dormant until some fundamental changes occur. HLT loans associated with large LBOs are typically part of a financing that includes junk bonds and thus may be evaluated on the basis of the public rating of the bonds.

The bulk of bank's corporate loan portfolio, however, consists of smaller loans to non-rated entities and thus is more difficult for outsiders to assess. No standard exists with which to compare internal ratings among banks, and useful data on the performance of these portfolios does not go beyond what must be disclosed in call reports. Organizations such as the Loan Pricing Corporation are attempting to gather the information necessary to jump-start this market, but to date they have not succeeded in satisfying investors, credit enhancers, and rating agencies.

What should be clear from this brief overview is that different markets are developing at different paces and for different reasons. Some markets, such as Spain, Hong Kong, Australia, Sweden, Brazil, and Argentina, have just emerged as important players. Some others are likely to surface in 1996. But what is certain is that securitization has gone global and American banks are the ones who made it possible.

NOTES

19. The goal was to stabilize the flow of funds into the residential mortgage market to enable individuals easier access to credit at a stable cost for the purchases of homes and to expand the number of participants to generate additional availability of funds in the credit market.

20. The Federal National Mortgage Association (Fannie Mae), a privately financed and managed association, developed the first secondary market for mortgages. Although Fannie Mae was initially authorized to purchase and sell only FHA mortgages, it has become active in purchasing VA and, beginning the 1970s, conventional loans. Actually, Fannie Mae does not create a pure secondary market because it deals only in mortgages on which forward commitments have been made through auction bidding.

Ginnie Mae, a government agency established in 1968, has the objective of making mortgages more liquid. Ginnie Mae acquires pools of FHA and VA mortgages from banks and other lenders and uses the pool to back its securities. Payment to Ginnie Mae securities holders are passed through from payment made on the underlying pools of mortgages, hence the name pass-through mortgage-backed securities (see section about different types of asset-backed securities in this Chapter). Freddie Mac, created in 1970, accomplishes for conventional loans what Ginnie Mae accomplishes for FHA and VA mortgages.

Like Ginnie Mae, Freddie Mac sells participations in mortgage pools and guarantees payment of interest and principal. Unlike Ginnie Mae, Freddie Mac deals in conventional mortgages and has truly advanced the marketability of these non-government-supported loans. Freddie Mac does, however, require private insurance on most mortgages in which it deals (Hempel, Coleman, and Simonson, 1990).

21. Many residential mortgages held by banks are conventional loans, meaning that they are not insured or guaranteed by a government agency. However, a growing proportion is not conventional and is supported by government agencies. The Federal Housing Administration insures and the Veterans Administration guarantees payment of principal and interest on certain qualifying residential mortgages originated by banks and other private lenders. These qualification features make it possible for lenders to accumulate a bundle of guaranteed or insured standardized mortgages or sale either to larger institutional investors, the Federal National Mortgage Association ("Fannie Mae" or FNMA), or the public by means of the Government National Mortgage Association (GNMA). The ability to package standardized loans helps banks to overcome the lack of marketability of small-denomination single loans whose characteristics would otherwise be highly dissimilar.

22. The 1986 Tax Reform Act eliminated the tax exemption on most state and local government issues purchased after August 1986. Realized appreciation or depreciation on these bonds' principal value, however, is subject to such taxes.

23. These mutual funds are managed for a fee. Money market mutual funds restrict their investment to short-term money market instrument with maturities less than one year. The typical fund holds a portfolio of Treasury bills, bank certificates of deposits, commercial paper, and bankers' acceptances. Some funds specialize in particular instruments such as Treasury bills (for very low-risk investors) or municipal notes, which are exempt for federal income taxes (for investors in high tax brackets). Most of them allow checks to be written on deposits with some restrictions. (Livingston, 1990). Thus, in many ways, large money market funds are like banks, although the formers are not insured by the FDIC. Maturities of assets and liabilities are usually matched and are either based on some agreed-upon future date when the fund will be liquidated, as in a closed-end fund, or on the preferences of the fund's investors, with assets liquidated as shareholders make withdrawals (Cumming, 1987).

24. Because returns on CDs have been so low, some banks have tried to make them more attractive by linking them to more profitable, yet riskier, indicators. Citibank and NationsBank, among other banks, offer stock-linked CDs based on Standard & Poor's 500 stock index performance. Blackfeet National Bank of

Montana is soon to offer a tax-deferred CD (Retirement CDs) that matures after the owner reaches age 65. Another twist is College-Tuition CD offered by College Savings Bank of New Jersey that offers an interest rate based on the inflation rate of college tuition. College-Tuition CDs are so successful that the bank built its entire business on an account that pays interest on tuition increases in 500 colleges. The Retirement CD that works like an annuity is considered to have so much potential that the insurance industry is threatening to go to court to stop banks from offering them. The Stock Linked CD, however, has had mixed response, mainly because of a declining stock market (For a more detailed description on these innovative instruments, refer to the Washington Post of February 26, 1994).

25. Until October 1989 there was no generally agreed benchmark to characterize an HTL beyond the understanding that the debt/equity ratio of the restructured corporation should significantly exceed historical standards. In that month, as part of efforts to tighten supervision, the three US national bank regulators—the Federal Reserve Board, the FDIC, and the Comptroller of the Currency—adopted a common broad definition for the purpose of banks' reporting requirements. The definition covers all buy-outs, recapitalization and acquisitions which either double the company's liabilities resulting in total liabilities/total assets ratios over 50% or in excess of 75%.

The three types of HLTs—buy-outs, acquisitions and recapitalization—are largely equivalent but differ somewhat in terms of the mechanics. In leverage buy-outs (LBOs), the transaction which has received the most attention, a corporation is purchased by a group of investors who establish a new ("shell") corporation with that sole purpose. If publicly quoted, the target company's shares are then removed from the stock market, i.e., the company is taken private. In contrast to LBOs, in leveraged acquisitions the acquirer is already an established corporation with other sources of revenues. In leveraged recapitalizations (recaps) a corporation retires part of its outstanding shares, substituting debt for equity. Typically, recaps are defensive measures against takeover threats. All three share two key characteristics. The first, and most obvious, is the small equity cushion of the restructured company. The second, partly the result of this small cushion, is the relatively complex structure of the debt (Borio, 1990). For a further description of HLTs, see DeAngelo and DeAngelo (1987), Doyle and Ammidon (1989), and Rizzi (1989).

26. Please refer to Chapter II, pp. 12+ for a definition of market efficiency and completeness.

27. Emphasis added.

28. The special reporting requirements for transfers involving residential mortgages were adopted so as not to hamper the development of the secondary mortgage market. That is, sales of residential mortgages entailed little or no retention risk by the selling institution.

29. Regulatory requirements for banks are contained in the instructions and glossary for the Call Reports issued by the Federal Financial Institutions Examination Council (FFIEC) and reflect consensus positions of the federal banking agencies.

30. This is in accordance with Regulation Y of the Federal Reserve Board and SEC requirements for public companies such as public bank holding companies.

31. These vehicles, known as captive finance subsidiaries, may be defined as wholly owned subsidiaries created to assist in the financing of the parent company. The parent company will usually transfer roughly equal amounts of receivables and debt to the subsidiary, thus removing them from the consolidated balance sheet. This method had proved effective in reducing debt-to-equity and other key ratios. The issuance of FASB No. 94 led certain companies to look for other means to achieve off-balance-sheet treatment for their receivables, namely, certain forms of securitization.

32. TB 85–2 also provides criteria that CMOs need to meet in order to obtain sales treatment.

33. The prohibition against multiple classes imposed under the IRS' so-called "Sears" regulations that were proposed in 1984 and finalized in 1986.

34. CMOs, which use the structure of 'owner trust' as the legal form of its special purpose vehicle (SPV), were introduced to, as will be detailed later, reduce the prepayment risk associated with pass-through mortgage-backed securities.

35. The most frequently discussed risk associated with investing in asset-backed securities is that of prepayment. In a scenario of falling interest rates, some borrowers may choose to prepay or refinance their obligations, in turn resulting in premature retirement of securities backed by those assets. The investor, then, a) does not realize the yield anticipated, and b), is faced with reinvesting at lower interest rates. Because the longer the maturity, the higher the prepayments risk, MBSs have been notorious in this respect. The development of CMOs is effectively a result of efforts made to minimize this risk.

36. For a detailed description of these instruments, refer to Bhattaya and Chin (1992) and Lee (1993).

37. The first CAR security was issued on May 15, 1985 by Valley National Financial Corp. It was the second non-mortgage-backed securities to be issued on the market (the first one was backed by leases on data processing equipment issued by Sperry Lease Finance Corp.). CARD issues didn't follow till January 19, 1987 by the Republic Bank of Delaware.

38. Sinking-fund provision requires the issuing firm to retire part of the bond issue at intervals stated in the bond debenture. There is evidence that sinking-fund bonds have lower yields than non-sinking fund issues. It is consistent with the view that a sinking-fund provision may signal lower default rate. The

availability of sufficient internal funds to meet the sinking-fund payment is a signal of high profitability. The availability of sufficient external funds is a signal that new lenders have confidence in the firm.

39. Larger volume of issues may make pay-throughs a more economical alternative.

40. Technically, this feature of MBSs is called negative convexity in contrast to positive convexity of non-callable bonds. Convexity measures the rate at which duration (weighted-average time to receipts of a bond's cash flow) changes in response to changes in interest rates. With positive convexity, the security becomes less price sensitive as interest rates rise. Negative convexity is the opposite: the security's duration lengthens when interest rates rise and shortens when they fall. Bonds that have fixed cash flows, such as Treasuries, have positive convexity. MBSs, which can be prepaid, often have negative convexity.

41. Because the timing of cash flow receipts significantly affects investment returns, MBS market participants spend considerable effort modeling prepayments, for prepayment assumptions are important in pricing all mortgage related securities. For details on MBS valuation given prepayment risks, consult the works of Fabozzi, 1992; Fabozzi, Ramsey and Ramirez, 1994; DeRosa, Goodman and Zazzarino, 1993; and Waldman, 1992.

42. This was done to comply with tax regulations, which stated that a trust generally could not qualify for grantor trust status if it issues multi-class interests that divide ownership of investment assets or the cash flows from such assets in a non-pro rata fashion.

43. Inverse floaters were introduced in October 1986.

44. Illustration appeared in Epstein's article (1993, p. 33).

45. So if one class has $10 million in inverse floater, we would expect to see $46 million of floaters.

46. This explains why holders of inverse floaters incurred huge losses after the increase in interest rates in May of 1994 by the Federal Reserve. The magnitude of losses, however, is contingent on the size of the multiplier.

47. Prepayments have the effect of shortening the life of the underlying mortgage bonds and duration.

48. MBS securities issued by government agencies have little credit risk, and therefore, do not require any credit enhancement mechanism.

49. Banks, major issuers of credit card-backed securities, have allowed their credit card loans back onto the balance sheet, for they no longer feel the need to securitize now that they have returned to healthier performances.

50. Between 1985 and 1988, about 25% of the volume of non-mortgage asset-backed securities was enhanced via LOCs alone. More than 43% of that volume was enhanced with LOC used with other types of credit support (Moss, 1989).

51. The majority of the larger domestic banks do not have the top credit rating necessary to add sufficient credit enhancement to an asset-backed issue.

52. On September 16th of 1992, with the pound sterling sinking, Britain raised interest rates from 10 percent to 12 percent, and later to 15 percent. After markets closed on that day, Britain—along with Italy which also had a sinking Lira—withdrew from the European exchange rate mechanism (ERM) and returned rates to 10 percent. Britain, who was a latecomer to the ERM, said that it would not rejoin unless the Bundesbank lowered further its Lombard rate, which rate was decreased by 0.5% in March of 1993.

53. Although granting an exception to one firm seems suspicious to outsiders, Japan's bureaucrats often operate this way when they want to loosen their grip on a particular market.

CHAPTER 4

Research Design and Methodology

In this chapter, the research design and methodology for the investigation of the differentiating characteristics between adopters and non-adopters of the technique of asset securitization are described.

Existing research has focused almost entirely on mortgage-backed securities and their derivatives, mostly valuation, pricing and prepayment forecasting at the market level (Chidambaran, 1994; Haroun, 1994; Buttimer, 1993; Jackson, 1991; Park, 1990; Shao, 1989; Gilley, 1988; and Miller, 1984)[54]. One exception has been the work of Lillaney, (1994), where all types of securitized assets were taken into account when investigating the benefits (in terms of stock prices) accrued to securitizors (banking and non-banking firms), to shareholders and to bondholders around the securitization period. But there has been practically no empirical work on asset securitization at the bank level or firm level in general.

RESTATEMENT OF RESEARCH HYPOTHESIS

The objective of this book is threefold:

1. to present the field and environment of asset securitization,
2. to identify the differentiating characteristics between securitizing and non-securitizing banks, and
3. to investigate the relationship between the level of assets securitization during the reporting period and the financial characteristics of the securitizing bank as reported on its financial statements.

For the purpose of this study asset securitization is defined as the repackaging of mortgage and non-mortgage loans into marketable instruments. The focus is on the asset securitization activities of the 200 largest U.S. commercial banks during the 1994—1995 reporting period. As of December 1995, there were 10,093 banks in the United States, with $4.5 trillion in total assets and three times as much in off-balance sheet activities. Of these 10,093 banks, only a small number (235) were involved at one time or another during the reporting year with the process of asset securitization (see Figure 4-1 below).

While securitizing banks represented only a small fraction of the population of U.S. commercial banks (2.3%), they controlled almost half (44.5%) of all U.S. commercial banking assets and 72% of the total amount of off-balance-sheet activities. The asset-backed securities (ABS) volume, on the other hand, amounted to less than 3% of total commercial banking assets. The market has seen a slow, but steady growth. It has advanced from a market principally made up of consumer obligations to one that covers a wide range of assets and is likely to continue its march down the balance sheet.

Figure 4-1: Asset Securitization by Commercial Banks: 1991–1995

	1995	1994	1993	1992	1991
Securitizing Banks					
Number of					
Banks	235	229	209	197	230
Assets ($mn)	2,019.27	1,708.00	1,460.72	1,342.77	1,268.85
ABS ($mn)*	128.28	84.73	78.91	75.76	74.98
OBS ($mn)**	9,987.62	8,575.76	6,608.34	4,642.39	3,514.08
ABS/Assets	6.4%	5%	5.3%	5.6%	5.9%
ABS/OBS	1.3%	1%	1.2%	1.6%	2.1%
OBS/Assets	495%	502%	446%	341%	277%
All Banks					
Number of					
Banks	10,093	10,512	11,020	11,515	11,970
Assets ($mn)	4,441.63	4,016.96	3,713.18	3,512.62	3,434.82
OBS ($mn)	13,964.84	12,344.77	9,230.33	6,580.39	5,455.12
ABS/Assets	2.9%	2.1%	2.1%	2.2%	2.2%
ABS/OBS	1%	0.7%	0.8%	1.2%	1.4%
OBS/Assets	314%	307%	249%	187%	159%

* ABS: Asset Backed Securities, including Mortgage-Backed Securities, as reported on Schedule RC-L.
** OBS: Off-balance-sheet Activities, including ABS, as reported on Schedule RC-L of the Call Reports.
Source: Call Report Tapes, The FDIC: 1991–1995.

RESTATEMENT OF RESEARCH QUESTIONS

The hypothesis of this research is:

Banks that adopt the technique of asset securitization are likely to differ from non-adopters on the basis of certain reported financial characteristics (size, level of international banking, level of wholesale business, capitalization, profitability, levels of diversification and loan charge-offs, funding costs, liquidity, and competitive advantage).

Stated otherwise, the focus of this research is on whether these aforementioned characteristics are related to the repackaging of bank loans into marketable assets. The null hypothesis is that there is no overall effect of securitization when group comparison is based on the specified financial variables. Should the findings lead to the rejection of the null hypothesis of no overall effect, one is led to test for significance at the univariate level, hence leading to the investigation of the following subsidiary research questions as grouped below.

Bank Characteristics:

R1   Are banks that engage in asset securitization, measured by the volume of repackaged mortgage and non-mortgage loans sold with and without recourse divided by bank's total assets, likely to have a larger size, measured by assets, than banks with no securitization activities?

Hester (1982, p.43) alluded to the possibility that financial innovation may have high set-up costs, and thus can be expected to occur in the portfolios of large institutions. In an empirical study of financial innovation by investment banks, Tufano (1989a, b) found that investment bankers estimate that a new financial product requires an investment of $50,000 to $5 million[55] and that the first firm to innovate bears substantially higher costs than subsequent imitators.

Large banks are also likely to be affected the most by changes in the competitive environment, namely the loss of their large corporate customers to financial markets, and the need to meet the BIS capital adequacy rules due to their diverse off-balance activities. In addition, large banks are likely to be exposed to more geographic markets and competitors. Therefore, they are more prone to investigate new avenues in meeting the challenges posed by the environment, such as the avenue of asset securitization.

Large banks are also likely to offer a wider range of products than smaller banks. Product diversification is likely to induce economies of scale and scope[56]. These economies are likely to provide banks with an added incentive to include more products in their portfolios. In their study of loan sales by commercial banks, Pavel and Phillis (1987) found the variable asset to have "the largest impact on a bank's probability to be a seller (of loans)." (p. 154)[57] Gorton and Haubrich (1987) in their essay "The Paradox of Loan Sales" noted that larger banks tended to sell more loans then relatively smaller banks. Pavel and Phillis, in the same research, associated size with sophistication. The larger the size of the bank, they advanced, the higher the level of sophistication of the management team. Subsequently, large banks are more prone to adopt new financial products, securitization in this case, then smaller size banks.

It is important to remember that the variable asset was used as a control variable for matching the group of securitizing banks with equally large banks (since only the top 200 commercial banks were included in the study) not involved with securitization. It may, therefore, be unlikely that the variable ASSET be a differentiating characteristic between the two groups at the univariate level. This does not mean, however, that the variable ASSET would not contribute to the overall securitization effect at the multivariate level[58].

R2   Are banks that engage in asset securitization (as defined above) likely to have relatively higher levels of international banking activities, measured by the ratio of international assets divided by total assets, than banks with no securitization activities?

R3   Are banks that engage in asset securitization likely to have higher levels of wholesale business than banks with no securitization activities?

There is no allusion in the literature that these variables carry any link to, or exert any weight in, bank's decision to securitize loans. Yet, the author chose to include these two measures in an attempt to build a profile of the securitizing bank, and to contribute to a better characterization of securitizing banks.

It can be argued that multinational banks are more prone to adopt innovation than purely domestic banks, especially if this innovation, like asset securitization, is likely to have acceptance in foreign markets[59]. Introduction of these innovations to foreign markets allows banks to spread the initial investments in both developing staff expertise as well as the system requisite for supporting that staff to a much larger customer base. Furthermore, the incentive to introducing these innovations to foreign markets is even higher knowing that not only management expertise has already been developed but also that it has the requisite knowledge in dealing with foreign markets. Hence, the volume of international banking is likely to be another characteristic of innovative banks[60].

The ratio of international assets to total assets is an indicator of the degree of internationalization of a bank (Holland, 1988). Banks with a high level of international business are likely to be more aggressive in their search for survival strategies, and, thus, more prone to adopt new forms of profitable intermediation.

The wholesale banking business as measured by the amount of commercial and industrial loans, government loans, and interbank lending— seems to be more affected by the erosion of traditional product and geographic market boundaries than the retail banking business (Channon, 1988; Holland, 1988; *The Economist,* 1992). As a result, banks with a substantial amount of wholesale business would appear to have more incentives to engage in non-traditional banking, namely asset securitization, than those mainly directed towards retail banking.

Bank Capitalization/Regulatory Taxes[61]
R4   Are securitizing banks likely to exhibit lower capital ratios than banks with no securitization activities?

Bank supervisory authorities in various countries have, in recent years, emphasized capital levels as a way to ensure bank safety and soundness. Capital levels are generally tied to asset levels which means banks have to maintain a minimum capital-to-asset ratio. Banks below or approaching the minimum capital level have an incentive to off-load their balance sheets by repackaging their booked loans into tradable securities. In doing so, banks reduce the size of their assets, thus enabling them to meet capital requirements. It has often been argued that asset securitization is principally a defensive reaction by banks to new capital requirement measures (Flannery, 1989; Greenbaum and Thakor, 1987; and Pavel and Phillis, 1987). Therefore, low capital ratios are likely to be associated with higher volumes of securitization.

Bank Profitability and Dependence Upon Fee Income
R5   Are securitizing banks likely to exhibit a higher degree of dependence on fee income, measured by the ratio of fee income divided by interest income, and higher return-on-asset ratios than banks with no securitization activities?

Banks would not engage in asset securitization unless asset securitization is perceived to be profitable. One question is whether the effect of asset securitization on overall banks' profitability can be measured. A less challenging, yet equally important, task is to see whether profitability differs between securitizing and non-securitizing banks and whether there is a positive correlation between the volume of securitized assets and banks returns.

There is no published empirical research linking returns to asset securitization[62]. It can, however, be argued that one direct effect of securitization is the generation of fee income on one hand and the induction of cost savings on the other (Federal Reserve Board, 1990a; *The Economist,* 1994, 1993c, and 1992; and Flannery, 1988, among others). Banks are increasingly shifting their attention and strategies toward fee-generating activities and less towards traditional banking, i.e., interest-income generating activities. Securitization is a fee-generating activity. Accordingly, banks with higher level of securitization are likely to have higher ratios of fee-income to interest income.

A key measure of bank performances is return on assets (Hempel et al., 1990, p. 58–59). Securitization, in and of itself, can enhance bank's return on assets. These returns are substantially augmented by the originator customarily being retained and paid a fee to service the assets supporting the related securities. By securitizing assets and removing them from their books, banks can either invest the proceeds in more lucrative ventures or begin the loan origination process again and use turnover and volume to generate profits. "Banks can enhance their returns on both assets and equity, as well as improve capital and leverage ratios, through the removal of assets from the books and recognition of fee income."[63] In addition, banks are able to realize some cost savings on loan warehousing.

Portfolio Quality
R6   Are securitizing banks likely to exhibit a lower loan portfolio quality, measured by the level of portfolio diversification and the ratio of net charge-offs to total loans, than those with no securitization activities?

It is often stated that one accruing benefit to banks from asset securitizing is increased portfolio diversification (Board of Governor's of the Federal Reserve System, 1990a; Pavel 1988; Pavel and Phillis 1987). Indeed, packaging a portion of the loans in which the bank is highly concentrated and taking it off its books should lead to a lower concentration and better diversification of the loan portfolio[64].

Lack of diversification of the loan portfolio of banks is often cited as one significant reason behind bank failure. Lack of diversification (or inability to diversify) geographically and across industries may be due to several factors. Among these factors are ties to the local economies (agricultural and energy sectors in decline in certain states), restrictions of certain banking laws (prohibition of, and limitations on, intra—and interstate branching), or simply lack of management expertise or unwillingness to diversify (Looney, Wansley, and Lane, 1987).

Securitization, according to the Federal Reserve Board (1990a, p. 6), may allow banks to alleviate some of these problems. Indeed, the ability to originate and then securitize assets may afford banks an ability to access a broader customer base without increasing its concentration in the particular area in which the bank is located. Concurrently, "dependency on local economies and their cycles may, then, be lessened in the securitization process" leading, eventually, to a more balanced loan portfolio, and subsequently, to a reduced risk of failure. This is in agreement with the argument presented by Golderberg (1988), Golderberg and Rogers (1988), and Ocampo and Rosenthal (1988) that securitization benefits loan originators by diversifying the default risk. Accordingly, banks that adopted the technique of asset securitization are likely to exhibit a lower degree of diversification (measured by $(\Sigma li^2)^{65}$ where l_i is the loan to asset ratio for loan type i, which takes on higher value for lower degrees of diversification[66]) than non-securitizing banks. Interpretation of the diversification measure, however, may be complicated by the fact that the observed level of diversification may be the result of previous loan repackaging activities of the bank.

On the other hand, there seems to be a shared belief that banks have an incentive to securitize their best assets and hold riskier assets on their balance sheets since the return on these assets is generally higher than that of high-quality low-risk assets (Golderberg, 1988; Ocampo and Rosenthal, 1988; Flannery, 1987). Supervising agencies such as the FDIC and the Board of Governors of the Federal Reserve System (1990a) expressed concern over the quality of assets remaining on the books of a bank engaging in securitization.

In order to get a triple A rating on their repackaged loans, banks, they argued, had an incentive to "sell only their best assets, thereby leaving the FDIC insuring a riskier asset structure." (Federal Reserve System, 1990a, p. 24) This behavior may somewhat be thwarted by the recent changes brought to the deposit insurance scheme whereby premiums are assessed based upon, among other things, the quality of the loan portfolio. It should be noted, however, that under the current scheme, the schedule of liability fees allows only a narrow range and a few discrete levels. (Epps, Pulley, and Humphrey, 1996, p. 699–721) As such, a bank may still find it advantageous to leave the FDIC insure its riskiest assets, even more so as the FDIC lowered the premium to most U.S. commercial banks to 4% as of December of 1995. (Journal of Accountancy, 1996, p.17–18)

In addition to the prospects of higher returns on lower quality assets, two cost factors entice banks to sell their best assets, thereby leaving the FDIC insuring a riskier asset structure. First, the better the quality of repackaged assets, the lesser the enhancement that is needed to realize an improved return, and the better the acceptance of the ABS issue among investors. Second, as deposit insurance premiums have recently been lowered for most U.S. commercial banks, it is more efficient, from the point of view of regulatory costs, to have capital and deposits fund riskier assets, which usually offer higher returns than less risky ones. Furthermore, there is the general belief that the market will only permit the sale of high quality repackaged assets (Lillaney, 1994. p.41).

Banks may choose to securitize their best assets in an attempt to redress for capital understatements caused by regulators, according to Flannery (1989) and Hassan (1993). Bank regulators force banks to write off bad loans while appreciating loans must be carried at book value. This generates an understatement of bank equity that is available for loan losses. The bank sells appreciating low-risk and high-value loans in order to realize capital gains that would balance the understatement brought to the book value of equity capital.

Based on the above-mentioned concerns, securitization is likely to result in a higher level of loan charge-offs (measured by the ratio of net charge-offs to total loans) due to the lower quality of the remaining assets in their portfolio. The level of loan charge-offs, therefore, may be expected to be higher for securitizing banks.

Liquidity

R7   Are securitizing banks likely to exhibit higher liquidity needs, measured by deposit to loan ratio, and dependence on volatile deposits, measured by the sum of brokered deposits, deposits in foreign offices, purchased repos, and all other short-term borrowed money to total assets, than non-securitizing banks?

Banks are enticed to use securitization as a funding mechanism, rather than deposits. Unlike deposits, funds collected through securitization are free from deposit insurance and reserve requirements. Greenbaum and Thakor (1987) examined the banking firms' choice between traditional deposits generation and asset securitization as alternate funding mode and found that, given an asymmetric information environment, banks would favor securitization for the best assets and deposit funding for the worst assets[67].

Boemio (1996) makes the difference between core deposits and volatile deposits (brokered funds and large denomination time deposits). Because of the subsidy attached to core deposits (through FDIC insurance), banks are able to attract funds at relatively attractive terms in order to fund assets in their portfolios. Using volatile deposits[68], on the other hand, can be costly, and therefore, act as an incentive to recur to securitization as an alternative. (Pavel and Phillis, 1987, p.147)

Cost of Funds
R8   Are securitizing banks likely to exhibit a higher cost of funds, measured by deposit interest expense to total interest expense and deposit interest expense to interest loan incomes ratios, than non-securitizing banks?

Banks that have to pay a higher cost to attract funds are likely to resort to asset securitization as a funding mechanism. It is likely that banks that have a high recurrence to market mediated funds (volatile deposits) would exhibit a higher funding cost. Certain banks experience shortages of funds and may find themselves forced to recur to intermediated funds in order to meet loan demand. Should it be the case, these banks are likely to pay higher interest on their borrowed funds. This would be reflected in a higher deposit interest expense relative to total interest expense. In this case, banks may find it more efficient to securitize assets rather then pay high funding costs.

The ratio of interest expense to loan income is an indication on how efficient a bank has been in the utilization of its borrowed funds, i.e., deposits. Banks that recur to intermediated deposits are likely to post higher funding costs, and thus, lower yield on their assets. Once more, securitization could be used as a means of reducing funding costs and improving the yield on assets.

Loan Origination and Competitive Advantage
R9   Are securitizing banks likely to make more use of their loan origination competitive advantage, measured by a higher loan growth

rate, a larger securitizable loan portfolio, and their prior experience with securitization, than non-securitizing banks?

The greater a bank's demand for loans, the more likely it is to securitize its assets. Indeed, securitization could be used as a funding mechanism for newly generated credit. It is a means of freeing money tied to previously originated loans in order to meet the demand for new loans. Hence, it is expected that the higher the level of loan growth over the period, the higher the likelihood of issuing asset-backed securities.

A higher loan growth rate may also be the result of a strategy followed by banks to use the origination competitive advantage they possess. Some banks may have a comparative advantage in originating loans, but not in warehousing them. Stricter capital requirements have made it increasingly expensive for banks to keep loans on the balance sheet. Credit securitization, as explained in earlier chapters, has allowed banks to reevaluate "each function of their value-added chain—origination, servicing, and funding—to determine where they possess a competitive advantage." (Kopff and Lent, 1988, p.14) and to specialize, whenever possible, in the function where they possess a competitive edge.

Another measure of competitive advantage, dubbed the 'learning curve', is banks' prior experience with the technique and technicalities of asset securitization. It is reckoned that banks with prior experience with asset securitization during the 1994 reporting period are more likely to securitize assets during 1995 than those who have not had the previous experience.

STUDY VARIABLES

Nine categories of bank characteristics are the focus of this study. These categories are: level of asset securitization, asset size, degree of international banking, degree of wholesale business, capital requirements, profitability, portfolio diversification, net charge-offs, loan growth over the period, and funding cost. The level of asset securitization is used as the dependent variable for the regression model, to be described later in this chapter (see Figure 4-2 for a listing and a brief description of the variables in the study).

Variable Definition

There has been a long tradition of using financial ratios when conducting research on firms' behavior. Whalen (1991); Asli (1989), Clarke (1988),

Gajewski (1988), Whalen and Thomson (1988), Cates (1985), Avery and Hanweck (1984), Khoury (1980), and Altman (1968)[69] used financial ratios in order to predict bankruptcy. Soybel (1992), Reiter and Zicbart (1991), Pinches and Mingo (1973), and West (1970) used them in order to determine bond ratings. Lillaney (1994), O'Connor (1973) used them to determine market returns, Zanakis and Walter (1994), Pantalone (1993), Mansour, Zangeneh and Zitz (1993), Merik, Leveen and Merik (1991), and Rose (1987)[70] to study mergers and acquisitions, and Pavel and Phillis (1987) to predict event occurrences[71]. Several of these studies involved commercial banks as well as other types financial institutions.

Level of Asset Securitization The level of asset securitization is measured by ratio of the volume of asset-backed securities to average assets. The volume of MABS is the sum of mortgage backed securities (FNMA and FHLMC residential mortgage loan pools and Farmer Mac agricultural mortgage loan pools, items 9.a,b, and c of Schedule RC-L) and securitized installment loans (auto loans, credit card and related plan receivables and all other consumer installment credits, including mobile home, recreational vehicle, and student loans, items 5.a, b and c of Schedule RC-L, Memoranda).

International Banking The level of international banking is measured by the ratio of International Assets divided by Total Assets. The volume of International Assets is made up of the following items in Schedule RC-C "Loan and Lease Financing": loans to banks in foreign countries; commercial and industrial loans to non-U.S. addressees; acceptances of other banks to other foreign banks; loans to foreign governments and official institutions; and lease financing receivables of non-U.S. addressees. Total asset size is provided by Schedule RC-Balance Sheet.

Wholesale Business[72] "[T]he wholesale banking business is viewed expansively as constituting the serving of commercial and industrial enterprises and government entities, and the provision of funds—other than those of a correspondent banking nature—to other financial institutions" (Holland, 1988, p. 179). Accordingly, the degree of involvement in wholesale business is assessed by the summation of 1), 2) and 3) all divided by total assets[73].

1. Commercial and industrial loans and lease financing receivables to U.S. addressees. These two items come from Schedule RC-C "Loan and Lease Financing Receivables";

2. Securities, both governmental and non-governmental, and loans to local governments. Item 1, Securities, is an element of the balance sheet. The second item 'Loans to local governments' is the sum of 1) non-rated obligations, other than securities, of state and political subdivisions in the U.S. and 2) other obligations, excluding securities, of states and political subdivisions in the U.S. Both items are from Schedule RC-C of the Call Report; and

3. Non-correspondent inter-bank business which is the sum of the following four items from Schedule RC-C: loans to U.S. branches and agencies of foreign banks; loans to other commercial banks in the U.S.; loans to other depository institutions in the U.S.; and acceptances of U.S. banks. All four items are derived from Schedule RC-C.

Capital Requirements Capital requirements have often been cited as the major drive behind asset securitization. The variable capital requirements is measured by the capital ratio, that is, total qualifying capital divided by adjusted assets. The numerator 'total qualifying capital (i.e., Tier-1 and Tier-2 capital) allowable under the risk-based capital guidelines' is derived from Schedule RC-R "Risk-Based Capital". The denominator is the sum of total assets, allowance for loan and lease losses, allocated transfer risk reserve (all balance sheet items) and net unrealized loss on marketable equity securities (Schedule RC-B, "Securities"). The computation of the ratio is based on the '1995 RBC Estimation Algorithm Draft' that is actually used by the Federal Reserve to assess bank capitalization. Notice that the FDIC and the Federal Reserve do not necessarily follow the same computational method[74] (Wilson, 1996).

Profitability Profitability is measured by the ratios of return on assets and fee income to net income. Income items in the numerators and the denominator are items of Schedule RI, "Income Statement".

Portfolio Quality

Portfolio Diversification The level of portfolio diversification is one of the two measures used to assess the quality of a bank's portfolio. For each bank, a diversification index is computed. This index is made up of the sum of loan to asset ratios for the different types of loans a bank carries on its books. These are loans secured by real estate, loans to depository institutions, agricultural loans, commercial & industrial loans, acceptances of other banks, consumer loans, loans to foreign governments, obligations of state and political subdivisions in the United States, other loans, and lease financing receivables). All of these items are recorded on Schedule RC-C, "Loan and Lease Financing Receivables". As stated earlier, the less diversified a bank is, the more likely that bank is to securitize its loans. The variable 'Loan diversification' takes on higher value for lower degrees of diversification.

Net Charge-offs The ratio of net charge-offs to total loans is the second proxy used to assess portfolio quality. Net charge-offs is an item of Schedule RI-B, "Charge-offs and Recoveries and Changes in Allowances for Loan and Lease Losses". 'Total loans' is an item of Schedule RC, "Balance Sheet".

Liquidity Needs Both items in the deposit to loan ratio are items of Schedule RC, "Balance Sheet". The ratio of dependence on borrowed money is measured by volatile deposits to total assets. Volatile deposits are the sum of brokered deposits, deposits in foreign offices, federal funds and repos purchased, and all other short-term borrowed money. Brokered deposits are a memorandum item of Schedule RC-E, "Deposit Liabilities". 'Deposits in foreign offices' is an item of Schedule RC-E, Part II and includes deposits in Edge and Agreement subsidiaries and IBFs. Federal funds and repos purchased and other short-term borrowed money are both items of Schedule RC, Liabilities".

Cost of Funds Items of the first cost measure, deposit interest expense to total interest expense, are reported on Schedule RC-I: "Income Statement". The denominator of the efficiency measure, deposit interest expense to loan interest income is item 1-g of Schedule RI.

Loan Growth Loan growth here is the rate of change of the volume of outstanding loans from one year to another. Total loans is an item of Schedule RC-C, "Loans and Lease Financing Receivables," of the Call Report.

Securitizable Loan Portfolio The securitizable loan ratio is measured by the sum of real estate loans secured by first liens, 1–4 residential properties, credit card plans, unused commitments in credit card lines, unused commitments in consumer loans, and unused commitments in home equity loans to total loans. The first two items in the numerators are part of schedule RC-C: "Loan and lease Financing Receivables". The unused commitment items are found in Schedule RC-L: "Off Balance Sheet Items".

HYPOTHESIS TESTING

Several motives explain the growth of the asset-backed securities market in general, and its popularity amongst commercial banks in particular. Based on these motives the following financial variables have been identified as plausible differentiating characteristics between securitizing and non-securitizing banks and likely to affect the volume of assets to be securitized during the period. These variables are:

- Financial characteristics (asset size, level of wholesale business, level of international banking),
- Capitalization level (risk-based capital ratio);

Figure 4-2: List of Variables in the Study[75]

Category	Variable	Expected Sign
Level of Asset Securitization in 1995 (Dependent Variable for regression analysis)	MABS95A = MABSs /Average Assets	(Regression)
Bank Characteristics		
· Size	Log (Assets)[1]	Positive
· International Banking	FARATIO. International Assets/TA	Positive
· Wholesale Business	WSRATIO is wholesale ratio sum. (commercial & industrial loans. govt & non-govt. securities. and non-correspondent interbank loans)/TA,	Positive
Bank Capitalization		
· Risk-Based Capital Ratio	KBCRATIO is the risk-based capital ratio. Qualifying capital/Total Adjusted Assets,	Negative
Bank Profitability		
· Fee Income Ratio	NIIRATIO Fee Income to Net Income,	Positive
· Return on Asset	RUA is the return on assets ratio,	Positive
Loan Portfolio Quality		
· Loan Diversification	L is the loan diversification index (L)[2], where LI is the loan to asset ratio for different loan types,	Positive
· Loan Charge-offs	NTLNLSK: Net Charge-offs/Total Loans,	Negative
Bank Funding Resources/Liquidity		
Funding resources	LIQ1: Deposits to Assets Ratio,	Negative
Market based Funding	LIQ2: Volatile Deposits to Total Deposits;	Positive
Cost of Funds		
Funding Cost	COSTR1: Dep. Interest Expense/Total Int Exp.;	Positive
Funding Efficiency	COSTR2: Dep. Int. Expense/Interest income,	Positive
Competitive Advantage		
· Securitization Potential	LOANLS. Securitizable Loans (Mortgage, Credit Card, Auto Loans respective Unused Commitments)/Total Loans & Leases;	Positive
· Loan Growth	LOANGR95. Loan Growth Rate during 1995,	Positive
· Learning Curve	MABS94A 1994 Securitized Assets/Av Assets	Positive

[1] Size is proxied by log(assets) in order to avoid the distortion of big numbers.

- Portfolio quality (diversification index, loan charge-off ratio);
- Profitability (return on assets, fee income to net income);
- Funding cost (deposit interest expense to total interest expense, deposit interest expense relative to loan income);
- Liquidity or ability to attract funds (volatile funds, deposits to loans);
- Use of banks' competitive advantage (size of its securitizable portfolio measured by volume of residential mortgages, auto loans and credit card plans and their respective unused commitments),
- Loan growth, and
- Prior involvement with asset securitization (dubbed the 'learning curve').

There are two main steps in the analysis of the securitization behavior of banks. First, MANOVA analysis is used to determine whether the two independent groups, securitizing and non-securitizing banks, differ based on the aforementioned variables. Differentiation between securitizing and non-securitizing banks is especially important to bank supervisors and bank regulators in regulating the innovative behavior of banks and addressing and controlling their risk-taking behavior. Investors will have a clearer understanding of the effect of securitization of the value of their investments/potential investments. Bank managers and prospective securitizors will make an educated decision on whether securitization is the tool to be used towards meeting certain bank objectives.

Second, a regression analysis is used in order to determine whether these same variables affect the decision about the volume of assets to be securitized during the period, and if so, the weight that is given to each variable in the decision making process.

Multivariate Analysis of Variance[76]

MANOVA: an Introduction Multivariate analysis of variance (MANOVA), an extension of the univariate analysis of variance technique (ANOVA), is a statistical technique that can be used to explore simultaneously the relationship between one (or more) categorical independent variable and two or more metric dependent variables[77].

To use the MANOVA technique, one only needs to know whether an event (securitization in this case) took place and then use a dichotomous value as the independent variable. Like ANOVA, MANOVA is concerned with differences between groups. ANOVA, a univariate procedure, is used to assess differences on a single metric dependent variable. MANOVA, on the other hand, is a multivariate procedure, and is used to assess group differences across multiple metric dependent variables simultaneously.

Both procedures are used to assess the statistical significance of differences between groups. In ANOVA, the null hypothesis tested is the equality of the means of the dependent variable across groups. In MANOVA, the null hypothesis tested is the equality of vectors of means on multiple dependent variables across groups, as illustrated in Figure 4-3 below[78].

Several statistical and conceptual benefits can be gained through the use of MANOVA. One major benefit is the ability to control for the overall, or experiment-wide, error rate. In the specific case of this study with nine dependent variables, running a series of nine separate ANOVAs would mean the probability of Type I error will lie somewhere between 5% (if all dependent variables are perfectly correlated) and 37% ($1-0.95^9$ if all independent variables are uncorrelated).

Thus, the series of t-tests leaves little control of the effective type 1 error. "If the researcher desires to maintain control over the experiment-wide error rate and there is at least some degree of inter-correlation among the dependent variables, then MANOVA is appropriate." (Hair et al., 1992, p.157)

Another statistical benefit resides in the ability of MANOVA to detect overall group significance that may go undetected by running a series of ANOVAs. Individual tests ignore the correlations among dependent variables and thus use less than the total information available for assessing overall group differences[79]. "In the presence of multicolinearity among the dependent variables, MANOVA will be more powerful than the separate univariate tests." (Hair et al., p.157) Such multicolinearity is actually sought after, for MANOVA requires that the dependent variables be conceptually linked. Consequently, one should be cautioned about throwing in unrelated variables simply because of MANOVA's ability to handle multiple dependent variables.

MANOVA Assumptions Three assumptions must be met in order for the multivariate procedure tests to be valid. These assumptions are 1) equality of variance-covariance matrices, 2) normality of the dependent variables, and 3) independence of the observations.

While the equivalence of the variance-covariance matrices is a concern, "its violation has minimal impact if the groups are of approximately of equal size."(Hair et al., p. 159) Groups are assumed to be of approximate size when the ratio of the size of the largest group to that of the smallest group is less than 1.5[80] (Stevens, 1992, p. 226; Wirtz, 1992 p.4). MANOVA is not greatly affected by violation of the assumption of normality (Hair et al., 1992 p. 160) if such violation is caused by skewness, as opposed to outliers[81] (Wirtz, 1992). In that case, departure from normality of the dependent variables can be remedied through data transformation. Positively skewed distributions are most effectively transformed by taking the logarithm of the variable, while negative skewness can be corrected by employing a square root transformation. In the case of a flat distribution, the most common transformation is the inverse $(1/X)$. Should departure from normality be caused by outliers, the researcher needs to use judgment whether deletion of the observations at hand would not distort the model.

Violation of the third assumption, and the most serious one, can occur in both experimental and non-experimental situations. In case of repeated measures, a time-ordered effect (serial correlation) may occur, even from different respondents, such as familiarity with an administered test. Non-experimental design violations can be caused by "extraneous and unmeasured effects [that] can affect the results by creating dependence among the respondents." (Hair et al., p.159) While it is easy to control, and therefore, remedy for factors causing dependence among observation in experimental designs, it is not always easy to identify the ones causing such dependence in observational, non-experimental ones.

MANOVA Hypothesis Testing For the purpose of this research, the objective for applying MANOVA is two-fold: 1) determine whether an overall difference exist between the two groups of securitizing and non-securitizing banks. Differentiation is based on the previously selected financial variables. Should such difference be detected, 2) determine at the univariate level which of these financial variables account for the difference between the two groups.

The null hypothesis is, therefore, stated as follows: Adopters and non-adopters of the technique of asset securitization are no different when compared on the basis of size, level of international banking, level of wholesale banking, capital ratio, profitability, portfolio quality (measured by portfolio diversification and the ratio of net charge-offs to total loans), liquidity, cost of funds and comparative advantage.

Testing for overall group differences at the multivariate level can be done through Roy's greatest characteristic root[82], Wilks's lambda (also known as the U statistic or the maximum likelihood criteria[83]), Hotelling's trace[84], and Pillai's Criteria[85]. Should the obtained significance level be below the pre-specified ($\alpha=0.05$), we reject the null hypothesis of equivalent mean vectors. Statistical packages, such as SAS and SPSS, have all of the aforementioned statistics and their associated probabilities as part of the output for MANOVA.

The fundamental distinction between these measures is "their assessment of differences across 'dimensions' of the dependent variables. Roy's greatest characteristic root, as the name implies, measures the differences on only the first canonical root (or Discriminant function)[86]" (Hair et al, p. 161). The other three measures, on the other hand, consider all characteristic roots[87] and can be approximated by an F statistic.

Generally, these tests lead to the same conclusions. However, Pillai is the test of choice when these criteria are ordered on the basis of power (ability to detect differences when they exist) and robustness (limited effect to departure from assumptions) (Wirtz, 1992, p.27)[88]. Roy's criterion is the one to be most severely affected by violations of the assumptions (Hair et al., p.161).

Should the overall MANOVA test lead to the rejection of the null hypothesis of no overall group differences, post-hoc tests are conducted at the univariate level. Control for type I error is obtained through the Bonferroni t-tests. A special option for this test is available under the SAS MANOVA procedure.

Regression Analysis

While MANOVA is used to determine whether there is an overall difference between securitizing and non-securitizing banks, regression analysis is conducted to assess the effect of each of these variables on the level of assets to be securitized for the period[89]. A bank is not only faced with the decision of whether or not to securitize assets, but it also must decide how much to securitize.

In order to understand the underlying factors in this decision, a regression model is estimated using the same data used for MANOVA analysis and based on the same bank characteristics used for MANOVA as independent variables. The dependent variable in this model is the dollar amount of securitized assets divided by total assets. The regression equation is:

$$MABSTAi = \beta_0 + \beta_1 X_{1i} + \beta_2 X_{2i} + \beta_3 X_{3i} + \beta_4 X_{4i} + \beta_5 X_{5i} + \beta_6 X_{5i} + \beta_7 X_{7i} + \beta_8 X_{8i} + \beta_9 X_{9i} + \beta_{10} X_{10i} + \beta_{11} X_{11i} + \beta_{12} X_{12i} + \beta_{13} X_{13i} + \beta_{14} X_{14i} + \beta_{15} X_{15i} + \epsilon i$$

where[90]:

Figure 4-3: Null Hypothesis Testing: ANOVA vs. MANOVA

ANOVA

H0: $\mu 1 = \mu 2 = \ldots = \mu k$.

Null Hypothesis (H0) = all the group means are equal, that is, they come from the same population.

MANOVA

$$
\text{Ho} = \begin{vmatrix} \mu 11 \\ \mu 21 \\ \\ \mu p1 \end{vmatrix} = \begin{vmatrix} \mu 12 \\ \mu 22 \\ \\ \mu p2 \end{vmatrix} = \ldots\ldots\ldots = \begin{vmatrix} \mu 1k \\ \mu 2k \\ \\ \mu pk \end{vmatrix}
$$

Null Hypothesis (H0) = all the group means vectors are equal, that is, they come from the same population.

μpk = mean of variable p, group k.

- **MABS95A** is the ratio of securitized assets (both mortgage and non-mortgage) to average assets during the 1995 reporting period.
- β_0 is a constant and $\beta_1 - \beta_{15}$ are regression coefficients;

Bank Characteristics
- X_1: LASSET is the variable for log(assets);
- X_2: FARATIO is the ratio of international assets to total assets;
- X_3: WSRATIO is a wholesale ratio measured by the sum of commercial & industrial loans, government and non-government securities, and non-correspondent interbank loans divided by total assets;

Bank Capitalization
- X_4: RBCRATIO is the risk-based capital ratio, that is, the ratio of qualifying capital to total adjusted assets;

Bank Profitability[91]
- X_5: NIIRATIO is the ratio of fee income to net income;

- X_6: ROA is the return on assets;

Loan Portfolio Quality
- X_7: L is the loan diversification index, that is, the $\sum L_i^2$, where L_i is the loan to asset ratio for different loan types;
- X_8: NTLNLSR is the ratio of net charge-offs divided by total loans and leases;

Bank Funding Resources/Liquidity
- X_9: LIQ1: Deposits to loan Ratio;
- X_{10}: LIQ2 is the ratio of volatile deposits to total assets;
Cost of Funds
- X_{11}: COSTR1: Deposit Interest Expense to Total Interest Expense;
- X_{12}: COSTR2: Deposit Interest Expense to Interest Loan Income;
Competitive Advantage
- X_{13}: LOANLS is the ratio of securitizable loans (mortgage loans, credit card receivables, and auto loans + respective unused commitments) to total loans and leases;
- X_{14}: LOANGR95 is the growth rate of loans during 1995;
- X_{15}: MABS94A is the ratio of assets previously securitized/average assets for the 1994 reporting period;
- ϵ_i is the error term.

The objective of the regression is to assess the relative contribution of each of the independent variables in explaining observed levels of asset securitization by banks. Hypothesis testing for overall significance and estimated coefficient significance is conducted through F and t scores, respectively.

DATA SOURCE

Data used for hypothesis testing are survey data for the population of US banks with domestic and foreign offices from the *"Consolidated Reports of Condition and Income"* for 1994–1995 time period filed with the Federal Deposit Insurance Corporation (FDIC), also known as Call Reports. The principal source of data on asset securitization activities of U.S. commercial multinational banks is *"Schedule L"* to the Call Reports, filed quarterly by banks. The second source is the *"Asset Sales Report"*, a weekly newsletter published by *American Banker–Bond Buyer*. Another source that follows new issues of ABSs is the *"Wall Street Journal"*[92] in its Credit Market and New Issues Section. The latter two sources report in a timely manner public issues of asset-backed security offerings and the terms relating to each one of them.

NOTES

54. One determinant risk associated with mortgage-backed securities and their derivatives, and not shared by non-mortgage backed securities, is prepayment risk. The difficulty in pricing these securities has generated a sheer amount of research on modeling and forecasting pre-payment rates given different interest rate and economic scenarios.

55. This investment includes (1) payment for legal, accounting, regulatory, and tax advice, (2) time spent educating issuers, investors, and traders, (3) investment in computer systems for pricing and trading, and (4) capital and personnel commitments to support market-making. In addition, investment banks that innovate are reported to pay $1 million annually to staff product development groups with two to six bankers.

56. No conclusive evidence has been presented, however, regarding the multi-product banks and probable costs/benefits accruing to these banks. For a detailed analysis to this effect, please refer to the work of Bentson, Berger, Hanweck, and Humphry, 1983.

57. The technique used in their investigation is Logit analysis. Both Pavel and Phillis and Gorton use a broad definition of loan sales, that is, outright sales and securitization. Because of the then recent and limited reporting requirements about securitization at the time, the data gathered was greatly limited to outright sales.

58. Please refer to the section about MANOVA where it is mentioned that even in the case of absence of *univariate* significance for all variables, we may still detect *overall, multivariate* significance. This reasoning holds for all of the subsequent variables in the study.

59. Please refer to the previous chapter regarding the diffusion of the technique of asset securitization to foreign markets and the involvement of US banks in such a process.

60. The author is aware that there will be cases where problems of multicolinearity may arise. Multicolinearity, however, is not an issue in the case of MANOVA. Please refer to the section about MANOVA.

61. The emphasis on capital requirements is due to the fact that there has been a shift away from reserve requirements toward capital monitoring. While reserve requirements are based on liabilities, capital requirements are based on

assets. It is believed, therefore, that capital ratio constitutes a better proxy for regulatory taxes then reserve requirements in the case of asset securitization.

62. Emprirical studies focused on gains in market value accruing to the securitizing entity following an issue of securitized assets on the market. The cost-return structure of securitization deals have never been a matter of investigation, even though it's been argued that the costs involved have deterred several entities from entering the market.

63. Federal Reserve Board, 1990a, p. 5.

64. It has been demonstrated both theoretically and empirically that a portfolio with a larger number of assets is less risky than a portfolio with fewer assets. Risk is quantified as the variability of the portfolio returns (i.e. standard deviation). Should this argument be applied to banks, banks have an incentive to diversify their lending activities geographically, by sector, and/or customer, for that should allow them to reach more stable returns on their assets. For a much more detailed analysis and illustrations of the benefits of diversification, see, among others, James C. Van Horne, 1984, pp. 55–65; Willian F. Sharpe, 1981; John Lintner, 1965, pp. 587–615; and Harry Markowitz, 1959.

65. This measure of portfolio diversification is based on the Herfindahl-Herschmin Index (HHI)-a "measure used by federal antitrust authorities to examine concentration in local banking markets and in markets in other industries. The HHI for a state is determined by calculating the percentage of deposits held by every depository institution in the state, then squaring these numbers and summing the results." The Federal Reserve Bulletin, 1996b, p.12–13.

66. Suppose two banks A and B with equal asset size (100) and equal loan size (60). Bank A has only one type of loans: Consumer loans = 60. Bank B has two types of loans: Consumer loans = 30,C&I = 30.

The diversification ratio for bank A = (60/100)2=0.36.

The diversification ratio for bank B = (30/100)2 + (30/100)2 = 0.18 (0.09 + 0.09) < 0.36. Therefore, the lower the number of assets in the loan portfolio, the higher the diversification ratio.

67. Because of the theoretical nature of their work, these findings were not supplemented by empirical evidence.

68. Shortages of savings and increased laon demand may cause banks to use brokered deposits.

69. This list is by no means exhaustive, but it is worth mentioning that Altman (1968), along with Beaver (1968), was one of the first to use financial ratios for corporate financial analysis in general and the prediction of corporate bankruptcy in particular.

70. Please refer to the work of Zanakis and Walter (1994) for an extensive literature review of statistical studies on mergers and acquisitions and takeovers in various sectors of the economy.

71. These involve the study of choices made (to sell or not sell assets, to securitize or not securitize, to list shares on the stock market or not to list, ...) by the group being studied, or events that have occurred (failed/did not fail, having one's securities downgraded/not downgraded, ...). Logit or Discriminant analyses are usually the statistical tools used to study these events.

72. The definition of this variable is based on Holland's work (1988, pp. 178–184).

73. The international aspect of the wholesale variable is reflected in the International Banking Variable.

74. The computation of the ratio is lengthy and involves the use of some 47 variables spanning the entire Call Report. Those interested in the computational algorithm could refer to Kevin Wilson at the Federal Reserve Board, Washington D.C.

75. Based on the works of Hassan (1993), Donahoo and Shaffer (1991), Holland (1988), Phillis (1988), and Pavel and Phillis (1987), The UBPR Report (1995), and Personal Interviews with Boemio (1996), Wilson (1996) and Berger (1994).

76. This section is based on the works of Demaris (1992), Hair et al. (1992), Jobson (1992), and Wirtz (1992).

77. Notice that with MANOVA, the roles of the dependent and independent variables are reversed. The independent variables of the regression analysis are the dependent variables for MANOVA and vice-versa.

78. In fact, as explained later, it is the equality of composites that is being tested, rather than the equality of mean vectors.

79. From a procedural standpoint, what happens with MANOVA is that "a 'composite' (a linear combination) dependent variable is created from the set of the dependent variables so as to *maximize group differences*; ANOVA is then performed on the composite dependent variable." (Wirtz, 1992, p.22, emphasis added). The weights in the composite are randomly assigned to the different dependent variables, and, therefore, are beyond the control of the researcher. Maximization of the group difference explains significance at the multivariate level when none exists at the univariate one.

80. In this study, the ratio of Nnon-securitizors/Nsecuritizors = 105/95=1.1, is below the 1.5 benchmark, making violation of this assumption of minimal concern.

81. What we're looking for is multivariate, not univariate, normality. Unfortunately, none of the major statistical packages (BMDP, SAS or SPSSX) have a test of multivariate normality (Stevens, 1992, p.248). Mardia (1974) has developed multivariate measures of skewness and kurtosis, however, the tests are not available for more than two variables, which severely limits its usefulness

(Kress, 1983, p. 420). All we can test for is univariate normality for several dependent variables. Note that multivariate normality means univariate normality for each dependent variable. Univariate normality, however, does not necessarily lead to a multivariate one. But that is the closest we can get to testing normality at the multivariate level.

82. The characteristic (determinant) root of a square matrix A is a value d such that $\det(A - dI) = \phi$, where I is the identity matrix and ϕ is the zero matrix. For a p x p matrix, there are, in general, p such roots, known also as Latent Roots or Eigenvalues. The corresponding row-vectors U or column-vectors V for which UA = dU or AV = dV are called characteristic vectors (Kendall and Buckland, 1971, p.22).

83. Wilks U statistic is defined as $Ut = \Pi^l_{i=1}Q_i$ where Q_i (i=1,2, . . . ,l) are the roots determinantal equation $\det(A - Q(A+C)) = \phi$, l the number of independent gamma variables, and Π a product notation. A is the within-groups multivariate dispersion matrix and C is the between-groups multivariate dispersion matrix with n_1 (number of groups – 1) and n_2 degrees of freedom respectively and $l=\min(p, n_1)$, where p is the number of dependent variables (Kandall and Buckland, 1971, p. 164 and Kres, 1983, p.5–6). The larger the between-groups dispersion, the smaller the value of Wilks' lambda and the greater the implied significance (Hair et. al., 1992, p.161).

84. Hotellings' Trace = Tr(A*C-1). A is the within-groups multivariate dispersion matrix and C is the between-groups multivariate dispersion matrix with n1 (number of groups-1) and n2 degrees of freedom respectively. T2 = Tr * n2.

85. Pillai criteria: Tr (A * (A+C)-1). A is the within-groups multivariate dispersion matrix and C is the between-groups multivariate dispersion matrix with n1 (number of groups-1) and n2 degrees of freedom respectively (Kres, 1983, p.6 and Wirtz, 1992).

86. Canonical root, also known as squared canonical correlations, provide an estimate of the amount of shared variance between the respective optimally weighted linear composites of criterion (dependent variables) and predictor (independent) variables. A discriminant function is a linear equation of the following form: $Z = \Sigma w_i x_i$ (i=1,. . ., n) where Z is the discriminant score, w_i is the discriminant weight given to x_i, and x_i is an independent variable. Please refer to Hair et al. (1992), chapters 3 and 5 respectively for a more detailed discussion of Multiple Discriminant Analysis and Canonical Correlation Analysis.

87. Total number of characteristic roots = min (p, k-1), where p is the number of dependent variables and k the number of groups in the study.

88. Notice, however, that "[m]ost of the published work on the power of these tests is based on simulation studies. These are inevitably of limited applicability, because the number of possible variables-the dimensionality, sample size

and eigenvalue structure—is so large. The same is true of studies of robustness."
(Krzanowski and Mariott, 1994, p.186)

89. It should be reiterated that MANOVA is a technique to asses group differences on a multivariate level based on whether or not an event takes place. Unlike regression analysis, it does not establish causality.

90. Ratio definition is based on the UBPR User's Guide (Federal Financial Institution Examination Council, 1995). The risk-based capital ratio, however, is still in its development stage. Finalization is expected by the end of this year. The author uses the Federal Reserve algorithm (Board of Governors of the Federal Reserve System, 1995) for the computation of RBCRATIO.

91. Cases of simulaneous determination between dependent and independent variables are likely to be present. As mentioned earlier (section 4–2, R6), loan portfolio quality is likely to affect securitization just as it is likely to be affected by it . That is also true of bank funding and securitizable loans.

92. The Wall Street Journal reports, in a new section: Asset-Backed Securities, developments and new issues of ABS on a regular basis.

CHAPTER 5

Findings and Conclusion

Three main areas are covered in this section of the book. First the sample in the study is presented with descriptive information regarding sample banks' involvement with securitization. Then the findings of the MANOVA procedure and the regression analysis are discussed. The section is then ended with a presentation of the conclusion to the research.

DATA DESCRIPTION

Participants in asset securitization were matched with non-securitizing banks of comparable size from the top 200 US commercial banks. The research sample includes 95 securitizing banks matched with 105 non-securitizing banks, a total of 200 banks (please refer to Figure 5-1 for the distribution of securitization among the top 200 banks). One bank (Wells Fargo Bank Arizona NA) had missing values and was deleted from the sample of non-securitizing banks (please refer to Figure 5-2 for a complete listing of banks in the study). Citibank NA, New York, was the largest bank at year-end 1995[93], with assets of $220.11 billion, and Bank of America NT&SA a distant second with $163.40 billion in assets. These two are the leading banks within their respective bank holding companies and have several affiliates within the top 200. The smallest bank was JP Morgan[94], Delaware, with $3.01 billion in assets. The top 200 banks had $2,946.85 billion in assets in 1995, compared with $2,694.44 billion at year-end 1994 (a 10% increase). Of the 200 largest commercial banks, six had no affiliation with bank holding companies (BHCs). These banks were American Express Centurion[95], Monogram

Figure 5-1: Distribution of Security Banks by Asset Size

Rank	Number	Assets	% of Total(1)	Cumul	MABS	% of Total(2)	Cumul
Top 100	60	1,758.14	87.07%	na	83.81	65.34%	na
101-200	35	166.28	8.23%	95.30%	25.5	19.88%	85.22%
201-300	19	42.324	2.10%	97.40%	15.65	12.20%	97.42%
301-400	13	16.64	0.82%	98.22%	1.75	1.36%	98.78%
401-600	17	14.22	0.70%	98.92%	0.45	0.35%	99.13%
601-800	12	6.18	0.31%	99.23%	0.14	0.11%	99.24%
801-1000	12	4.43	0.22%	99.45%	0.1	<0.01%	99.24%
1001-2000	34	8.37	0.41%	99.86%	0.81	0.63%	99.87%
2001-3000	11	1.37	0.07%	99.93%	0.01	<0.01%	99.87%
3001-5000	10	0.89	0.04%	99.97%	0.01	<0.01%	99.87%
5001-8464	11	0.41	0.02%	99.99%	0.04	0.03%	99.90%
Total	234	2,019.27	100%(3)		128.26		100%(3)

(1): % of Total   Assets of Securitizing Banks within Rank/Assets of All Securitizing Banks
(2): % of Total   Securitized Assets By Banks Within Rank/Securitized Assets By All 234 Banks
(3): May Not Add Up Due to Rounding

Source: The FDIC Tapes Dec. 1994-1995

CCB of Georgia[96], Greenwood Trust, First USA, Household Bank Nevada, and Capital One Bank. The latter four were aggressive securitizors as they averaged an ABS to asset ratio of 117%, much higher than the securitizing sample mean of 12.5%, or that of the securitizing population mean of 11.8%.

Bank holding companies differed considerably in the way they structured their business internally in the pursuit of their securitization objectives. Citicorp, for instance, had limited purpose banks as well as retail affiliates. Two of its affiliates, Citibank Nevada and Citibank South Dakota, are limited purpose banks and had a tremendous impact on the securitization market, its development and its growth. Its commercial bank affiliates, on the other hand had either minor involvement (Citibank NA, the largest affiliate within the group) or no involvement at all (Citibank New York, Citibank Delaware) with asset securitization.

Several other bank holding companies are multi-bank holding companies with no clear specialization except may be by region. State legislative actions and falling interstate barriers have allowed several banks to expand into neighboring states at first and then nationwide. Most of these interstate BHCs tend to be in retail banking, therefore, involved with securitization on a rather sporadic, non-specialized way. NationsBank, for instance, has five affiliates among the top 200 banks and none of them has a high level of concentration in credit card, auto or mortgage loans. Accordingly, they have minor involvement with asset securitization. This is also true of Bank of America, which, with six affiliates within the top 200, has no securitized assets.

With $17.5 billion in securitized assets, MBNA America NA (ranked 55) was the leading bank in asset securitization, followed by Citibank Nevada ($15.2 billion) and First USA Bank ($11.7 billion). The banks with the highest relative securitization level were First USA Bank (a ratio of ABS to assets of 166%), Citibank Nevada (162%), Capital One (157%), MBNA America Bank (144%), and Greenwood Trust Co. (114%). All of these banks dealt exclusively with credit card securitization for they were limited purpose banks. Citibank, Nevada and MBNA America are affiliates within bank holding companies and have a mission to warehouse credit card business of the holding company. First USA and Capital One (a new comer to the market) have no affiliation with any bank holding company and are important players in the market.

The market for securitized bank assets was characterized by restored confidence in its safety after the 1994 interest rate hikes initiated by the Federal Reserve. Another feature of the market is its high degree of concentration, and hence, the under-utilization of this technique by the majority of U.S. banks despite its well publicized benefits and established technology. The volume of securitized assets increased by 51% between 1994 and 1995, the largest one-year increase ever recorded for commercial banks. Concentration in the securitization market was two fold: among banks and by product. The top five securitizing banks (MBNA America, Citibank Nevada, Greenwood Trust, First USA, and Citibank South Dakota) totaled $65.2 billion in securitized assets, representing 50.8% of all securitized assets in 1995 and 59.6% of securitized assets by the top 200 banks. As shown in Figure 5-2 below, such high degree of concentration is further evidenced by the distribution of securitization activities across the commercial banking industry. Eighty five per cent of all securitization activities happened within the top 200 banks, 99% within the top 600 banks, and less than 1% was accounted for by the remaining 9,500 banks. Similar proportions were seen in 1994.

Credit card receivables dominated the market in 1995, as they did in 1994, with 87% and 86% market share in 1995 and 1994, respectively (please refer to Figure.5-3). Citibank, between its two affiliates (Citibank Nevada and Citibank South Dakota) accounted for 22% of the overall credit card securitization market. MBNA America Bank accounted for another 16%. This fastest growing segment of the market was fueled by the proliferation of credit card debt. Indeed, the typical American uses four credit cards, gets solicited for 6 more each year and is using these cards more often for purchases (*The Wall Street Journal*, Oct.30; 1995). A very distant second is the mortgage-backed securities market, with less then 8% in market share. The auto loan segment remained flat, capturing less than 4% of the total volume of ABS market.

Sixteen financial ratios (including the one used as a dependent variable for the regression analysis) were used in the analysis as measures of various financial characteristics of securitizing banks (please refer to Figure 5-4 below). The multivariate analysis of variance, MANOVA, method was used to test for overall group significance. The data was for 1995. After concluding that the mean vectors are not equivalent, other more specific comparisons, called post hoc tests, were conducted. The four test criteria (Wilks' Lambda, Hotelling-Lawley Trace, Pillai's Trace, and Roy's Greatest Root) for overall significance are part of the SAS output for MANOVA. Significance at the univariate level is also provided by the SAS output for MANOVA.

The second step in the analysis was to isolate the group of securitizing banks and to regress the level of assets securitized during 1995 on the aforementioned financial characteristics. In this case, lagged ratios pertaining to the year 1994 were used. The rational behind this decision is to allow for the temporal order between the act of securitization and the securitization effect on financial characteristics[97]. Parameter estimates, t-scores and corresponding probabilities are all provided through the output for the SAS regression procedure.

FINDINGS

The MANOVA Procedure

In this section, the hypothesis of overall difference is tested. The financial ratios were used as an input to the SAS-MANOVA computer program. MANOVA statistics obtained will be presented later in this section.

Testing for MANOVA Assumptions The initial step in running MANOVA is to test for the tenability of the assumption of normality of the dependent variables in the study. While MANOVA is not greatly affected by departure from normality, the Box-test for the homogeneity of covariance matrices is quite sensitive to such departure (Wirtz, 1992, Hair et al., 1992 and Stevens, 1992). SAS Univariate procedure offers two ways (aside from the graphical ones: stem-leaf and Box plot) to test for univariate normality[98]: the Shapiro-Wilk test with the associated significance probability and the skewness and kurtosis coefficients. An indication of non-normality is a high degree of skewness. If the data are highly skewed to either the left or the right, the distribution is asymmetrical and does not have the standard bell-shaped curve. The coefficient of kurtosis measures the heaviness of the tails of a distribution. A normal distribution will have a kurtosis of coefficient of 3. Values higher than 3 indicate leptokurtosis (peaked distribution) whereas values lower than 3 indicate platykurtosis (flattened distribution) (Stevens, 1992, p. 255).

The latter two coefficients are used in this study, for they allow the separation of these two types of non-normality, whereas the Shapiro-Wilk statistic combines them (Stevens, 1992, p. 253). The reason such separation is sought is due to the fact that skewness does not have an effect on power, while kurtosis does. One, therefore, needs to worry more about violations due to kurtosis, especially platykurtosis (Stevens, 1992, p.253–4). The skewness and kurtosis coefficients are displayed in Figure 5-5 below.

For a sample size of 200 and $\alpha=0.05$, the significance level is $Sk_{crit} = |0.280|$ (Pearson and Hartley, Table 34B, p. 183). That is, if $\{-0.280 <$

Skewness Coefficient > 0.280}, we fail to reject the null hypothesis of no skewness. If the skewness coefficient lies outside the significance interval, the null hypothesis of no skewness is rejected in favor of the alternative hypothesis. As shown in Figure 5-5 below, the ROA ratio is the only ratio for which we are more then 95% confident that it has a symmetrical distribution. We reach the same results at the 1% level. All tests are significant except for the ROA ratio (for $\alpha=0.01$, $Sk_{crit} = |0.403|$).

For a sample size of 200 and ($=0.05$, the critical value for leptokurtosis (upper value) $Kr_{crit,lept} = 3.57$. Thus, if the value of kurtosis is higher then 3.57, we conclude leptokurtosis exists. This is the case of foreign asset ratio, RBC ratio, diversification index, fee income ratio, ROA, deposit to asset ratio, securitizable loan ratio, loan growth ratio, funding efficiency ratio, and prior securitization ratio.

The critical value for platykurtosis (lower value) $Kr_{crit, plat} = 2.51$ (Pearson and Hartley, 1956, Table 34C, p. 184). If the kurtosis value is less than 2.51, we conclude that platykurtosis exists. This is the case of Log (asset), Wholesale ratio, Loan-to-Asset ratio, Volatile deposit ratio, and Funding Cost ratio.

The non-normal nature of the cross-sectional distribution of financial ratios has long been documented (So, 1987; Lee, 1985; Bedingfield et al., 1985; and Deakin, 1976). These results were, therefore, expected. Several transformations were attempted in order to remedy the problems of skewness and kurtosis, with little improvement.

In the case of positive skewness (i.e., skewness>0.280), the log transformation[99] was performed on the following variables: foreign asset ratio, risk-based capital ratio, loan growth ratio, diversification index, loan to deposit ratio, volatile deposit ratio, net charge-off ratio, securitizable asset ratio, cost efficiency ratio and prior securitization ratio. All the transformed variables had a significant skewness value. For those with negative skewness (skewness<–0.280), the square root was taken. That was the case of the wholesale ratio, the net income ratio, the loan to asset ratio, and the cost of fund ratio. Once more, all the transformed variables had significant skewness coefficients.

Similar steps were undertaken to deal with the problem of kurtosis (all variables had kurtotic distributions). Again, no gains were achieved in this area, which leads the author to believe that the non-normality of these financial ratios may be caused by the violation of the assumption of proportionality, as explained below. This is in accordance with the findings of So (1987), who, like Deaken before her (1976), has found that many ratios still deviate significantly from the normal distribution after removal of outliers, logarithm and square root transformations.

Figure 5-2: Listing of Banks in the Study, 200 Largest Banks, 1995.

Name	BHC	FED	Assets ($mm)	Securitization in 1995 ($mm)	% of Assets (1995)	Securitization in 1994 ($mm)	% of Assets (1994)
Citibank NA	Y	Y	220110.00	3134.00	1.42%	3456.00	1.64%
Bank of America NT&SA	Y	Y	163398.00	59.00	0.04%	100.00	0.07%
Chemical Bank	Y	Y	147120.00	29.00	0.02%	108.00	0.08%
Morgan Guaranty TC of NY	Y	Y	143397.40	0.00	NA	0.00	NA
Chase Manhattan Bank NA	Y	Y	100352.00	1965.00	1.96%	834.30	0.89%
NationsBank NA	Y	Y	79179.16	74.28	0.09%	0.00	NA
Bankers Trust Co	Y	Y	79080.00	1.00	0.001%	2.00	0.00%
First NB of Chicago	Y	Y	49360.47	11.53	0.023%	13.65	0.03%
Wells Fargo	Y	Y	49091.76	0.00	NA	0.00	NA
NationsBank of Texas NA	Y	Y	48368.45	251.06	0.52%	53.57	0.14%
Bank of New York	Y	Y	42711.91	158.97	0.37%	0.00	NA
PNC Bank NA	Y	Y	41905.46	56.08	0.13%	70.26	0.16%
First NB of Boston	Y	Y	40273.93	6.81	0.00%	9.00	0.00%
NationsBank NA South	Y	Y	37609.62	275.77	0.73%	0.00	NA
First Union NB of Florida	Y	Y	36591.49	35.23	0.10%	20.34	0.07%
Mellon Bank NA	Y	Y	35565.12	156.49	0.44%	186.49	0.57%
First Fidelity Bank NA	Y	Y	32686.86	121.10	0.40%	138.88	0.41%
NBD Bank	Y	Y	29461.64	0.00	NA	0.00	NA
Natwest Bank NA	Y	Y	28489.10	0.00	NA	0.00	NA
Comerica Bank	Y	Y	28394.04	4.01	0.01%	4.97	0.02%
First Union NB of NC	Y	Y	27415.42	12.00	0.04%	16.27	0.07%
Wachovia Bank of NC NA	Y	Y	26825.19	0.00	NA	0.00	NA
First Interstate Bank of CA	Y	Y	26555.76	1.42	<0.001%	1.81	NA
State Street Bank&Trust Co	Y	Y	25558.10	0.00	NA	0.00	NA
Society National Bank	Y	Y	22307.49	1180.14	5.29%	690.42	2.81%
Corestates Banks NA	Y	Y	21577.88	6.83	0.03%	123.19	0.56%
Marine Midland Bank	Y	Y	20342.47	211.79	1.04%	280.39	1.53%
Texas Commerce bank NA	Y	Y	19990.22	0.00	NA	0.00	NA
Union Bank	Y	N	19646.41	0.00	NA	0.00	NA
BanK One Texas NA	Y	Y	18797.76	903.55	4.81%	198.35	1.09%
Norwest Bank of Minnesota NA	Y	Y	18233.56	27.34	0.15%	33.01	0.20%

Figure 5-2 (*Continued*): Listing of Banks in the Study, 200 Largest Banks, 1995.

Name	BHC	FED	Assets ($mm)	Securitization in 1995 ($mm)	% of Assets (1995)	Securitization in 1994 ($mm)	% of Assets (1994)
Fleet NB of Connecticut	Y	Y	18129.50	62.83	0.35%	124.23	0.73%
Wachovia Bank of Georgia NA	Y	Y	17345.53	0.00	NA	0.00	NA
Seattle-First National Bank	Y	Y	17151.00	0.00	NA	0.00	NA
First Bank NA	Y	Y	16376.00	19.45	0.12%	27.84	0.10%
Bank of America Illinois	Y	N	16171.00	0.00	NA	0.00	NA
Branch Banking&Trust Co.	Y	N	15991.53	91.40	0.57%	48.13	0.52%
Key Bank of New York	Y	Y	15372.76	33.82	0.22%	237.91	1.59%
Northern Trust Co.	Y	Y	15230.54	0.00	NA	0.00	NA
Fleet Bank	Y	Y	14621.32	0.00	NA	0.00	NA
Huntington National Bank	Y	Y	14424.54	22.27	0.15%	20.42	0.17%
Integra Bank	Y	Y	13978.57	29.31	0.21%	29.75	0.39%
Fleet NB of Massachusetts	Y	Y	13867.73	0.00	NA	87.00	0.60%
Crestar Bank	Y	Y	13557.74	0.00	NA	0.00	NA
First Am Bank—Michigan NA	Y	Y	13338.29	579.95	4.35%	0.00	NA
Midlantic Bank NA	Y	Y	13289.59	100.35	0.76%	99.04	0.77%
United Jersey Bank	Y	Y	13129.43	0.00	NA	0.00	NA
Banc One Arizona NA	Y	Y	13080.76	200.50	1.53%	219.84	1.84%
Banco Popular de Puerto Rico	Y	N	12931.00	0.00	NA	0.00	NA
Citibank South Dakota NA	Y	Y	12697.89	9226.05	72.66%	9293.82	85.38%
Trust Co Bank	Y	Y	12459.20	0.00	NA	0.00	NA
Meridian Bank	Y	Y	12439.77	328.69	2.64%	166.70	1.30%
Harris Trust&Savings Bank	Y	Y	12247.56	0.00	NA	0.00	NA
MBNA America Bank NA	Y	Y	12162.77	17258.74	144.09%	10353.71	116.07%
United States NB of Oregon	Y	Y	12126.00	5.00	0.04%	11.00	0.10%
First Union NB of Georgia	Y	N	12116.07	2013.78	16.62%	15.12	0.17%
Bank of Hawaii	Y	N	11827.45	363.66	3.08%	0.00	NA
Fleet National Bank	Y	Y	11693.03	0.00	NA	0.00	NA
Lasalle National Bank	Y	Y	11216.06	0.00	NA	0.00	NA
Boatmens NB of St Louis	Y	Y	11180.06	291.92	2.61%	0.00	NA
American Express Centurion	N	N	11173.43	0.00	NA	0.00	NA
Baybank National Association	Y	Y	11128.43	31.90	0.29%	34.62	0.36%

Figure 5-2 (*Continued*): Listing of Banks in the Study, 200 Largest Banks, 1995.

Name	BHC	FED	Assets ($mn)	Securitization in 1995 ($mn)	% of Assets (1995)	Securitization in 1994 ($mn)	% of Assets (1994)
First Tennessee Bank NA	Y	Y	11127.23	682.07	6.13%	607.70	6.05%
Southtrust Bank of AL NA	Y	Y	11121.60	0.00	NA	0.00	NA
Fleet Bank of MA NA	Y	Y	11037.14	38.73	0.35%	46.36	0.48%
First Union NB of Virginia	Y	Y	11032.72	0.00	NA	0.00	NA
Chase Manhattan Bank USA	Y	N	10889.33	4625.00	42.47%	3000.00	29.53%
Central Fidelty NB	Y	Y	10755.00	0.04	<0.001%	20.68	0.21%
Signet Bank	Y	Y	10727.03	218.93	2.04%	5145.12	76.20%
National City Bank	Y	Y	10316.76	64.31	0.62%	0.78	<0.01%
Greenwood Trust Co.	N	N	10113.81	11561.86	114.09%	8183.04	94.61%
Amsouth Bank of Alabama	Y	Y	9826.42	0.00	NA	0.66	<0.01%
Old Kent Bank	Y	Y	9748.23	231.56	2.38%	0.00	NA
Michigan National Bank	Y	Y	9385.51	91.09	0.97%	97.51	1.18%
Citibank Nevada NA	Y	Y	9369.61	15163.26	161.83%	12651.95	136.36%
First Alabama Bank	Y	N	10280.11	2.85	0.03%	3.55	0.04%
NBD Bank NA	Y	Y	10182.14	0.00	NA	0.00	NA
Manufacturers &Traders Tr Co.	Y	Y	10179.17	17.30	0.17%	15.89	0.18%
FCC National Bank	Y	Y	9211.57	7985.71	86.69%	6366.67	96.39%
Fifth Third Bank	Y	Y	9032.36	1.40	0.02%	1.70	0.02%
First American NB	Y	Y	9009.34	0.00	NA	0.00	NA
Bank of New York Delaware	Y	N	8795.04	0.00	NA	412.50	5.43%
Bank of America Arizona	Y	N	8761.23	0.00	NA	27.24	0.32%
First Interstate Bank of AZ NA	Y	Y	8758.26	6.61	0.08%	7.19	0.10%
European American Bank	Y	Y	8565.81	0.00	NA	0.00	NA
First NB of Maryland	Y	Y	8460.70	11.02	0.13%	13.91	0.19%
Star Bank NA	Y	Y	8388.68	3.78	0.05%	4.67	0.06%
Bank of California NA	Y	N	8041.49	0.00	NA	0.00	NA
Bank of Tokyo Trust Co.	Y	N	7931.92	0.00	NA	0.00	NA
Bank of America NA	Y	Y	7739.75	0.00	NA	0.00	NA
Key Bank of Washington	Y	N	7720.33	1.12	0.01%	1.79	0.02%
Bank One Columbus NA	Y	Y	7669.20	3494.41	45.56%	1173.95	15.42%
Sanwa Bank of California	Y	N	7627.88	0.00	NA	0.00	NA

Figure 5-2 (Continued): Listing of Banks in the Study, 200 Largest Banks, 1995.

Name	BHC	FED	Assets ($mm)	Securitization in 1995 ($mm)	% of Assets (1995)	Securitization in 1994 ($mm)	% of Assets (1994)
Citibank of NY State	Y	N	7476.60	0.00	NA	0.00	NA
Bank South	Y	Y	7356.65	1.58	0.02%	13.25	0.19%
Fleet Bank NA	Y	Y	7321.41	0.00	NA	0.00	NA
Bank of America TX	Y	Y	7286.61	0.00	NA	0.00	NA
First Am Bank-Ill NA	Y	Y	7243.48	0.00	NA	0.00	NA
Hibernia NB	Y	Y	7192.07	0.00	NA	0.00	NA
Firstar Bank of Milwaukee NA	Y	Y	7130.39	287.57	4.03%	29.94	0.47%
Wachovia Bank of SC NA	Y	Y	7127.58	0.00	NA	0.00	NA
First USA Bank	N	N	7056.64	11730.91	166.24%	5513.02	92.02%
US Bank of Washington NA	Y	N	7054.84	0.00	NA	0.00	NA
Colorado National Bank	Y	Y	7024.52	0.00	NA	0.00	NA
National City Bank Kentucky	Y	N	6981.79	0.00	NA	0.30	<0.01%
First Citizens Bank &Trust Co.	Y	N	6956.35	0.00	NA	0.00	NA
Norwest Bank of Colorado NA	Y	N	6647.21	610.53	9.19%	229.90	5.87%
First Interstate Bank of OR NA	Y	Y	6617.20	0.00	NA	0.00	NA
Bank of Indianapolis NA	Y	Y	6,484.86	182.63	2.82%	169.70	2.79%
First Security Bank of UT NA	Y	Y	6296.99	91.36	1.45%	0.93	0.02%
Compass Bank	Y	Y	6263.77	0.00	NA	0.00	NA
Premier Bank NA	Y	Y	6257.61	18.70	0.30%	23.75	0.44%
New Jersey NB	Y	N	6245.05	0.00	NA	0.00	NA
First Hawaiian Bank	Y	N	6198.47	318.05	5.13%	5.38	0.09%
First Interstate Bank of TX NA	Y	Y	6940.19	0.00	NA	0.00	NA
Mercantile BK of St Louis NA	Y	Y	6875.30	0.00	NA	0.00	NA
National City Bank of Columbus	Y	Y	6763.93	389.01	5.75%	90.16	1.52%
Nationsbank of Delaware	Y	N	6712.52	1429.79	21.30%	1330.00	27.03%
NBD Bank	Y	N	6193.50	0.00	NA	0.00	NA
Provident Bank	Y	Y	5951.55	0.00	NA	0.00	NA
Suntrust Bank Central FL NA	Y	Y	5748.14	0.00	NA	0.00	NA
National City Bank Indiana	Y	N	5623.04	0.00	NA	0.00	NA
Summit Bank	Y	N	5615.46	0.96	0.02%	206.44	3.81%
First Interstate BK of WA NA	Y	Y	5519.06	0.00	NA	0.00	NA

Figure 5-2 (*Continued*): Listing of Banks in the Study, 200 Largest Banks, 1995.

Name	BHC	FED	Assets ($mn)	Securitization in 1995 ($mn)	% of Assets (1995)	Securitization in 1994 ($mn)	% of Assets (1994)
Centura Bank	Y	Y	5327.30	1.32	0.03%	1.39	0.03%
Norwest Bank Sout Dakota NA	Y	Y	5241.20	0.00	NA	0.00	NA
Wilmington Trust Co.	Y	N	5237.54	0.00	NA	0.00	NA
NationsBank of Tennessee NA	Y	Y	5230.82	0.00	NA	0.00	NA
First NB Bank of Commerce	Y	Y	5207.88	0.00	NA	0.00	NA
Dauphin Deposit B&T Co	Y	Y	5186.37	1.08	0.02%	1.21	0.02%
Bank IV National Association	Y	Y	5063.56	19.76	0.39%	39.87	0.75%
Chemical Bank NA	Y	Y	5045.91	379.76	7.53%	51.09	2.08%
PNC Bank Kentucky Inc	Y	Y	5045.42	0.00	NA	0.00	NA
Trustmark National Bank	Y	Y	4983.22	0.00	NA	0.00	NA
Central Carolina B&T Co	Y	N	4966.87	0.00	NA	0.00	NA
Barnett Bank of South FL NA	Y	Y	4957.79	0.00	NA	0.00	NA
Magna Bank NA	Y	Y	4,913,97	0.00	NA	0.00	NA
Boston Safe Deposit&Trust Co	Y	N	4876.36	0.00	NA	0.00	NA
Sumitomo Bank of CA	Y	N	4855.98	0.00	NA	0.00	NA
Bank One Milwaukee	Y	Y	4677.93	0.00	NA	0.00	NA
West One Bank Idaho	Y	Y	4659.89	0.00	NA	0.00	NA
Barnett Bank Broward City NA	Y	Y	4639.54	0.00	NA	0.00	NA
Zions First National Bank	Y	Y	4309.95	459.59	0.11%	448.73	12.09%
Wells Fargo Bank AZ NA	Y	N	4307.54	0.00	NA	0.00	NA
Banco Santander Puerto Rico	Y	N	4281.92	0.00	NA	0.00	NA
Bank One Kentucky NA	Y	Y	4271.75	0.00	NA	0.00	NA
Bank of New York	Y	Y	4193.30	0.00	NA	0.00	NA
Boatmens First NB of KS City	Y	Y	4160.07	0.00	NA	0.00	NA
City Bank of Oklahoma NA	Y	Y	4144.48	11.31	0.27%	11.20	0.29%
National Bank	Y	Y	4138.47	0.00	NA	0.00	NA
Bank of America Nevada	Y	Y	4099.55	0.00	NA	22.68	0.54%
Riggs NB of Washington DC	Y	Y	4091.88	0.00	NA	0.00	NA
Capital One Bank	N	Y	4590.66	7189.09	156.60%	0.00	NA
Valley National Bank	Y	Y	4572.76	0.00	NA	0.00	NA
Industrial Bk of Japan Tr Co	Y	N	4534.43	0.00	NA	0.00	NA

Figure 5-2 (*Continued*): Listing of Banks in the Study, 200 Largest Banks, 1995.

Name	BHC	FED	Assets ($mn)	Securitization in 1995 ($mn)	% of Assets (1995)	Securitization in 1994 ($mn)	% of Assets (1994)
Deposit Guaranty NB	Y	Y	4479.71	0.00	NA	0.00	NA
Bank of the West	Y	N	4359.68	27.13	0.62%	38.35	0.95%
First National Bank	Y	Y	4059.29	0.00	NA	0.00	NA
First Security Bank of ID NA	Y	Y	3991.97	129.80	3.25%	0.00	NA
PNC Bank Ohio NA	Y	Y	3977.97	7189.09	156.60%	0.00	NA
Household Bank Nevada NA	N	Y	3973.63	1248.92	31.43%	1633.00	55.15%
M&I Marshall & Ilsley Bk	Y	Y	3960.80	69.69	1.76%	0.00	NA
Bank One Dayton NA	Y	Y	3951.85	45.28	1.15%	22.12	0.67%
Israel Discount Bank of NY	Y	N	3851.61	0.00	NA	0.00	NA
First Interstate BK of NV NA	Y	Y	3846.22	0.00	NA	0.00	NA
Southtrust Bank of GA NA	Y	Y	3840.29	21.65	0.56%	26.35	0.78%
Branch B&T Co of SC	Y	N	3818.55	0.00	NA	0.00	NA
Bank of America Oregon	Y	N	3679.96	21.56	0.59%	33.94	1.01%
Key Bank of Maine	Y	N	3676.72	0.00	NA	0.00	NA
Barnett Bank of Cntl FL NA	Y	Y	3631.00	0.00	NA	0.00	NA
Comerica Bank TX	Y	N	3622.46	0.00	NA	0.00	NA
Norwest Bank AZ NA	Y	Y	3604.13	0.00	NA	0.00	NA
Society NB Indiana	Y	Y	3590.11	0.00	NA	0.00	NA
Citizens Bank of Maryland	Y	N	3564.25	9.88	0.28%	25.82	0.78%
One Bank&Trust Co	Y	N	3519.88	0.00	NA	0.00	NA
Barnett Bk of Pinellas Cnty	Y	Y	3477.64	23.66	0.68%	31.68	0.86%
Citibank Delaware	Y	N	3476.51	0.00	NA	0.00	NA
Colonial Bank	Y	Y	3442.21	184.12	5.35%	0.00	NA
Fleet Bank–NH	Y	Y	3223.42	69.89	2.17%	49.46	2.82%
Norwest Bank Wyoming NA	Y	Y	3212.78	0.00	NA	0.00	NA
First Union NB of SC	Y	Y	3161.26	35.51	1.12%	7.82	0.33%
Rhode Island Hospital TR NB	Y	Y	3152.66	0.00	NA	0.00	NA
National City Bank Northeast	Y	Y	3151.86	0.00	NA	0.00	NA
First VA Bank	Y	Y	3133.98	0.00	NA	0.00	NA
Suntrust Bank South FL NA	Y	Y	3118.06	0.00	NA	0.00	NA
Bank One Colorado NA	Y	Y	3104.33	159.46	5.14%	66.42	4.74%

Figure 5-2 (*Continued*): Listing of Banks in the Study, 200 Largest Banks, 1995.

Name	BHC	FED	Assets ($mn)	Securitization in 1995 ($mn)	% of Assets (1995)	Securitization in 1994 ($mn)	% of Assets (1994)
Monogram CCB of Georgia	N	N	3431.21	0.00	NA	0.00	NA
Southtrust Bank of FL NA	Y	Y	3430.34	0.00	NA	0.00	NA
United Carolina Bank	Y	N	3420.65	0.00	NA	0.00	NA
Suntrust Bank of Nashville NA	Y	Y	3408.42	0.00	NA	0.00	NA
Barlett Bank Jacksonville NA	Y	Y	3407.84	0.86	0.03%	1.22	0.04%
North Fork Bank	Y	N	3282.45	5.25	0.16%	6.45	0.24%
PNC Mortgage Bank NA	Y	Y	3250.11	81.32	2.50%	53.78	1.70%
First National Bank of Omaha	Y	Y	3042.36	43.00	1.41%	0.00	NA
Commerce Bank NA	Y	Y	3019.01	0.00	NA	0.00	NA
JP Morgan Delaware	Y	N	3010.46	0.00	NA	0.00	NA
Total Top 200	**2946.85**	**109.31**	**75.10**				
All Banks	**4441.63**	**128.28**	**84.73**				
% of Total	**0.66**	**0.85**	**0.89**				

BHC: Yes if a member of a Bank Holding Company, No, otherwise.
Fed: Yes if a membership of the Federal Reserve System, No, otherwise.
%Assets: Ratio of asset-backed securities to total assets for the year.
Source: FDIC Tapes, Dec 1995, 1994.

Figure 5-3:US Commercial Bank Securitization by Asset Type

	1995		1994	
	All Banks	**Top 200**	**All Banks**	**Top 200**
Number	234	95	229	89
CARDs[100] ($bn)	111.53	94.68	72.71	65.16
& %	86.9%	86.6%	85.8%	86.6%
CARs[101] ($bn)	4.77	4.34	2.22	1.25
& %	3.7%	3.9%	2.6%	1.7%
MBS ($bn)	9.45	7.89	7.52	6.83
& %	7.4%	7.2%	8.9%	9.1%
Other ($bn)	2.51	2.40	2.28	1.82
& %	2.0%	2.2%	2.7%	2.4%
Total ($bn)	128.28	109.31	84.73	75.07

Lacky So (1987) and P. Barnes (1982) attributed such results to the violation of the basic assumption of ratio analysis, that is, the assumption of *proportionality*. For instance, if the ROA ratio was found to be non-normal, then the relationship between the two variables in the ratio (assets and net income) may be either *nonlinear* or an *intercept term exists* when one variable is regressed on the other one in the ratio. No corrective measures were offered to deal with non-proportionality. Adjusting the confidence interval, however, may lead to more reliable results.

As mentioned above, the Box test is very sensitive to departure from multivariate normality. The Box-test of homogeneity of the covariance matrices was significant at the 5% level. The computed chi-square was 1261.47 with an associated probability of 0.0001. The good news is that heterogeneity has a slight effect on α when the samples have equal sizes (or a ratio of larger sample size to smaller sample size less then 1.5). Actual α seems always to increase slightly over the nominal α. Thus, even with non-normal multivariate normality and heterogeneity, the inference about overall securitization effect should only be slightly affected.

MANOVA Results The four multivariate statistics in Figure 5-6 indicate that the overall financial characteristics of the two groups are significantly different at the 0.01% level. The univariate statistics based on the Bonferroni t-tests[102], show that six out of 15 variables differentiated between the securitizing and the non-securitizing banks. These variables

Figure 5-4: MANOVA Results, Expectations vs. Results

Variable Definition	Financial Ratio	Expected Direction[1]	Result
Bank Characteristics			
• Size	Log (Assets);	Higher	Higher
• International Banking	FARATIO: International Assets/TA;	Higher	Insignificant
• Wholesale Business	WSRATIO is a wholesale ratio: sum (commercial & industrial loans, govt. & non-govt. securities, and non-correspondent interbank loans)/TA;	Higher	Lower
Bank Capitalization			
• Risk-Based Capital Ratio	RBCRATIO is the risk-based capital ratio: Qualifying capital/Total Adjusted Assets;	Lower	Lower
Bank Profitability			
• Fee Income Ratio	NIIRATIO: Fee Income to Net Income;	Higher	Insignificant
• Return on Asset	ROA is the return on assets ratio;	Higher	Insignificant
Loan Portfolio Quality			
• Loan Diversification	L is the loan diversification index: $\sum(li^2)$ where li is the loan to asset ratio for different loan types;	Higher	Insignificant
• Loan Charge-offs	NTLNLSR: Net Charge-offs/Total Loans;	Lower	Insignificant
Bank Funding Resources/Liquidity			
• Funding resources	LIQ1: Deposits to Assets Ratio;	Lower	Lower
• Market Based Funding	LIQ2: Volatile Deposits to Total Deposits;	Higher	Insignificant
Cost of Funds			
• Funding Cost	COSTR1: Dep. Interest Expense/Total Int. Exp.;	Higher	Insignificant
• Funding Efficiency	COSTR2: Dep. Int. Expense/Int. Loan Income;	Higher	Insignificant
Competitive Advantage			
• Securitization Potential	LOANLS: Securitizable Loans (Mortgage, Credit Card, Auto Loans + respective Unused Commitments)/Total Loans & Leases;	Higher	Higher
• Loan Growth	LOANGR95: Loan Growth Rate during 1995;	Higher	Insignificant
• Learning Curve	MABS94A: 1994 Securitized Assets/Av. Assets	Higher	Higher

[1] Tests for directionality are conducted at the univariate level.

are Log(asset), the Wholesale ratio, the Risk-Based Capital ratio, the Deposit to Loan ratio, the Securitizable Loan ratio, and the Level of Securitization during 1994.

Research Question 1

R1　Are banks that engage in asset securitization, measured by the volume of repackaged mortgage and non-mortgage loans sold with and without recourse divided by bank's total assets, likely to have a larger size, measured by assets, than banks with no securitization activities?

Based on the reported mean values, securitizing banks have a significantly higher volume of assets. On average, securitizing banks carried twice as much assets as non-securitizing banks. The author, although expecting such result, had some reservation as far as the differentiating potential of this variable. Indeed, size was used as a control variable in order to match the group of securitizing banks with non-securitizing banks. A closer look at the data revealed that, even though both the securitizing and non-securitizing banks were all large banks (with assets exceeding $3 billion each), 65% of all securitization activities was undertaken by banks within the top 100 banks. These banks controlled 85% of the assets of all banks within the sample (please refer to Figure 5 2 above).

Phillis and Pavel (1987, p. 151), in their analysis of loan sale behavior of commercial banks, took size as an indication of the level of sophistication of bank management. Should that be the case, securitizing bank managers appear to be more sophisticated than those of non-securitizing banks. Rebecca Demsetz (1994, p.5), in her loan sales analysis, attributed the strong relationship between loan sales and asset size to both supply considerations (for example, fixed costs associated with secondary market activity) and/or demand considerations (such as reputational requirements most easily met by large institutions).

Research Question 2
R2 Are banks that engage in asset securitization (as defined above) likely to have relatively higher levels of international banking activities, measured by the ratio of international assets divided by total assets, than banks with no securitization activities?

The level of international banking activities was not a differentiating factor between the two groups. This result could be attributed to the fact that securitization has mainly reported on domestic assets, as opposed to international assets.

Research Question 3
R3 Are banks that engage in asset securitization likely to have higher levels of wholesale business than banks with no securitization activities.

Securitizing banks had a significantly lower wholesale ratio. The author included this variable with the intent of bringing a fuller picture of the differentiating characteristics between the two groups, the expectation being that securitizing banks would have a significantly higher level of wholesale banking. One reason that could explain this result is the way banks in general and bank holding companies in particular structure their business. The most active banks in the securitization market are all limited-purpose banks with an almost exclusive concentration of their loan portfolio in consumer loans and an average ratio of securitized assets to total assets of 130%. These banks are MBNA of Delaware, Citibank Nevada, Citibank South Dakota, First USA, Greenwood Trust, FCC National Bank, and Capital One.

Research Question 4

R4   Are securitizing banks likely to exhibit lower capital ratios than banks with no securitization activities?

Securitizing banks on average had significantly lower risk-based capital ratios than non-securitizing banks. In fact, securitizing banks kept the same level of capitalization as in 1994[103]. As expected, capitalization was a significant differentiating characteristic between the two groups, which is in accordance with the widely shared belief that compliance with regulatory requirements (capital requirements in this case) has been an important motive behind banks' adoption of financial innovation in general and asset securitization in particular. How much bearing capital requirements had on securitization will be investigated in the regression analysis section.

R6   Are securitizing banks likely to exhibit a lower loan portfolio quality, measured by the level of portfolio diversification and the ratio of net charge-offs to total loans, than those with no securitization activities?

The observed high degree of concentration in securitizing banks' loan portfolios may cause the loan diversification index to be significantly higher for these banks[104]. The mean value was higher, but not significantly higher (please refer to Figure 5-6 above). Non-securitizing banks are as diversified as securitizing banks, although not necessarily in the same lines of business. It has already been established that non-securitizing banks have a significantly higher wholesale business ratio, wholesale business

Financial Innovation in the Banking Industry

Figure 5-5: Testing for Normality

Variables	Skewness	Kurtosis
Log Assets	1.28	1.79
Foreign Asset Ratio	4.33	21.68
Wholesale Ratio	-0.71	0.58
Risk-Based Capital Ratio	3.32	17.69
Diversification Index	2.72	7.38
Net Charge-off ratio	3.29	12.33
Fee Income Ratio	-4.01	54.72
ROA	0.133**	10.11
Deposit to Loan Ratio	1.58	8.97
Volatile Deposit to Asset Ratio	1.29	1.39
Securitizable Loan Ratio	4.29	20.09
Loan Growth Ratio	6.24	44.69
Funding Cost Ratio	-1.25	1.63
Funding Efficiency Ratio	3.87	25.24
1994 Securitization Ratio	3.24	9.74

*   Significant at the 5% α level

** Significant at the 1% α level

being defined as the sum of loans to local governments, interbank loans, C&I loans and securities held in their portfolios.

A closer look at the portfolio composition of both securitizing and non-securitizing banks has revealed that the latter carried significantly more C&I loans and municipal loans, two main components in the computation of the wholesale ratio, on their books than their securitizing counterparts[105]. Securitizing banks, on average, have 23% of their loan portfolio in C&I and municipal loans, compared with 28% for non-securitizing banks. Higher concentration in the wholesale business may have had a balancing effect on securitizing bank's higher concentration in consumer loans, thus bringing the diversification index to comparable levels.

Interpretation of the diversification measure in this case is somewhat complicated by the fact that the observed level of diversification at 1995 year end may be the result of securitization achieved in the previous pe-

Figure 5-6: MANOVA Results

Dependent Variable	Mean: (Securitizors)	Mean: (Non-Securitizors)	Univariate F-Value	Sig. Level	Bonferroni t-test
Assets($bn)	19.792	9.917	7.30	0.0075	A-B
Foreign Asset Ratio	0.0152	0.0069	3.67	0.0570	A-A
Wholesale Ratio	0.3281	0.3748	5.42	0.0210	A-B
RBC Ratio	0.1554	0.1785	16.66	0.0001	A-B
Diversification Index	0.2198	0.1915	1.18	0.2796	A-A
Net Charge-off Ratio	0.0061	0.0045	1.66	0.1995	A-A
Fee Income Ratio	1.1901	1.6647	0.33	0.5650	A-A
ROA	0.0129	0.0121	0.66	0.4168	A-A
Deposit to Loan Ratio	1.0412	1.1901	4.82	0.0293	A-B
Volatile Deposit Ratio	0.2415	0.2162	1.00	0.3181	A-A
Securitizable Loan Ratio	2.3922	1.0949	7.04	0.0086	A-B
Loan Growth Ratio	74.800	89.150	0.69	0.4080	A-A
Funding Cost Ratio	0.6533	0.6930	1.76	0.1856	A-A
Funding Efficiency Ratio	0.4808	0.4160	3.07	0.0811	A-A
1994 Securitization	0.1037	0.0007	11.78	0.0007	A-B

Multivariate Tests of Significance

	Value	F-Value	Significance
Wilks' Lambda	0.7744	3.5537	0.0001
Pillai's Trace	0.2255	3.5537	0.0001
Hotelling's-Lawley Tr	0.2913	3.5537	0.0001
Roy's Greatest Root	0.2913	3.5537	0.0001

riod, or even throughout 1995. If the motive behind securitization was a better diversified portfolio, then we may be led to conclude that securitization was effective in reaching such a goal. For, overall, both groups exhibit similar diversification patterns. Investigating the validity of such a claim would require the isolation of the effect of securitization from that of all banks' activities that may affect portfolio diversification. Suffice it to say that the diversification index in 1995 was not significantly different from that of 1994 for the group of securitizing banks.

The same financial characteristics were used in order to run a separate MONOVA on the securitizing group with time as the main effect.

This procedure involves a repeated measure MANOVA with banks acting as their own control group and being measured on the same dependent variables at the end of each reporting period). The objective was to test whether there was an overall difference between the financial characteristics at 1994 year-end and those exhibited at 1995 year—end. The test was significant at the 0.02% level (F=2.53). Pairwise post-hoc tests revealed there was no significant change in the level of diversification between the two periods. Does this negate the plausible effect of securitization on diversification? Once more, one need to isolate the effect of securitization from that of the different asset-liability management techniques available to banks in their portfolio management.

The net charge-off variable, the second variable in the loan portfolio quality category, did not reveal to be significant at the univariate level. Regulators have often stated that banks may be securitizing their best assets, leaving the riskier ones on their books. By doing so, banks reduce the amount of credit enhancement that is needed in the securitization process. Credit enhancement protection is usually set at three to four times the expected default rate. The higher the quality of the loan being securitized, the lower the default rates, hence, the lower the credit enhancement protection that is needed. The findings of the current study do not confirm these claims. Securitization did not add to the riskiness of the remaining loan portfolio of securitizing banks.

On average, securitizing banks exhibited no different level of loan charge-offs than their non-securitizing counterparts. Banks realize that they may realize some extra savings in the short-run, but will find their deteriorating loan portfolio quality reflected in higher cost of debt and equity in the future. Furthermore, the asset securities market is a multi-period framework where most originators return to the market to securitize more assets. The originator is likely to want to preserve its reputation, even though the underlying security is no longer its direct obligation, but that of the special purpose vehicle that is the issuer. This is in agreement with Malitz' suggestion (1989) that this concern for reputation governs the behavior of firms and lowers the agency cost of debt. John and Nachman (1985) and Diamond (1989) also show that a firm's reputation has value, especially in a multi-period framework, where firms must return to the financial markets for financing in different periods.

Only two financial characteristics differed from the previous period. These are the Level of Securitization to Average Assets and the Funding Efficiency ratio (that is, Deposit Interest Expense to Loan Interest Income). Securitizing banks securitized significantly more assets in 1995 then they did in 1994. Indeed, the 1995 volume of securitized assets was 50% higher then that of 1994. However, they were significantly less efficient in the use of their funds. They reported higher Deposit Interest Expenses per dollar of earned Loan Income (0.41 in 1995 versus 0.36 in 1994).

Research Questions 7 and 8

R7   Are securitizing banks likely to exhibit higher liquidity needs, measured deposit to asset, and volatile to total deposit ratios, than non-securitizing banks?

R8   Are securitizing banks likely to exhibit a higher cost of funds, measured by deposit interest expense to total interest expense and deposit interest expense to interest loan income ratios, than non-securitizing banks?

The ratios of 1995 funding efficiency for the two groups were not significantly different in 1995 at the 5% α level. They were, however, significantly different at the 10% α level. At this level, securitizing banks were significantly more efficient in the use of their borrowed funds. The average Deposit Interest Expense to Loan Interest Income ratio was .41 versus .48 in 1995 and .36 versus .43 in 1994 for securitizing and non-securitizing banks, respectively. It is probable that Funding Efficiency was negatively affected by the interest rate hikes registered in May of 1994. It should be noted that their profitability did not decline because of such increase in their cost of funding relative to their loan returns, nor was there a significant decline in their fee income ratio.

The other cost ratio in the model, deposit interest expense to total interest expense was not adversely affected by the increase in interest rates, nor was there a significant difference between the two groups. For the group of securitizing banks, the mean of the ratio was slightly lower in 1995 than that reported in 1994. On average, this group also reported cost of funding relative to overall interest expenses then the group of non-securitizing banks both in 1994 and 1995.

The above results could be construed either as the attempt of securitizing banks to control costs by recurring less to deposits as a source of funds (the Deposit To Loan ratio is significantly lower for securitizing banks) and using securitization instead as a funding mechanism. The effect is not significant because securitization is yet to become an important line of business for these banks. Another explanation would be that securitization, regardless of the motive behind it, is starting to have an effect on the cost structure, which effect would become more significant as banks securitize more assets.

It is often argued that securitization is a cheaper source of funds and that banks who have a high funding cost are likely to use securitization as a funding alternative. It is also argued that banks that are likely to have a high cost of funds are those that are likely to have a higher recourse to market intermediated funding as opposed to traditional deposits. However, the volatile deposit variable (volatile deposit to total asset ratio) was not significant either. Securitizing banks did not have a higher level of volatile deposits, which may explain why they did not have on average higher deposit interest expenses relative to overall interest expenses, as revealed by the results. On average, they were as efficient as their counterparts in funding their lending activities. This may lead to the inference that neither funding nor funding costs were a problem area for securitizing banks in the top 200 and, therefore, may not have been a motive behind asset securitization.

That funding was not an underlying factor behind securitization may not exactly be the case, for one of the two liquidity measures, deposit to loan ratio, revealed to be a differentiating characteristic between the two groups. Securitizing banks had a significantly lower deposit to loan ratio than their counterparts in the other group, which was expected. This could be construed as an indication that securitizing banks, unlike their counterparts in the control group, are relying on securitization to fund part of their lending activities.

Whether that was part of the decision to rely less on deposits and more on securitization for funding purposes may warrant further investigation. Whatever the case may be, we would need more than reported financial data to shed light on this question.

Research Question 9

R9   Are securitizing banks likely to make more use of their loan origination competitive advantage, measured by a higher loan growth rate, a larger securitizable loan portfolio, and their prior experience with securitization) than non-securitizing banks?

The securitizable loan ratio was significantly higher for securitizing banks than for non-securitizing banks, which again was expected. The variable securitizable loans is defined as the sum of bank loans that have been traditionally converted into asset-backed securities (consumer and mortgage loans) plus unused commitments pertaining to these loans.

Boemio (1996) predicted that this variable may reveal to be one of the most significantly differentiating characteristics between securitizors and non-securitizors. Banks that have come to realize the benefits of securitization, and these are likely to be the ones with prior experience with securitization, are most likely to increase their commitments (used and unused) within these respective lines of business in anticipation of their future securitization activities.

Just as expected, a most significant differentiating characteristic is 1994 securitization level. On average, banks that securitized assets during 1994 had a significantly higher level of securitization in 1995. In fact, certain banks, like Citibank and MBNA, have built a niche for themselves and have been involved with securitization from the outset. In addition, except for six banks[106], all banks that securitized during 1994 did securitize assets in 1995. The withdrawal of these banks did not seem to have much of an effect on the market, for they had an extremely marginal involvement with asset securitization.

The third variable in the Competitive Advantage category, Loan Growth, did not show a significantly differentiating financial characteristic. The assumption was that banks had a competitive advantage in loan origination, and therefore, would recur to increase their loan portfolio to back up their securitization activities. A plausible reason for that not being the case may be the fact that the observed level of loans at the end of the period is net of the amount of assets that have been securitized during the period. However, readjusting the amount of loans for securitization still did not yield a significant difference between the two groups[107]. This may lead to believe that the observed result was due to an ill-defined variable. For the purpose of securitization, banks are likely to limit the increase in origination to loans that have traditionally been securitized. Most loans on bank's balance sheet do not fall into that category, even though experimentation is underway to generalize the process to all loan types. Should the variable Loan Growth be redefined to include growth in securitizable loans only, we may be able to detect significant difference between the two groups.

One variable in the model that is close to the above definition is the Securitizable Loan variable. The Securitizable Loan variable measures the ratio of the sum of Credit Card Installments, Mortgage Loans, Auto Loans, and other types of consumer loans plus their respective Unused Commitments divided by Total Loans. This variable was found to be a significant differentiating characteristic between the two groups at the pairwise post-hoc Bonferroni test.

Boemio (1996) projected that interpretation of the variable loan growth would be complicated by the fact that non-securitizing banks may equally increase their overall loan portfolio, but for different reasons, thus, overshadowing the increase in securitizable loan origination by securitizing banks. In fact, non-securitizors may even increase their booking of securitizable loans for reasons other than securitization.

Research Question 5

R5   Are securitizing banks likely to exhibit a higher degree of dependence on fee income, measured by the ratio of fee income divided by interest income, and higher return-on-asset ratios than banks with no securitization activities?

Neither one of the return characteristics were significant at the univariate level. Both the Return On Asset ratio (measured by the ratio of Net Income to Total Assets) and the Fee Income ratio (measured by Non-Interest Income divided by Net Income) were not significant as differentiating characteristics of securitizing banks. It is likely that the lack of significance of the ROA ratio is due to the fact that, on average, securitizing banks are significantly larger than non-securitizing banks, thus increasing the size of the denominator, and decreasing that of the ROA ratio. One, therefore, can make the inference that on average, securitizing banks exhibit higher returns (i.e. net income levels) then their counterparts. While it is unlikely that these higher returns could be attributed solely to securitization, it is conceivable that securitizing banks may be more innovative in nature, and thus more prone to adopt new income generating avenues. For instance, if the involvement with off-balance activities was indicative of innovativeness/ aggressiveness, securitizing banks carry twice as much off-balance sheet activities relative to assets as their non-securitizing counterparts[108].

The lack of significance of the second return measure is probably more indicative of the lack of direct contribution of securitization to returns. Banks that engage in asset securitization do not generate significantly higher fee income than non-securitizing ones. Assessing the unique contribution of securitization to non-interest income in particular, and to returns in general, would require to control for all income generating activities of the securitizing bank. While this is beyond the scope of this research, it is likely that the reason for lack of significance is simply due to the rather small levels of securitization, whether in comparison to total assets or to off-balance sheet activities.

In summary, the hypothesis tested in this section is that the overall financial characteristics of the securitizing banks are significantly different from the overall financial characteristics of the non-securitizing banks. The multivariate test statistics indicate that the overall characteristics are significantly different at the 1% level. The univariate statistics showed that the two groups are significantly different at the 1% level in terms of Asset Size, Wholesale Business, Level of Capitalization, Level of Deposits, Level of Securitizable Loans, and Prior-Year Level of Experience. According to these results, Funding Costs, Returns, and Portfolio Quality, as defined in the study, were not key differentiating characteristics, as postulated by theory.

Regulatory Taxes, in the form of capital requirements, and Funding, measured by the Deposit to Asset ratio, however, were significant. Securitizing banks exhibited lower Capitalization and lower Deposit to Loan levels. They also had higher proportions of Securitizable Loans on and off the balance sheet (in the form of credit card and mortgage loans on the balance sheet and unused commitments off the balance sheet) and higher Level of Securitization during the previous period. It should be noted that these banks did not have a higher increase in their Loan Portfolio. They were probably wary not to unduly increase the size of their assets that could further lower their capitalization levels. Instead, they resorted to higher levels of unused commitments, mostly in Credit Card Receivables, while keeping their loan portfolios within comparable levels with those of non-securitizing banks.

Regression Analysis

The decision to securitize assets is followed by the decision of how much to securitize in one particular period. In order to understand the underlying factors in this decision, a regression model was estimated based on the same variables used for the MANOVA procedure and using 1994 data for securitizing banks. Assumptions of normality, homoscedasticity, and independence of the error terms need to be observed in order to insure the stability of the regression coefficients and the tenability of the regression findings. None of these assumptions holds in the case of the sample in the study, which greatly limits the ability to generalize the findings. The non-normal distribution of the error terms limits the use of the findings to draw inferences about the underlying population. The presence of multicolinearity between the independent variables makes the regression coefficient unstable. This study is about the securitization behavior of the top 200 commercial banks in the United States and may have limited bearing on the securitization behavior of the population of U.S. commercial banks. The banks in the study do not represent a random sample of the 10,500 U.S. commercial banks. They, however, constitute an important mass in the banking industry. They control around 44% of all commercial banking assets in the United States and are likely to control an even larger share of the banking business as the industry goes through intensified consolidation, mergers and acquisitions.

Regression Results

The dependent variable in the model is the dollar amount of loans securitized during 1995 divided by 1995 average assets. The independent variables are as defined for the MANOVA analysis, except that they pertain to the year 1994 in order to allow for the temporal effect of the independent variables on the 1995 level of securitization. The SAS regression procedure was selected. The results of the procedure are presented in Figures 5-7 below[109]. The model is significant at the 0.01% level. The adjusted R-squared of the regression model is 0.90, meaning that 90% of the variation of the dependent variable is accounted for by the variables found to be significant in the model. The observed explanatory power of the model is, however, tainted by the presence of multicolinearity among the independent variables which is known to inflate R-squared (Maddala, 1977, p. 185).

Five of the fifteen variables were significant at the 5% level. Three more were significant at the 10% level. These results were not exactly consistent neither with the MONOVA findings nor with expectations. Variables that were found to be differentiating characteristics with the MANOVA procedure were not necessarily the ones that exerted a significant weight in determining the amount of assets to be securitized. Whereas Cost, Return, and Funding variables were hardly significant differentiating characteristics between the two bank groups in the MANOVA procedure, they revealed to be significant factors in the decision of how much to securitize during the period. None of the bank characteristics (measured by Size, International Banking and Wholesale Banking) had a significant impact on the level of securitization of the banks in the sample. Yet, two of them were significant in the MANOVA procedure.

Return-on-Asset ratio, Interest Deposit Expense to Total Interest Expense, Deposit to Loan ratio, Volatile Deposit ratio, Securitizable Loan ratio, and Prior Involvement With Asset Securitization had the expected impact on the proportion of loans that banks securitized in 1995 and were all significant at the 5% level. As expected, the Loan Charge-Off ratio, significant only at the 10% level, exerted a negative impact on securitization. Net Charge-offs, and thus, the ability of banks to service loans, seemed to have a tempering effect on asset securitization. Banks with higher levels of net charge-offs were likely to securitize fewer assets. The second measure of portfolio quality, Diversification, did not reveal to be significant at the 5% level. Diversification was not only equivalent among the two groups of banks at the MANOVA level, but had no significant impact on the securitization decisions.

The Loan Growth variable had no significant impact on the securitization decision. As noted in the MONOVA section, the loan items in this ratio are aggregate loan amounts including all loan types as opposed to securitizable loan amounts. As such, the level of outstanding loans and securitized assets do not have a direct link to one another.

The variable Securitizable Loans, however, is positively related to asset securitization and is highly significant. This variable measures the outstanding amount of Securitizable Loans scaled by Total Loans. The positive relationship indicates that banks are likely to use their comparative advantage in the origination of securitizable loans in order to increase their participation in asset securitization.

Banks, it seems, have a strategy of controlling the size of their overall loan portfolio and not unduly accelerate its growth except in areas where securitization is anticipated. This is in agreement with both the MANOVA results where the securitizing and non-securitizing banks recorded similar loan growth rates, and the regression analysis, where this variable had an insignificant relationship to Loan Securitization.

The fact that banks are limiting the expansion of their loan portfolio to securitizable assets was evidenced by the significant, positive relationship of the securitizable loan variable to the dependent variable. Concurrently, these banks were trying to limit their funding through deposits by issuing more asset-backed securities, as demonstrated by the negative sign of the coefficient of the Deposit to Loan ratio.

Cost of Funding itself exerted a positive impact on the level of securitized assets. Banks with higher costs would tend to securitize more assets, which again, may explain why banks would seek to limit funding through deposits and use their comparative advantage in originating and securitizing certain loan types as an alternative. The Return On Asset ratio also exerted a significant positive impact on banks to securitize more assets. The Fee Income ratio, significant only at the 10% level, had a positive impact

Figure 5-7: Regression Analysis, Expectations and Results.

Variable Definition	Expected Sign	Results	Coefficient	T Score	Pr(t)
Intercept		Insignif.	-0.351	-1.273	0.207
Bank Characteristics					
• Size	Positive	Insignif.			
• International Banking	Positive	Insignif.			
• Wholesale Business	Positive	Insignif.			
Bank Capitalization					
• Risk Based Capital Ratio	Negative	Insignif.			
Bank Profitability					
• Fee Income Ratio	Positive	Positive	0.0065	1.722	0.089*
• Return on Asset	Positive	Positive	5.331	2.041	0.0446
Loan Portfolio Quality					
• Loan Diversification	Positive	Insignif.			
• Loan Charge-offs	Negative	Negative	-4.950	-1.877	0.0643*
Bank Funding Resources/Liquidity					
• Funding resources (dep. to asset ratio)	Negative(?)	Negative	-0.201	-2.626	0.0104
• Market Based Funding (volatile dep. ratio)	Positive	Positive	0.404	2.779	0.0068
Cost of Funds					
• Funding cost (dep interest exp/total int exp)	Positive	Positive	0.526	4.107	0.0001
• Funding Efficiency (dep int exp/loan int income)	Positive	Insignif.			
Competitive Advantage					
• Securitization Potential (securitizable loans/assets)	Positive	Positive	0.011	2.480	0.0153
• Loan Growth	Positive	Insignif.			
• Learning Curve (1994 level of securitization)	Positive	Positive	0.869	11.076	0.0001

Model Significance: Adjusted R^2: 0.9045

F-Value: 59.73   Pr (F): 0.0001

* Significant at the 10% confidence level.

on the level of securitization. Securitization is a fee-income generating
activity and it has been documented that banks have been shrinking their
loan portfolio in favor of non-traditional banking activities.

The regulatory tax variable, the risk-based capital ratio, did not have
a significant impact on the level of securitization. This result is especially
interesting when evaluating the role of bank capital, since capital constraints are so commonly offered as a motive for commercial bank asset
securitization. The author hypothesized that capital constrained banks
use securitization in order to receive servicing and origination fees without increasing the size of their loan portfolio[110]. A closer look at the data
revealed that all banks were well above the minimum capital requirement of 8%. For the sample of the securitizing banks in the study, the average capital ratio was 12.11% in 1995 versus 12.05% in 1994. The
lowest ratio was 9.12% and it was reported by NationsBank of Texas. It
is apparent that these banks were within comfortable range of the regulatory requirements, which may explain why capital was not a motivating
factor behind asset securitization for the particular group in the study.

To further investigate the relationship between capital and securitization, deviation from the minimum capital requirements was entered in
the regression model instead of the level of capitalization. The same results were obtained. Capitalization, or deviation from it, does not appear
to be a motive behind securitization. The MANOVA results, on the other
hand, indicated that, on average, securitizing banks had a significantly
lower capital ratio[111]. It is again probable that the effect of capitalization
on securitization was overshadowed by a third factor, an overall bank
strategy, that is affecting both securitization and capitalization concurrently. It is most probable that banks have attained the current levels of
Capitalization through other means than securitization, probably by controlling the growth of their loan portfolio, as advanced earlier. Several
studies (Griswold, Karels, and Lavin, 1996; Collins, Shackelfford, and
Wahlen, 1995; Wall and Peterson, 1995; Peek and Rosengren, 1995a)
suggested a strong link between capital regulatory requirements and loan
shrinkage for banks. Some regions in the U.S. suffered a credit crunch
because of banks' reduced lending (Peek and Rosengren, 1995b).

The alternative explanation is that securitization and capitalization
were both affected by the same overall bank strategy. This strategy consists of

• Attempting to limit loan growth in order to improve capitalization,
• Cut costs by reducing deposit taking activities,

- Improve returns by engaging in more fee generating activities such as asset securitization (securitizing banks have a significantly higher level of off-balance sheet activities relative to assets when compared with non-securitizing banks), and
- Prepare for such activity by increasing their holdings of securitizable loans.

To adopt such reasoning would undermine the cause and effect relationship[112] that was presumed to exist between the dependent variable and some of the explanatory variables in the regression. Further investigation is needed to see where asset securitization fits into overall strategy formulation of banks, and what weight it has, if any, in the pursuit of banks' overall objectives. Some limited-purpose banks, be they bank holding companies affiliates or independent banks, seem to have made it their objective to specialize in securitization (mostly that of credit cards) and designed their business strategy accordingly. These banks greatly influenced the development and growth of the ABS market. Abnormal high levels of securitization, measured by Securitized Assets to Total Assets, may be indicative of market share and leadership goals rather then mere tactics in portfolio and capital management. Modest to low levels of securitization, as was the case for the majority of securitizing banks in the sample, may be indicative of banks using securitization as a management towards achieving some cost, return, portfolio, liquidity and/or funding objectives. An area of future research would be to investigate the reasons for the under-utilization of the technique of securitization by the population of US commercial banks.

The level of securitization during 1994 had the largest impact on the level of assets to be securitized in 1995, with the largest t score (11.317). This variable was also found to be the most differentiating characteristics of securitizing banks. This finding is in agreement with Lillaney (1994), Diamond (1989) and John and Nachman (1985) statement that securitization is a multi-period framework, where securitizing firms are likely to return to the market for more securitization.

Because of the observed high explanatory power of this variable, a separate regression was run with the dependent variable being the first difference between 1995 securitization level and that of 1994. The explanatory power of the model fell from 90% to 25% (please refer to Figure 5-7 and 5-8 for a comparison of the models results). The results were comparable except for the return-on-asset variable. Under the new model this variable was no longer significant. Is this to indicate that the increment over the level of 1994 securitization was not affected by return motives but solely because of liquidity, cost, and return considerations? In any case, overall, these results confirm the hypotheses that operational consideration and possessed comparative advantage in loan origination are the motive behind asset securitization. But most of all, securitization is a multi-period framework, where securitizing firms are likely to return to the market for more securitization.

AREAS OF FUTURE RESEARCH

This research has focused on the Securitization activities of the 200 largest commercial banks in the United States. A natural next step is to extend this research to securitization of the non-banking sector as well as to securitization in foreign markets where acceptance of the technique has been growing. It has already been noticed in prior chapters that this technique has gained popularity not only among banks in developed nations, but in developing nations as well. It is true that the technique is not as widespread and that issues are still sporadic at best. Regulatory and accounting professions are still lagging, if not lacking, in most countries. In fact, in some countries, such as France, existing securities and monetary regulations were an impediment to the development of the technique and it was not until these laws were amended that certain assets were securitized for the first time. In other markets, securitization existed for a long time, albeit in a different form, which, again, thwarted the diffusion of the technique as know in the United States into those markets.

This research dealt with securitization at the bank level. It has already been noted that some special purpose banks within bank holding companies (BHCs) carry an abnormally high level of asset securitization. This could indicate that the securitization decision is made at the headquarters level, not the subsidiary level. Should this be the case, a study of securitization at the bank holding level is worth conducting. In this research, a bank holding company would be treated as one single, integrated banking organization. Berger, kashyap, and Scalise (1995), in a comprehensive and impressive empirical research about the evolution of the U.S. banking industry over the past fifteen years, adopted this approach based on both regulatory and business considerations.

The legislation requires cross-guarantees whereby all banks within a holding company may be held liable for any deposit insurance funds that are used to assist any other bank within the holding company. Similarly, the Federal Reserve's requires the holding company to stand ready to provide financing whenever any of its banks becomes distressed (the source-of-strength policy). The top-tier holding company is effectively made to be the risk management unit by regulation.

From an operational standpoint, most multi-bank holding companies are in fact managed on a consolidated basis. Strategy formulation, important business decision, and policies and procedures are typically made at the holding company level, observe Berger et al (1995). In many cases subsidiaries simply carry out these strategies. This may explain the observed specialization of some of the affiliates within the organizations in the study. Although beyond the scope of this research, an analysis of strategy formulation and organizational structures within BHCs is likely to shed light on the adoption process of the technique of securitization and eventually that of financial innovation in general.

What it most important is that analysis at the bank level of a large holding company could lead to distortions because holding company affiliates often exchange portfolio instruments. Because of legal lending limits, the largest loans are likely to be booked in the largest bank in the holding company, even when issued elsewhere within the organization. Similarly, large New York City banks often book their fee-generating activities at the Delaware affiliates of their holding company because of the state low taxes on fee income. Thus looking at the holding company rather then at an individual bank within a multi-bank holding company may give a more accurate description of the securitization process. Even more interesting would be to see whether the conclusions reached at the bank level would still hold at the bank holding level.

RESEARCH CONCLUSIONS

In this section, the author has studied the financial characteristics of the 200 largest commercial banks that securitized assets during 1995 using MANOVA and regression techniques. One major problem frequently associated with the use of financial ratios as measures of financial characteristics has been the non-normal distribution of the financial ratios. The findings of this research, while applicable to other large securitizing banks not included in the study, can not be generalized to the population of US commercial banks or the population of securitizing banks elsewhere without many reservations.

The market for asset securitization is highly concentrated, dominated by a few limited purpose banks that seem to have adopted the strategy of making securitization their main line of business. The impact of these banks on the market has been well documented. The market itself is dominated by securitized credit card installment loans. The sample is characterized by great disparities, not only in the level of securitization (it ranges from less then 4 thousandths of a percent to 166% of total assets), but in their lines of business as well.

The analysis revealed the financial characteristics of the two groups in the study to be significantly different at the 1% level. At the univariate level, securitizing and non-securitizing banks differed in terms of assets, wholesale business, risk-based capital ratio, deposit to loan ratio, securitizable loan ratio and 1994 securitization level. None of the cost, return, or portfolio variables were found to significantly differentiate between the two groups. Securitizing banks were neither more profitable, more cost efficient, nor better diversified then non-securitizing banks.

The findings, however, seem to support the theory that securitization is being used as an alternative to deposit funding. Securitizing banks reported a significantly lower level of deposit to loan ratio. Findings also indicate that regulation, in the form of capital requirements, plays an important role in explaining which banks are likely to securitize assets. A bank's comparative advantage in originating loans, as measured by the securitizable loan variable, also plays an important role in its securitization process.

The most differentiating characteristic, however, is prior involvement with securitization. Banks that securitized assets in the previous period are the ones most likely to securitize assets in the current reporting period. The number of securitizing banks has been growing slowly, but steadily, over the past five years. Interest rate hikes of 1994, while abating general confidence in the mortgage-backed securities market, gave the non-mortgage sector a renewed belief in its potential as well as safety. Yet, the market for commercial bank assets has been underutilized. Only a small fraction of commercial banks have adopted this technique, which, overall, captured less then 3% of total commercial banking assets at year-end 1995.

Securitized Assets to Total Assets was the dependent variable in the regression model in this study. Bank characteristics, measured by bank size and the ratios of international banking and wholesale business, had no weight on the securitization decision, neither did capital requirements. Instead, the decision as to how much to securitize was dictated by operational considerations (cost, return and liquidity), loan origination comparative advantage, and familiarity with the technique of securitization, that is prior involvement with the technique. These findings are all

Figure 5-8: Regression Results with First Difference

Variable	Parameter Estimate	T for H0: Parameter=0	Prob >|T|
Intercept	-0.333	-1.177	0.2426
Size	-0.002	-0.136	0.8923
Inter. Banking	-0.389	-0.792	0.4306
Wholesale Bus.	0.029	0.227	0.8213
RBC Ratio	1.019	1.421	0.1591
Fee Income	0.006	1.515	0.1337
ROA	1.785	1.221	0.2257
Diversif.	-0.273	-1.692	0.0945
Charge-Offs	-4.954	-1.857	0.0670
Funding Resour.	-0.222	-2.919	0.0046
Market Funding	0.385	2.627	0.0104
Funding Cost	0.556	4.332	0.0001
Funding Eff.	0.123	0.903	0.3694
Loan growth	0.000	0.072	0.9429
Sec. Loans	0.001	2.127	0.0365

R-square: 0.3692	Adj R^2: 0.2574
F Value: 3.302	Prob>F: 0.0004

in agreement with the cost of funding hypothesis, the liquidity hypothesis, and the comparative advantage hypothesis. The banks in the study securitized more assets when faced with higher Return On Assets, higher Fee Income ratio, lower level of Net Charge-Offs, lower level of Loans to Assets, lower Deposit to Loan ratio, higher level of Deposit Interest Expense to Total Interest Expense, higher level of Securitizable Loans to Total Loans, and higher Level of Securitization during 1994.

The fact that the capital ratio had no significant relationship to the securitization level was contrary to the capital constraint hypothesis. The absence of such a relationship may be due to the simple fact that the banks in the study are well capitalized. It could also be due to the fact that banks do not rely on securitization to improve capital. They may use securitization to improve returns, to reduce cost of funding, to improve their liquidity, to take advantage of a comparative advantage in the issuance of certain types of loans, but not to improve capital. It is also probable that the decision to participate in securitization was initially dictated by capital requirements, but as banks reached satisfactory levels of capitalization, that motive was overshadowed by other business strategy and considerations, such as liquidity, costs and returns.

As noted earlier, it is most probable that the securitization decision is made at the bank holding company's level, as opposed to the commercial bank level. The existence of highly specialized securitizing units within the organization of certain bank holding companies support this observation. These units tended to carry highly concentrated loan portfolios in consumer (i.e., securitizable) loans. Out of the 95 securitizing banks in the sample, only four had no affiliation with bank holding companies. These banks were also highly specialized in issuing and securitizing consumer loans.

FINAL NOTES

This research has been an examination of the securitization activities of the largest 200 commercial banks in the United States. The technique of securitization by commercial banks is still in its growth stage. Banks have been rather shy in approaching the market, and if it weren't for some key players that polarized the market, the market would have probably waned at its inception. Although diffusion has been rather limited amongst commercial banks, it is expected to grow both among banks and down the balance sheet as more and more loans will come to be securitizable. Currently, a variety of loans are being securitized. Credit card loans accounted for more then 85% of all securitized assets by the commercial banking industry as well as the top 200 banks in the study. The next largest category of loans to be securitized by banks was mortgage loans, accounting for 7.5% of securitized assets, followed by auto loans. Auto loans contributed less then 4% to the pool assets securitized by commercial banks at 1995 year-end.

During the 1994–1995 period, the volume of asset-backed securities grew faster then did the assets of the banking industry. Asset growth for the largest 200 banks was 10%, while that of securitized assets grew at a 46% rate, a rate that is typical of a product that is at the growth stage of its life cycle. Yet, these banks securitized an average of less then 4% of their total assets. The commercial banking industry as a whole securitized an even smaller portion (3%) of their assets during the reporting period of 1995.

The research conducted in this book indicates that capital requirements, and therefore the Basle Committee, may have played an important role in the decision to securitize assets. However, one is to surmise recourse to asset securitization in compliance with regulatory capital requirements has waned as banks drew farther from the 1992 deadline. Indeed, costs, returns, funding, liquidity, and the comparative advantage in the origination of securitizable assets all weighed on the securitization decision of the banks in the study, in accordance with postulated theory. The findings, however, do not corroborate concerns over banks securitizing their best assets. Higher levels of loan charge-offs appear to act as a deterrent for banks to securitize more assets. Investors and rating agencies are likely to look unfavorably at securities of a bank with low portfolio quality even though these securities are issued by a trust or a special purpose corporation. Furthermore, increased riskiness of the loan portfolio may lead to increased costs of capital and borrowing for the bank.

It has been argued that securitization, rather then promoting certain risk-taking behavior by bank management, is likely to have positive implications on bank soundness. Securitization allows banks to profit from what they do best, that is originate and service loans rather then warehouse them. That not only reduces the implications of default risk, but also could be deemed a safer alternative to certain fee-generating off-balance sheet and derivative activities. This is especially true as the Basle Committee and the Federal Reserve define and refine new rules for the measurement of market risk and capitalization.

NOTES

93. Citibank's leadership position is bound to end after the finalization of the merger between Chase Manhattan and Chemical bank on the first week of April of this year (Bloomberg Business News (1996), Interview with Thomas Labrecque, Chairman of Chase Manhattan, (March 27th) Channel 22, 6:30am.

94. JP Morgan is a bank Subsidiary of Morgan Guaranty Trust Co. of NY.

95. A Subsidiary of American Express Corp., it specializes in credit card issuance.

96. Also specializes in credit card issuance.

97. Regression analysis assumes causality. Causality is based on 1) temporal order (hypothesized cause must precede hypothesized effect; 2) covariation (hypothesized cause must covary with hypothesized effect; and 3) spuriousness (observed covariation between cause and effect can not be explained by a third factor that causes both of them (Wirtz, 1989).

98. As mentioned in the methodology chapter, none of the major statistical packages (SAS, SPSSx, or BMDP (recently acquired by SPSS)) have a test of

multivariate normality. Mardia (1974) has developed multivariate measures of skewness and kurtosis. These measures are, however, limited to two variables.

99. Please refer to the methodology chapter about appropriate variable transformations in cases of non-normality.

100. CARDs: Solomon Brothers' acronym for Certificates for Amortizing Revolving Debts.

101. CARs: Solomon's acronym for Certificates for Automobile Receivables

102. The Bonferroni t-test is designed to control for the experimentwise error when conducting the post-hoc tests. Please refer to Hair et al. (1992, p. 170–171) for an enumeration of the different tests available on SAS and SPSS that allow to control the a level. A more detailed explanation is presented in the SAS/STAT User's guide, 1989, p. 914–917.

103. Based on the same model described above where time was the main effect in the MANOVA analysis.

104. Remember that a high diversification index is an indication of low diversification level.

105. The ratio ((C&I loans + Municipal Loans)/Total Loans) was significantly higher at the 5% level for non-securitizing banks. No significance was inferred for the ratio of Total Securities to Assets between the two groups, leading to the conclusion that the reason for the observed difference in wholesale business was due to larger involvement of the non-securitizing banks in C&I Loans and Municipal Loans.

106. Amsouth's two affiliates within the top 200, Amsouth Bank of Alabama and Amsouth Bank of Florida, both marginally involved with securitization in 1994, completely withdrew from the market in 1995. Bank of America, with 7 affiliates within the top 200, greatly reduced its involvement with the market. Its Arizona and Nevada affiliates withdrew from the market. Its leading affiliate had a marginal involvement in 1994 and further reduced the volume of securitization in 1995, so did its Oregon affiliate. Bank of New York, on the other hand, seems to have shifted its securitization department from its affiliate in Delaware towards its leading bank in New York. Once more, involvement had been marginal in 1994 and even more so in 1995. Its third affiliate, Bank of New York New Jersey, was not involved with securitization either year. National City Bank has regrouped all of its securitization activities within its leading bank, National City Bank of Ohio. In any case, its Kentucky affiliate had a rather insignificant amount of securitized assets in 1994 (5 thousandth of a percent its asset size).

107. The variable loan growth was redefined to include securitized amounts as the numerator and then reentered in the MANOVA model. The overall significance of the model hardly changed (F statistic still equals 3.56) and the post hoc test for the modified loan growth variable was found to be insignificant at the 5% level.

108. The ratio of Off-Balance-Sheet activities to Total Assets was 210% and 99% for the securitizing and non-securitizing banks, respectively. These means were significantly different at the 5% level, meaning that securitizing banks had a much higher degree of involvement with off-balance sheet activities. For the group of securitizing banks in the study, securitization in itself did not constitute a significant proportion of their Off-Balance Sheet activities (1.15%). It could be surmised that, while it is not yet a significant line of business, securitization may be indicative of an innovative managerial style, and therefore, would have more of a synergetic (economies of scope) effect, rather than a direct one, on bank returns and costs.

109. The dependent variable in this model is truncated, that is, left-censored at zero. In these cases, the appropriate estimation technique to be used is the Tobit model (named after J. Tobin) for truncated dependent variables. For further information on this topic, please refer to Maddala (1977, pp. 162–170) in his discussion of Limited Dependent Variables and to SAS/Stat User's Guide (1990. pp.999, 1024) for computer-aided analysis. Because the Tobit procedure produced the same results as the regression technique, the author chose to report those of the latter. In addition, the SAS Tobit procedure (a special case of the 'Lifereg' procedure) has limited options and is rather limited in its output compared to that of the regression.

110. Several authors have made the same hypothesis about capital and loan sales (Demsetz, 1994; Pennacchi, 1988; and Pavel and Phillis, 1987).

111. Please refer back to the section about the MANOVA results.

112. Spuriousness is one of three components of Causality. Spuriousness means that the observed covariation between cause and effect can not be explained by a third factor that causes both of them.

Appendix A

Schedule RC-L—Off-Balance Sheet Items

Please read carefully the instructions for the preparation of Schedule RC-L. Some of the amounts reported in Schedule RC-L are regarded as volume indicators and not necessarily as measures of risk.

		C460 ◄
	Dollar Amounts in Thousands	Bil Mil Thou

1. Unused commitments:
   a. Revolving, open-end lines secured by 1–4 family residential properties, e.g., home equity lines .... — **1.a.**
   b. Credit card lines .... — **1.b.**
   c. Commercial real estate, construction, and land development:
   (1) Commitments to fund loans secured by real estate .... — **1.c.(1)**
   (2) Commitments to fund loans not secured by real estate .... — **1.c.(2)**
   d. Securities underwriting .... — **1.d.**
   e. Other unused commitments .... — **1.e.**
2. Financial standby letters of credit and foreign office guarantees .... — **2.**
   a. Amount of financial standby letters of credit conveyed to others .... — **2.a.**
3. Performance standby letters of credit and foreign office guarantees .... — **3.**
   a. Amount of performance standby letters of credit conveyed to others .... — **3.a.**
4. Commercial and similar letters of credit .... — **4.**
5. Participations in acceptances (as described in the instructions) conveyed to others by the reporting bank .... — **5.**
6. Participations in acceptances (as described in the instructions) acquired by the reporting (nonaccepting) bank .... — **6.**
7. Securities borrowed .... — **7.**
8. Securities lent (including customers' securities lent where the customer is indemnified against loss by the reporting bank) .... — **8.**
9. Mortgages transferred (i.e., sold or swapped) with recourse that have been treated as sold for Call Report purposes:
   a. FNMA and FHLMC residential mortgage loan pools:
   (1) Outstanding principal balance of mortgages transferred as of the report date .... — **9.a.(1)**
   (2) Amount of recourse exposure on these mortgages as of the report date .... — **9.a.(2)**
   b. Private (nongovernment-issued or -guaranteed) residential mortgage loan pools:
   (1) Outstanding principal balance of mortgages transferred as of the report date .... — **9.b.(1)**
   (2) Amount of recourse exposure on these mortgages as of the report date .... — **9.b.(2)**
   c. Farmer Mac agricultural mortgage loan pools:
   (1) Outstanding principal balance of mortgages transferred as of the report date .... — **9.c.(1)**
   (2) Amount of recourse exposure on these mortgages as of the report date .... — **9.c.(2)**
10. When-issued securities:
    a. Gross commitments to purchase .... — **10.a**
    b. Gross commitments to sell .... — **10.b**
11. Spot foreign exchange contracts .... — **11.**
12. All other off-balance sheet liabilities (exclude off-balance sheet derivatives) (itemize and describe each component of this item over 25% of Schedule RC, item 28, "Total equity capital") .... — **12.**
    a. — **12.a.**
    b. — **12.b.**
    c. — **12.c.**
    d. — **12.d.**
13. All other off-balance sheet assets (exclude off-balance sheet derivatives) (itemize and describe each component of this item over 25% of Schedule RC, item 28, "Total equity capital") .... — **13.**
    a. — **13.a.**
    b. — **13.b.**
    c. — **13.c.**
    d. — **13.d.**

FFIEC 031
Page RC-15

Legal Title of Bank

25

FDIC Certificate Number

Schedule RC-L—Continued

C481 ◄

Dollar Amounts in Thousands Off-balance Sheet Derivatives Position Indicators	(Column A) Interest Rate Contracts Tril Bil Mil Thou	Column B) Foreign Exchange Contracts Tril Bil Mil Thou	(Column C) Equity Derivative Contracts Tril Bil Mil Thou	(Column D) Commodity and Other Contracts Tril Bil Mil Thou	
14. Gross amounts (e.g., notional amounts) (for each column, sum of items 14.a through 14.e must equal sum of items 15, 16.a, and 16.b):					14.a.
a. Futures contracts	*CFD 8693	*CFD 8694	*CFD 8695	*CFD 8696	14.b.
b. Forward contracts	*CFD 8697	*CFD 8698	*CFD 8699	*CFD 8700	
c. Exchange-traded option contracts:					14.c.(1)
(1) Written options	*CFD 8701	*CFD 8702	*CFD 8703	*CFD 8704	14.c.(2)
(2) Purchased options	*CFD 8705	*CFD 8706	*CFD 8707	*CFD 8708	
d. Over-the-counter option contracts:					14.d.(1)
(1) Written options	*CFD 8709	*CFD 8710	*CFD 8711	*CFD 8712	14.d.(2)
(2) Purchased options	*CFD 8713	*CFD 8714	*CFD 8715	*CFD 8716	14.e.
e. Swaps	*CFD 3450	*CFD 3826	*CFD 8719	*CFD 8720	
15. Total gross notional amount of derivative contracts held for trading	*CFD A126	*CFD A127	*CFD 8723	*CFD 8724	15.
16. Total gross notional amount of derivative contracts held for purposes other than trading:					16.a
a. Contracts marked to market	*CFD 8725	*CFD 8726	*CFD 8727	*CFD 8728	16.b.
b. Contracts not marked to market	*CFD 8729	*CFD 8730	*CFD 8731	*CFD 8732	

FFIEC 031
Page RC-1f

26

Schedule RC-L—Continued

Dollar Amounts in Thousands Off-balance Sheet Derivatives Position Indicators	(Column A) Interest Rate Contracts Bil Mil Thou	(Column B) Foreign Exchange Contracts Bil Mil Thou	(Column C) Equity Derivative Contracts Bil Mil Thou	(Column D) Commodity and Other Contracts Bil Mil Thou	
17. Gross fair values of derivative contracts:					
a. Contracts held for trading:					
(1) Gross positive fair value	8723	8734	8738	8739	17.a.(1)
(2) Gross negative fair value	8737	8738	8739	8740	17.a.(2)
b. Contracts held for purposes other than trading that are marked to market:					
(1) Gross positive fair value	8741	8742	8743	8744	17.b.(1)
(2) Gross negative fair value	8745	8746	8747	8748	17.b.(2)
c. Contracts held for purposes other than trading that are not marked to market:					
(1) Gross positive fair value	8749	8750	8751	8752	17.c.(1)
(2) Gross negative fair value	8753	8754	8755	8756	17.c.(2)

Memoranda

	Dollar Amounts in Thousands	Bil Mil Thou	
1.–2. Not applicable			
3. Unused commitments with an original maturity exceeding one year that are reported in Schedule RC-L, items 1.a through 1.e. above (report only the unused portions of commitments that are fee paid or otherwise legally binding)		3833	M.3.
a. Participations in commitments with an original maturity exceeding one year conveyed to others	3834		M.3.a
4. To be completed only by banks with $1 billion or more in total assets: Standby letters of credit and foreign office guarantees (both financial and performance) issued to non-U.S. addressees (domicile) included in Schedule RC-L, items 2 and 3, above		3377	M.4.
5. To be completed for the September report only: Installment loans to individuals for household, family, and other personal expenditures that have been securitized and sold without recourse (with servicing retained), amounts outstanding by type of loan:			
a. Loans to purchase private passenger automobiles		2741	M.5.a
b. Credit cards and related plans		2742	M.5.b
c. All other consumer installment credit (including mobile home loans)		2743	M.5.c

Appendix B

Legal Title of Bank

FDIC Certificate Number |_____

| 33 |

Schedule RC-R—Risk-Based Capital

This schedule must be completed by all banks as follows: Banks that reported total assets of $1 billion or more in Schedule RC, item 12, for June 30, 1994, must complete items 2 through 9 and Memoranda items 1 and 2. Banks with assets of less than $1 billion must complete items 1 and 2 below or Schedule RC-R in its entirety, depending on their response to item 1 below.

1. Test for determining the extent to which Schedule RC-R must be completed. To be completed only by banks with total assets of less than $1 billion. Indicate in the appropriate box at the right whether the bank has total capital greater than or equal to eight percent of adjusted total assets ....

	C480	◄
	YES	NO
RCFD 6056			1.

For purposes of this test, adjusted total assets equals total assets less cash, U.S. Treasuries, U.S. Government agency obligations, and 80 percent of U.S. Government-sponsored agency obligations plus the allowance for loan and lease losses and selected off-balance sheet items as reported on Schedule RC-L (see instructions).

If the box marked YES has been checked, then the bank only has to complete item 2 below. If the box marked NO has been checked, the bank must complete the remainder of this schedule.

A NO response to item 1 does not necessarily mean that the bank's actual risk-based capital ratio is less than eight percent or that the bank is not in compliance with the risk-based capital guidelines.

	(Column A) Subordinated Debt[1] and Intermediate Term Preferred Stock			(Column B) Other Limited-Life Capital Instruments		
Item 2 is to be completed by all banks.						
Dollar Amounts in Thousands	Bil	Mil	Thou	Bil	Mil	Thou
2. Subordinated debt[1] and other limited-life capital instruments (original weighted average maturity of at least five years) with a remaining maturity of:						
a. One year or less	RCFD 3780			RCFD 3786			2.a.
b. Over one year through two years	RCFD 3781			RCFD 3787			2.b.
c. Over two years through three years	RCFD 3782			RCFD 3788			2.c.
d. Over three years through four years	RCFD 3783			RCFD 3789			2.d.
e. Over four years through five years	RCFD 3784			RCFD 3790			2.e.
f. Over five years	RCFD 3785			RCFD 3791			2.f.
3. Not applicable						

	(Column A) Assets Recorded on the Balance Sheet			(Column B) Credit Equivalent Amount of Off-Balance Sheet Items[2]		
Items 4–9 and Memoranda items 1 and 2 are to be completed by banks that answered NO to item 1 above and by banks with total assets of $1 billion or more.						
	Bil	Mil	Thou	Bil	Mil	Thou
4. Assets and credit equivalent amounts of off-balance sheet items assigned to the Zero percent risk category:						
a. Assets recorded on the balance sheet:						
(1) Securities issued by, other claims on, and claims unconditionally guaranteed by, the U.S. Government and its agencies and other OECD central governments	RCFD 3794						4.a.(1)
(2) All other	RCFD 3795						4.a.(2)
b. Credit equivalent amount of off-balance sheet items				RCFD 3796			4.b.

[1] Exclude mandatory convertible debt reported in Schedule RC-M, item 7.
[2] Do not report in column B the risk-weighted amount of assets reported in column A.

FFIEC 031
Page RC-24

34

Schedule RC-R—Continued

	(Column A) Assets Recorded on the Balance Sheet	(Column B) Credit Equivalent Amount of Off-Balance Sheet items[1]
Dollar Amounts in Thousands	Bil Mil Thou	Bil Mil Thou

5. Assets and credit equivalent amounts of off-balance sheet items assigned to the 20 percent risk category:

  a. Assets recorded on the balance sheet:

    (1) Claims conditionally guaranteed by the U.S. Government and its agencies and other OECD central governments .... RCFD 3796   5.a.(1)

    (2) Claims collateralized by securities issued by the U.S. Government and its agencies and other OECD central governments; by securities issued by U.S. Government-sponsored agencies; and by cash on deposit .... RCFD 3798   5.a.(2)

    (3) All other .... RCFD 3800   5.a.(3)

  b. Credit equivalent amount of off-balance sheet items .... RCFD 3801   5.b.

6. Assets and credit equivalent amounts of off-balance sheet items assigned to the 50 percent risk category:

  a. Assets recorded on the balance sheet .... RCFD 3802   6.a.

  b. Credit equivalent amount of off-balance sheet items .... RCFD 3803   6.b.

7. Assets and credit equivalent amounts of off-balance sheet items assigned to the 100 percent risk category:

  a. Assets recorded on the balance sheet .... RCFD 3804   7.a.

  b. Credit equivalent amount of off-balance sheet items .... RCFD 3805   7.b.

8. On-balance sheet asset values excluded from the calculation of the risk-based capital ratio[2] .... RCFD 3806   8.

9. Total assets recorded on the balance sheet (sum of items 4.a, 5.a, 6.a, 7.a, and 8, column A) (must equal Schedule RC, item 12 plus items 4.b and 4.c) .... RCFD 3807   9.

Memoranda

Dollar Amounts in Thousands	Bil Mil Thou

1. Current credit exposure across all off-balance sheet derivative contracts covered by the risk-based capital standards .... RCFD 3784   M.1.

	With a remaining maturity of		
	(Column A) One year or less	(Column B) Over one year through five years	(Column C) Over five years
2. Notional principal amounts of off-balance sheet derivative contracts[3]:	Tril Bil Mil Thou	Tril Bil Mil Thou	Tril Bil Mil Thou
a. Interest rate contracts	RCFD 3809	RCFD 8766	RCFD 8767	M.2.a.
b. Foreign exchange contracts	RCFD 3812	RCFD 8769	RCFD 8770	M.2.b.
c. Gold contracts	RCFD 8771	RCFD 8772	RCFD 8773	M.2.c.
d. Other precious metals contracts	RCFD 8774	RCFD 8775	RCFD 8776	M.2.d.
e. Other commodity contracts	RCFD 8777	RCFD 8778	RCFD 8779	M.2.e.
f. Equity derivative contracts	RCFD A000	RCFD A001	RCFD A002	M.2.f.

[1] Do not report in column B the risk-weighted amount of assets reported in column A.
[2] Include the difference between the fair value and the amortized cost of available-for-sale securities in item 8 and report the amortized cost of these securities in items 4 through 7 above. Item 8 also includes on-balance sheet asset values (or portions thereof) of off-balance sheet interest rate, foreign exchange rate, and commodity contracts and those contracts (e.g., futures contracts) not subject to risk-based capital. Exclude from item 8 margin accounts and accrued receivables as well as any portion of the allowance for loan and lease losses in excess of the amount that may be included in Tier 2 capital.
[3] Exclude foreign exchange contracts with an original maturity of 14 days or less and all futures contracts.

Bibliography

Albert, Howard W. (1991), "Asset Securitization Benefits All banks," *The Bankers Magazine* (November/December): 16–20.

Aliber, Robert Z., (1984), "International Banking: A Survey," *Journal of Credit, Money, and Banking*, November: 661–678.

———, (1976), "Toward a Theory of International Banking," *Federal Reserve Bank of San Francisco Economic Review*, Spring: 5–8.

———, (1975), "International Banking: Growth and Regulation," *Columbia Journal of World Business*, Winter: 9–15.

Altman, Edward I. (1968), "Financial Ratios, Discriminant Analysis, and the Prediction of Corporate Bankruptcy." *Journal of Finance* (September): 589–609

American Banker–Bond Buyer (1992), *Securitization Directory and Handbook*.

American Banker–Bond Buyer (Weekly Issues), *Asset Sales Report*, 1990–Nov. 1996, Weekly Issues.

Ames, Chris (1993), "Introduction to Collateralized Mortgage Obligations," *Lehman Brothers Market Introduction Series: No.3,* (August).

Askari, Hossein (1991), *Third World Debt and Financial Innovation: The Experience of Chile and Mexico*, The Organization for Economic Co-Operation and Development.

Asset Finance Group—The First Boston Corporation- (1989), "Overview of Assets and Structures," in *The Asset Securitization Handbook*, Phillip L. Zweig, editor, Illinois: Dow-Jones Irwin.

Association of Reserve City Bankers, *Strategic Issues in Banking*, Arthur Anderson & Co. 1988.

Avery, Robert B. and Allen N. Berger (1991), "Risk-Based Capital and Deposit Insurance reform," *Journal of Banking and Finance*, Vol 15: 847–874.

Avery, Robert B. and Allen N. Berger (1990), "Loan Commitments and Bank Risk Exposure," *Federal Reserve Board, Manuscript* (June).

Avery, Robert B. and Gerald A. Hanweck (1984), "A Dynamic Analysis of Bank Failures," in *A Conference Proceedings on Bank Structure and Competition*, Federal Reserve Bank of Chicago (April 23–25): 380–395.

Bank For International Settlements (1986), *Recent Innovations in International Banking*, Basle: Switzerland, April.

Bank for International Settlements (1986b), *The Management of Banks' Off-Balance-Sheet Exposures: A supervisory Perspective*, Committee on Banking Regulation and Supervisory Practices (March 17).

The Banker (1994), "Two-Way Openings: Divisions Between Banks And Securities Houses Are Being Broken Down," (Jan.): 52–5.

Barnea, D. (1902), "Methodological Implications of Non-normally Distributed Financial Ratios." *Journal of Business Finance and Accounting* (Summer): 51–62.

Barth, James R., Dan R. Brumbaugh, Daniel Sauerhaft, and George H. K. Wang (1985), "Thrift Institution Failures: Causes and Policy Issues," in *A Conference Proceedings on Bank Structure and Competition*, Federal Reserve Bank of Chicago (May): 1–3.

Dass, Isabel (1990). "Internationalizing the Pfandbrief," *Institutional Investor,* May: 119–123.

Beaver, William H. (1968), "Alternative Financial Ratios as Predictors of Failure." *Accounting Review* (January): 113–122.

Bedingfield, J., P. Reckers and A.J. Stagliano (1985), "Distributions of Financial Ratios in the Commercial Banking Industry." *Journal of Financial Research* (Spring): 77–81.

Ben-Horim, Moshes and Silber William L. (1977), "Financial Innovation: A Linear Programming Approach," *Journal of Banking and Finance*, 1: 277–296.

Bentson, George J., Robert A. Eisenbeis, Paul H. Horvitz, Edward, J. Kane and George J. Kaufman, (1986) *Perspective on Safe and Sound Banking*, Cambridge, Mass., MIT Press.

Bentson, George J; Allen N. Berger; Gerald A. Hanweck; and David B. Humphry (1983), "Economies of Scale and Scope in Banking," *Research Paper in Banking and Financial Economics, Board of Governors of the Federal Reserve System.*

Benveniste, Lawrence M. and Allen N. Berger (1987), *Securitization With Recourse: An Instrument that Offers Uninsured Bank Depositors Sequential*

Claims, Finance and Economics Discussion Series No. 97, Washington, D.C.: Board of Governors of the Federal Reserve System.

Berger, Allen N., Anil K. Kashyap, and Joseph M. Scalise (1995) "The transformation of the U.S. Banking Industry: What a Long Strange Trip It's Been." *Brookings Papers on Economic Activities,* n2: 55–218.

Berger, Allen N. and Gregory F. Udell (1991), *Securitization, Risk, and the Liquidity Problem in Banking,* Finance and Economics Discussion Series No. 181, Washington, D.C.: Board of Governors of the Federal Reserve System.

Bicksler, J., and A. H. Chen (1986), "An Economic Analysis of Interest Rate Swaps," *Journal of Finance,* 41 (July), 645–55.

Board of Governor's of the Federal Reserve System (1995), *1995 RBC Estimation Algorithm Draft* (May 3) Revised. Washington, D.C.: 16pp.

Board of Governors of the Federal Reserve System (1994), *Risk Based Capital Requirements: Recourse and Direct Credit Substitutes,* (May 25): Washington D.C.: 116pp.

Board of Governor's of the Federal Reserve System (1994), *Capital Adequacy Guidelines,* (May). Washington, D.C.: 68pp.

Board of Governors of the Federal Reserve System, Supervision and Regulation Task Force on Securitization (1990a), *An Introduction to Asset Securitization,* Washington, D.C.

Board of Governors of the Federal Reserve System, Supervision and Regulation Task Force on Securitization (1990b), *Accounting Issues Relating to Asset Securitization,* Washington, D.C.

Board of Governors of the Federal Reserve System, Supervision and Regulation Task Force on Securitization (1990c), *Examination Guidelines for Asset Securitization,* Washington, D.C.

Board of Governors of the Federal Reserve System (1989), *The International Banking Act Package,* April.

Boemio, Thomas (1996), Personal Interview (February 23), Board of Governors of the Federal Reserve System. Washington D.C.

Boemio, Thomas R. and Gerald A. Edwards Jr. (1989), "Asset Securitization: A supervisory Perspective," *Federal Reserve Bulletin*: 659–669.

Boot, Arnoud W.A. and Anjan V. Thakor (1991), "Off-Balance Sheet Liabilities, Deposit insurance and Capital Regulation," *Journal of Banking and Finance,* Volume 15: 825–46.

Borg, Bella, Brian Lancaster, and Jane Tang (1992) "Inverse Floating Rate CMOs," in, *The Handbook of Mortgage-Backed Securities,* Fabozzi, Frank J., Editor 3rd. edition. Chicago, IL: Probus Publishing Company, pp 483–518.

Borio, C.E.V. (1990), *Banks' Involvement in Highly Leveraged Transactions*, Basle: Bank for International Settlements.

Bradlee, Michael G., Carol A. Wambeke, and David A. Whibdee (1991), "Risk Weights, Risk-Based Capital and Deposit Insurance," *Journal of Banking and Finance*, No. 15: 875–893

Brimmer, Andrew F., and Frederick R. Dahl (1975), "Growth of American International Banking: Implication of Public Policy," *Journal of Finance*, May: 341–363.

Bryan, Lowell L. (1989) "Introduction," in *The Asset Securitization Handbook*, by Phillip L. Zweig, editor, Illinois: Dow-Jones Irwin.

Buttimer, Richard Joseph, Jr. (1993), *The Pricing of Mortgage-Derivative Securities: A Comparison of Interest Rate Models*. PhD, University of Georgia.

Cantor, Richard and Ronald Johnson (1992), "Bank Capital Ratio, Asset Growth and the Stock Market." *Federal Reserve Bank of New York* (Autumn): 10–24.

Carter, Michael (1989), "Financial Innovation and Financial Fragility," *Journal of Economic Issues* (September):779–793.

Cates, David C. and Henry A Davis (1987), *Off-Balance-Sheet Banking and the Changing Nature of Financial Risk*, Philadelphia: Robert Morris Associates.

Cates, David C. (1985), "Bank Risk and Predicting Bank Failure," *Issues in Bank Regulations*, Autumn. 10–20.

Caves, Richard E. (1971), "International Corporations: The Industrial Economics of Foreign Investment," *Economica*, February: 1–27.

Chang, Chih-Cheng (1989), *Cost Synergies in the Commercial banking Industry: An Econometric Examination*, Ph.D., University of Illinois at Urbana-Champaign.

Channon, Derek F. *Global Banking Strategy*, New York: John Wiley and Sons, 1988.

Channon, Derek, F. *The Service Industry: Strategy, Structure, And Financial Performance*, London: Holmes & Meier Publishers, Inc., 1978.

Chidambaran, Nemmara Krishnamurthy (1994), Path-Dependent Contingent Claims (Portfolio Insurance). Ph.D, NYU: School of Business Administration.

Cho, Kang Rae (1983). *A Study on Multinational Banks (MNBs): Their Identities and Determinants*. Ph.D Dissertation, University of Washington.

——— (1985), *Multinational Banks: Their Identities and Determinants*. Ann Arbor, MI.: UMI Research Press.

Clarke, Robert L. (1988) "Why Banks Fail?," *Texas Banking* (April): 35.

Collins, Julie H., Douglas A. Shackelford and James M. Wahlen (1995), "Bank Differences in the Coordination of Regulatory Capital, earnings, and taxes." *Journal of Accounting Research* (Autumn): 263–291.

Cooper, Ian (1986), "Innovations: New Market Instruments," *Oxford Review of Economic Policy*, Vol. 4 No. 2 (Winter): 1–17.

Cross, Howard and George H. Hempell (1980), *Management Policies for Commercial Banks*, Englewood Cliffs, N.J.: Prentice-Hall.

Cumming, Christine (1987), "The Economics of Securitization," *FRBNY Quarterly Review* (Autumn): 11–23.

Dale, Richard (1986), *The Regulation of International Banking*. Englewood Cliffs, NJ: Prentice Hall.

Deaken, E.B. (1976), "Distributions of Financial Accounting Ratios: Some Empirical Evidence." *The Accounting Review* (Jan): 90–6.

DeAngelo, H and L. DeAngelo (1987), "Management Buyouts of Publicly traded Corporations, " *Financial Analysts Journal* (May-June): 38–49.

Demaris, Alfred (1992), *Logit Modeling: Practical Applications*. Sage University Paper Series on Quantitative Applications in the Social Sciences # 86, Newbury park, CA.

Dermiguc-Kunt, Asli (1989), "Deposit-Institution Failures: A Review of the Literature," *Economic Review Federal Reserve Bank of Cleveland* (4th Quarter): 2–18.

DeRosa, Paul, Laurie Goodman and, Mike Zazzarino (1993), "Duration Estimates on Mortgage-Backed Securities." *Journal of Portfolio Management* (Winter): 32–38.

Diamond, Douglas (1989), "Reputation Acquisition in the Debt Market." *Journal of Political Economy*: 828–862.

Donahoo, Kathleene K. and Sherrill Shaffer (1991), "Capital Requirements and the Securitization Decision," *Quarterly Review of Economics and Business* (Winter): 12–23.

Doyle, B.M. and H. Ammidon (1989), *The Anatomy of a Leveraged Buyout— Profile, Process, Capitalizations and Implications*, New York: Saloman Brothers (April).

Dufey, G. and Giddy Ian (1978), *The International Money Markets*, Englewood Cliffs, N.J.:Prentice-Hall Inc.

Dunning, John H. (1977), "Trade, Locations of Economic Activity, and the Multinational Enterprise: A Search for an Eclectic Approach," In *The International Allocation of Economic Activity*, edited by Bertil Ohlin et al.,: 395–418. London: Macmillan.

—— (1979), "Explaining Changing Patterns of International Production: In Defense of the Eclectic Theory," *Oxford Bulletin of Economics and Statistics*, November: 269–95.

—— (1980), "Toward an Eclectic Theory of International Production," *Journal of International Business Studies*, January:9–31.

Dunning, John and Alan Rugman (1985), "The Influence of Hymer's Dissertation on the Theory of Foreign Direct Investment," *American Economic Review*, May: 228–32.

The Economist (1995a), "Banking Supervision : Do-it-Yourself Regulation." Apr 15: 70–71.

The Economist (1995), "Small Loans, Big Problems," (Jan. 28): 73.

The Economist (1995), "Finding the Right Chemistry," (September 2): 67–8.

The Economist (1995), "Cleaning up the Mess: Banks in Trouble," (September 2): 68.

The Economist (1994), "Going for Goldman. (Goldman Sachs chosen for Japanese securitization deal with Nippon Shinpan)," (July 30) p. 71.

The Economist (1994), "International Banking Survey: Recalled to Life," (April 30): 1–42.

The Economist (1993a), "A Survey of Investment Management: Only Perform," (November 27): 1–30.

The Economist (1993b), "A Survey of the Frontiers of Finance: The Mathematics of Markets," (October 9): 1–22.

The Economist (1993c), "International Banking Survey: A Comedy of Errors," (April 10): 1–38.

The Economist (1992), "World Banking Survey: Banks Meet the Marketplace," (May 2): 1–50.

Elderfield, Matthew (1996), "Basle Accord : Financial Market Risk Capital Standards Published." *Financial Regulation Report*, Jan/Feb: 7–10.

Ellspermann, W. R. (1988), "Supporting growth Through Asset Securitization," *Bank Administration* (October): 24+.

Epps, T.W., Lawrence B. Pulley, and David B. Humphrey (1996), "Assessing the FDIC's Premium and Examination Policies using Soviet Put Options." *Journal of Banking and Finance* (May): 699–721).

Epstein, Lee (1993), "Basis Points: Topsy-Turvy World of Inverse Floaters," *Corporate CashFlow* (February): 33–4.

Euromoney (1995), "The Big Banks are Back" (May): 26–9.

Euromoney (1995), "Regulatory Overload: Capital Adequacy," (June): 115–120.

Euromoney (1994), "US Focus on Structured Deals," (Sept.): 328–9.

Euromoney (1991), "Security in Big Numbers," (March): 37–40.

Euromoney (1989)," Asset Securitisation: Changing the Face of Lending," A Special Insert (August): 1–28.

Euroweek (1995a), International Structured Finance Supplement (July): 1–26.

Euroweek (1995b), "Indosuez, Bear in New Packaging of French Mortgages," (July 28) : 63.

Euroweek (1995c), "UK financiers welcome credit card bond debut by top US name MBNA," (July 21): 38.

Fabozzi, Frank J. (1992), Editor, *The Handbook of Mortgage-Backed Securities*, 3rd. edition. Chicago, IL: Probus Publishing Company.

Fabozzi, Frank J., Chuck Ramsey, and Frank R. Ramirez (1994), *Collateralized Mortgage Obligations: Structures and Analysis*, 2nd ed. Buckingham, PA: Frank J. Fabozzi Associates.

Federal Financial Institutions Examination Council (1995), *A Users's Guide for the Uniform Bank Performance Report*. March, Washington D.C.

Federal Reserve Board and Bank of England (1987) "Agreed Proposal of the United States Federal Banking Supervisory Authorities and the Bank of England on Primary Capital and Capital Adequacy Assessment"

Federal Reserve Bulletin (1996a), Tables I.54, "Mortgage Debt Outstanding" and I.55, "Consumer Installment Loans," (October): A38–9.

Federal Reserve Bulletin (1996b), Tables I.54, "Mortgage Debt Outstanding" and I.55, "Consumer Installment Loans," (March): A38–9.

Federal Reserve Bulletin (1996c), "Trends in the Structure of Federally insured Depository Institutions, 1984–1994." (January): 1–15.

Federal Reserve Bulletin (1992), Tables I.54, "Mortgage Debt Outstanding" and I.55, "Consumer Installment Loans," (September): A36–7.

Federal Reserve Bulletin (1992a), "Development in the Prices of Credit Card Services," (September): 652–666.

Feeney, P.W. (1989), *Euronotes: Risk and Pricing*, Ph.D. University of North Wales, Bangor (UK).

Fieleke, Norman (1977), "The Growth of U.S. Banking Abroad: An Analytical Survey," In Federal Reserve Bank of Boston, Conference series, *Key Issues in International Banking* 18:9–40.

Financial Standard Accounting Board (1990), *SFAS No. 105: Disclosure of Information About Financial Instruments with Off-Balance-Sheet Risk and Financial Instruments with Concentrations of Credit Risk* (March).

Financial Times (1996), "Asia-Pacific: Tokyo plans 'Big Bang' by 2001," (Nov. 11).

Financial Times (1993a), "Financial Times Survey: International Capital markets," (October 28).

Financial Times (1993b), "Financial Times Survey: Derivatives," (October 20).

Financial Times (1992a), "Ignorance and Other Failures of the Regulators" (December 7).

Financial Times (1992b), "Bank Tries to Boost Prospects for UK Securitisation," (December 7).

Financial Times (1991), "Asset Backed Finance" (Wednesday June 19).

Finnerty, John D. (1988), "Financial Engineering in Corporate Finance: An Overview," *Financial Management* (Winter): 14–33.

Flannery, Mark J. (1989), "Capital Regulation and Insured Banks' Choice of Individual Loan Default Risk," *Journal of Monetary Economics* (September): 235–258.

Flannery, Mark J. (1987), "Deposit Insurance Capital Regulation, and the Choice of Bank Loan Default Rates." *Working Paper, University of North Carolina at Chapel Hill* (February).

Flury, Bernhard and Hans Riedwyl (1988), *Multivariate Statistics" A Practical Approach*. UK. Cambridge, the University Press.

Flood, Mark D. (1992), "Two Faces of Financial Innovation," *Federal Reserve Bank of St. Louis* (September/October): 3–17.

Freeman, C. (1982) *The Economics of Innovation*. London:F. Pinter

Fugal, Herbert (1992), "German ABS Market Slow to Get Started," in *Asset securitization: Theory and Practice in Europe*, Charles Stone, Anne Zissu, and Jess Lederman, editors, London: Euromoney Publication.

Gajewski, Gregory R. (1988), *Bank Risk, Regulator Behavior and Bank Closure in the Mid-1980s: A Two-Step Logit Model*, PhD. Dissertation, The George Washington University.

Gamble, Richard H. (1990), "Recipe for an Off-Balance-Sheet Diet: The Green Goes in the Side Dish," *Corporate CashFlow* (August): 28–32.

Giddy, Ian H. (1981), "The Theory of Industrial Organization of International Banking," In the *Internationalization of Financial Markets and National Policies*, edited by Robert Hawkins & al. NY, JAI Press.

Gilley, Brian Alan (1988), *A Regional Model of MBS Prepayment Rates*. PhD, University of South Carolina.

Goldberg, Ellen, Edward I. Altman, and Edward E. Furash (1984), *Off-Balance-Sheet Activities of Banks: Managing the Risk/Reward Trade-Offs*, Robert Morris Associates.

Goldberg, Lawrence G., and Anthony Sounders (1980), "The Causes of U.S. Bank Expansion Overseas: The Case of Great Britain," *Journal of Credit, Money, and Banking*, November :630–643.

Goodhart, Charles (1986), "Financial Innovation and Monetary Control," *Oxford Review of Economic Policy* (Winter): 79–102.

Goodman, John L. (1992), *Market Power and the Pricing of Mortgage Securitization*, Finance and Economics Discussion Series, No. 187, Washington, D.C.: Board of Governors of the Federal Reserve System.

Goodman, Laurie S., (1984), "Comments on International Banking: A Survey," *Journal of Credit, Money, and Banking*, November: 678–690.

Goudreau, Robert E. and B. Frank King (1990), "Recovering Bank Profitability: Spoiled Again by Large Banks' Loan Problem," *Economic Review (Federal Reserve Bank of Atlanta* (May/June): 30–34.

Gray, Jean M., and H. Peter Gray (1981), "The Multinational Bank: A Financial MNC?," *Journal of Banking and Finance*, March: 33–63.

Greenbaum, S.I. and A.V. Thakor (1987), "Bank Funding Modes: Securitization versus Deposits," *Journal of Banking and Finance* (September): 379–401.

Greenbaum, S.I. and C.F. Haywood (1974), "Secular Changes in the Financial Services Industry," *Journal of Money, Credit and Banking* (May).

Greenspan, Alan (1988), "Innovation and Regulation of Banks in the 1990s," Remarks Before the American Bankers Association, Honolulu, Hawaii (October 11).

Grivoyannis, Elias Constantine (1989), *Current Issues of Monetary Policy in the U.S. and Japan: Predictability of Money Demand (United States)*, Ph.D., New York University.

Griswold, Melissa, Gordon V. Karels, and Angeline M. Lavin (1996), "Risk-Based Capital Standards or Bank Exams: Which have more Effect on Bank Portfolios." *Journal of Commercial Lending*, (January): 49–56.

Grubel, Herbert G. (1977), " A Theory of Multinational Banking," *Banca Nationale del Lavoro Quarterly Review*, December: 349–63.

Guo, Chen (1989) *Pricing Interest Rate Contingent Claims*, Ph.D., Queen's University at Kingston (CA).

Guttery, Randall S. and Ed McCarthy (1995), "Real Estate Derivative Assets" CMOs, IOs, POs, and Inverse Floaters," *Real Estate Finance* (April 24): 18–29.

Hair, Joseph F. Jr., Rolph E. Anderson, Ronald L. Tatham, and William C. Black (1992), *Multivariate Data Analysis with Readings*, New York: Macmillan Publishing Company.

Haroun, Mansour (1994), *Mortgage Choice and Asset Pricing*. PhD, University of Chicago.

Hassan, M. Kabir (1993), "Capital Market Tests of Risk Exposure of Loan Sales Activities of Large U.S. Commercial Banks," *Quarterly Journal of Business and Economics* (Winter): 27–49.

Haubrich, Joseph G. (1995), "Derivative Mechanics: The CMO," *Economic Commentary, the Federal Reserve Bank of Cleveland* (September 1).

Heimann, John G. (1987), "Financial Innovation: Opportunities, Risk and Regulation," *Proceedings of a Conference on Bank Structure and Competition.* Federal Reserve Bank of Chicago: 27–31.

Hempel, George H., Alan B. Coleman, and Donald G. Simonson (1990), *Bank Management: Text and Cases*, New York: John Wiley & Sons.

Hester, D. D. (1982), "On the Adequacy of Policy Instruments and Information When the Meaning of Money is Changing," *American Economic Review*, 72(2): 42.

Holland, David (1988c) *An Examination of Off-Balance-Sheet Activities: Case of the U.S. Banks*, Ph.D., the George Washington University.

Hopper, Gregory P (1996), "Value At Risk : A New Methodology For Measuring Portfolio Risk." *Business Review (Federal Reserve Bank of Philadelphia)* Jul/Aug: 19–31.

Houpt, James V. (1980), "Foreign Ownership and the Performance of United States Banks," *Board of Governors of the Federal Reserve System Staff Studies* 109, July.

Houthakker, Hendrik S., (1984), "Comments on International Banking: A Survey," *Journal of Credit, Money, and Banking*, November: 684–690.

Hymer, S. (1976), *The International Operations of national Firms: A Study of Direct Foreign Investment*. Cambridge, Mass.: The MIT Press.

Hyre, Lakbir and L. Pendergast (1993), "Guide to CMO Market Place," *Prudential Securities Financial Strategies Group* (January): 13–28.

Ingram, Virginia Carol (1990), *Financial Innovation as a Response to Regulation: The Case of Variable Rate Preferred Stock*, Ph.D., Georgia State University.

Jackson, T. Steven (1991), *A Statistical Analysis of Federal Home Loan Mortgage Corporation: Mortgage-Backed Securities Unscheduled Prepayments*. MS, University of Nevada: Reno.

Jarsulic, Marc, editor (1985), *Recent Economic Thought: Money and Macro Policy*, Boston: Kluwer Nijhoff Publishing.

Jobson, J.D. (1992), *Applied Multivariate Data Analysis, Volume II: Categorical and Multivariate Methods*, New York: Springer-Verlag.

John, Kose and Eli Ofek (1993), "Source of Gains in Asset Sales: Fit or Focus?" *Stern School of Business, NYU* (May): 1–30.

Johnson, Mark (1989), "Asset Securitization: Changing the Face of Lending," *Euromoney, Special Supplement* (August): 1–28.

Johnston, R. B. (1982), The Economics of the Euro-Market: History, Theory, and Policy. New York: St. Martin Press.

Journal of Accountancy (1996), "Banking: U.S. Bank's Insurance Lowered; SAIF Institutions unchanged," (January): 17–18.

Julapa, Rungkasiri (1989), *Bank Participation in the Swap Market: Credibility and Regulatory Effects*, Ph.D. New York University.

Kane, Edward J. (1984), "Microeconomic and Macroeconomic of Financial Innovation," in *Financial Innovation*, the Federal Reserve Bank of St. Louis: 3–20.

——— (1981), "Accelerating Inflation, Technological Innovation, and the Decreasing Effectiveness of Banking Regulation," *Journal of Finance*, (May): 355–367.

——— (1977), "Good Intentions and Unintended Evil: The Case Against Selective Credit Allocation," *Journal of Money, Credit and Banking*, (October): 55–69.

Kahn, Sharon (1995), "IFC Magic," *Global Finance* (Aug) : 22–23.

Kane, Gregory D. (1995), "Accounting for Securitized Assets: Are There Strings that Should Determine the Treatment?" *The CPA Journal* (July): 44–7.

Kavanagh, Barbara (1992), "Asset-Backed Commercial Paper," *Federal Reserve Bulletin* (February): 107–16.

Keeley, M.C. and F.T. Furlong (1990), "A Reexamination of Mean-Variance Analysis of Bank Capital Regulation," *Journal of Banking and Finance,* (January) 69–84.

Keeton, W.R. (1988), "Substitutes and Complements in Bank Risk-Taking and the Effectiveness of regulation," *Federal Reserve Bank of Kansas City, Working Paper* (Dec).

Kelly, Janet (1977), *Bankers and Borders: The Case of American Banks in Britain*. Cambridge, MA: Ballinger.

Kendall, Maurice G. and William R. Buckland (1971), *A Dictionary of Statistical Terms*. 3rd. Edition, the Internatinal Statistical Institute. NY: Hafner Publishing Company Inc.

Khambata, Dara (1989), "Off-Balance-Sheet Activities of US Banks: An Empirical Evaluation," *Columbia Journal of World Business* (Summer): 3–13.

Khoury, Sarkis J. (1990) *The Deregulation of the World Financial Markets*, Quorum Books, Connecticut: Greenwood Press Inc.

——— (1980), *Dynamics of International Banking.* New York: Praeger Publishers.

——— (1979), "International Banking: A Special Look at Foreign Banks in the U.S.," *Journal of International Business Studies*, Winter: 36–52.

Kim, Eung Jin (1989), *The Selection of a Framework for Intermediate Monetary Policy Targets in a Changing Financial Environment*, Ph.D., Clark University.

Kim, D. and A.M. Santomero (1988), "Risk in Banking and Capital Regulation,: *Journal of Finance*, Vol. 1219–1233.

Kinderlberger, Charles P. (1969), *American Business Abroad: Six Lectures on Direct Investments*, New Haven, Conn.: Yale University Press.

Koehn, M. and A.M. Santomero (1980), "Regulation of Capital and Bank Risk," *Journal of Finance*, Vol. 35: 1235–1244.

Kopff, Gary J. and Jeremy Lent (1988), "Securitization: Taking the Business Off the Balance Sheet," *The Bankers Magazine* (November/ December): 14–18.

Kose, John and David Nachman (1985), "Risky Debt, Investment Incentives and Reputation in a Sequential Equilibrium." *Journal of Finance*: 863–878.

Kravitt, Jason H.P., Ian R. Coles, and C Mark Nicolaides (1991), "Coping With Cross-Border Securitisation," *International Financial Law Review* (November): 34–38.

Kress, Heinz (1983), *Statistical Tables for Multivariate Analysis: A Handbook with References and Applications*, New York: Springer-Verlag Publications.

Kuhn, Robert Lawrence, editor (1990), *Mortgage and Asset Securitization*, Homewood, Ill.: Dow-Jones Irwin.

Lavin, David (1992), "FAS 105: The Future of Disclosure Standards for Financial Instruments," *The National Public Accountant* (November): 14–17.

Lawson, Catherine L. (1988), Financial *Innovation as a Response to Financial Instability*, Ph.D., University of Colorado at Boulder.

LDC Debt Report (1996), "Wave of Latin Securitization Just the Start," (Nov. 4).

Lee, C. (1985), "Stochastic Properties of Cross-Sectional Financial Data." *Journal of Accounting Research* (Spring): 213–27.

Lees, F. A. (1974), *International Banking and Finance*. London and New York: Macmillan.

Lefebvre, Olivier (1988), "Securitisation: Definition, Instruments et Tendences," *Bulletin the L'IRES, Université Catholique de Louvain, Institut de Recherches Economiques (Belgium) No 128* (November):1–50.

Lillaney, Sanjay Haridas (1994), *Asset-Backed Securities: Theory and Evidence*. Ph.D., Rutgers, State University of NJ.

Linderberg, Eric B., and Stephen A. Ross (1981), "Tobin's q Ratio and Industrial Organization," *Journal of Business*, January: 1–32.

Lintner, John (1965) "Security Prices, Risk and Maximal Gains from Diversification," *Journal of Finance*, 20 (December): 587–615.

Livingston, Miles (1990), *Money and Capital Markets: Financial Instruments & Their Uses*, New Jersey: Prentice Hall.

Looney, Stephen W., James W. Wensley, and William R. Lane (1987), "An Examination of Bank Failure Misclassifications Using the Cox Model," *Proceedings of a Conference on Bank Structure and Competition*. Federal Reserve Bank of Chicago: 214–229.

Lunnerberg, Clifford E. and Robert D. Abbott (1983), *Elementary Multivariate Analysis for the Behavioral Sciences: Applications of Basic Structure*, NY: the Elsevier Science Publishing Co., Inc.

McConnell, John J. and Manoj Singh (1994), "Rational Prepayments and the Valuation of Collateralized Mortgage Obligations," *Journal of Finance* (July): 891–921.

Machayya, Madanda Ganapathy (1989) *Efficiency of the Currency Swap Market: Theoretical Pricing and Empirical Evidence*, Ph.D., New York University.

Maddala, G.S. (1977), *Econometrics*, New York: McGraw Hill Inc. 516pp.

Malitz, Ileen B. (1989), "A Re-Examination of the Wealth Expropriation Hypothesis: The Case of Captive Finance Subsidiaries," *Journal of Finance*: 1039–1047.

Manly, Bryan F.J. (1986), *Multivariate Statistical Methods: A Primer*, UK: Chapman and Hall Ltd.

Mansour I., Hammed Zangeneh and Mark S. Zitz (1993), "The Association Between Bank's Performance Ratios and Market Determined Measure of Risk." *Applied Economics* (Dec): 1503–1510.

Meric, Gulser, Serpil S. Leveen and Ilhan Meric (1991), "The Financial Characteristics of Commercial Banks Involved in Interstate Acquisitions." *The Financial Review* (Feb): 75–90.

Markowitz, Harry M. (1959), *Portfolio Selection: Efficient Diversification of Investments*. New York: John Wiley & Sons, Inc.

Marshall, John F. and Vipul K. Bansal (1992), *Financial Engineering: A Complete Guide to Financial Innovation*, New York Institute of Finance, Allyn and Bacon Inc..

Miller, John U. (1984), *The Pricing of GNMA Modified Pass-through Securities. The Multi-Period Valuation of Stochastic Mortgage Payments*. PhD, University of Houston.

Miller, Merton H. (1991), *Financial Innovations and Market Volatility*, Cambridge, Oxford: Basil Blackwell.

Miller, Merton H. (1986), "Financial Innovation: The Last Twenty Years and the Next," *Journal of Financial and Quantitative Analysis* (December): 459–71.

Milligan, John W. (1988), "The Pioneer of Corporate Debt Guarantees," *Institutional Investor* (April): 197.

Minsky, Hyman P. (1984) "Financial Innovations and Financial Instability: Observation and Theory," in *Financial Innovations*. Federal Reserve Bank of St. Louis: 21–41.

Minsky, Hyman P. (1957), "Central Banking and Money Market Changes," *Quantitative Journal of Economics* (May): 171–87.

Mohammadioun, Mina (1989), *Prediction of the Velocity of Money in the Presence of Financial Innovation and Deregulation: Application of Time Varying Parameter Models*, Ph.D., the University of Texas at Austin.

Mortgage Banking (1996) , "The MBS Goes Global," (May): 78–87.

Moss, Barbara (1989), *The Benefits and Risks of Asset Securitization for Commercial Banks*, Federal Reserve Bank of Richmond.

Munter, Paul (1992), "The Financial Instruments Project Marches On," *The CPA Journal* (July): 30–36.

Murray, John D., (1984), "Comments on International Banking: A Survey," *Journal of Credit, Money, and Banking*, November: 691–695.

Napoli, Janet and herbert L. Baer (1991), "Disintermediation Marches On," *Chicago Fed Letter* (January): 1–4.

Nikkei English News (1996), "Securitization of Bad Loans Increases at City Banks," (Nov. 11).

Nigh, Douglas; Kang Rae Cho, and Suresh Krishnan (1986), "The Role of Location-Related Factors in U.S. Banking Involvement Abroad: An Empirical Examination," *Journal of International Business Studies*, Fall: 59–72.

Ocampo, Juan M. (1989), "Breaking Down the Lending Function: The ABCs of Asset Securitization," *The Bankers Magazine* (May/June): 5–9.

O'Connor, M. (1973), "On the Usefulness of Financial Ratios to Investors in Common Stock." *The Accounting Review* (1973): 339–352.

Ostcr, Avi R. and Barry W. Wood (1992), "Trade Receivable Financing Gear up," *Standard & Poor's CreditWeek* (February): 45–47.

Pantalone, Coleen C. and Marjorie B. Platt (1993), "Impact of Acquisitions on Thrift Performances." *Financial Review* (Nov): 493–522.

Park, Tae Hyung (1990), *Adjustable Rate Mortgages and Mortgage-Backed Securities*. PhD, The University of Michigan.

Park, Yoon S. and Jack Zwick (1985), *International Banking in Theory and Practice*, Addison-Wesley.

Parks, James T. (1991), "The ABCs of CMOs, REMICs and IO/POs: Rocket Science Comes to Mortgage Finance," *Journal of Accountancy*, (April): 41–51

Pasquinelli, Joseph L. (1991), "FAS 105: An Industry Perspective," *Management Accounting* (July): 41–43.

Pavel, Christine A. (1989), *Securitization: The Analysis and Development of Loan Backed/Asset Backed Securities Market* Chicago: Probus Publishing.

Pavel, Christine A. and David Phillis (1987), "Why Commercial Banks sell Loans: An empirical Analysis," *Proceedings of a Conference on Bank Structure and Competition*. Federal Reserve Bank of Chicago: 145–165.

Peek, Joe and Eric Rosengren (1995a), "Bank Regulators and the Credit Crunch." *Journal of Banking and Finance*, (June): 679–692.

Peek, Joe and Eric Rosengren (1995b), "Bank Regulatory Agreement in New England." *New England Economic Review*, (May/June): 15–24.

Pennacchi, George G. (1987), "Advantages and Optimal Structuring of Bank Loan Sales," *Working Paper, University of Pennsylvania* (August).

Perlmuth, Lyn (1995), "Pumping Up the ABS," *Institutional Investor* (May): 36.

Pinches, G.E. and K.A. Mingo (1973), "A Multivariate Analysis of Industrial Bonds Ratings," *Journal of Finance* (March): 1–18.

Podolski, T. M., (1986), *Financial Innovation and the Money Supply*, Oxford: Basil Blackwell: 106.

Powell, F.C. (1982), *Statistical Tables for the Social, Biological and Physical Sciences*. U.K.: Cambridge University Press.

Project & Trade Finance (1996), "IFC Puts Faith in Securitization," (Feb.) p. 26.

Radcliffe Report (1959a), *Committee on the working of the Monetary System: Report*, London.

Radcliffe Report (1959b), *Committee on the Working of the Monetary System: Principal Memoranda of Evidence*, Vol.3, Part XIII, London.

Randall, Jeffrey (1990), "Captive Finance Subsidiaries: A Method for Off-Balance-Sheet Financing," *Secured Lender* (Nov/Dec): 66–70+.

Reiter, Sara A. and David Zicbart (1991), "Bond Yields, Ratings and Financial Inoformations: Evidence From Public Utility Issues." *Financial Review* (Feb): 45–73.

Rhodes, Stephen A. and Donald T. Savage (1991), "Post Deregulation Performances of Large and Small Banks," *Issues in Bank Regulation* (Winter): 20–31.

Rice, Jim and David Mullarky (1992), "Laying the Foundations," *Euromomey* (April): 90,91.

Rizzi, J.V. (1989), "Managing the Risks of LBO Lending," *The Bankers Magazine* (September-October): 9–10.

Rose, Sanford (1993), "The Bittersweet Future of Loan Securitization," *Journal of Retail Banking*, (Spring): 29–32.

Rose, P.S. (1987), "The Impact of Mergers in banking: Evidence From a Nationwide Sample of Federally Chartered Banks." *Journal of Economics and Business* (Nov): 289–313.

Rosenthal, James A. and Juan M. Ocampo (1988), *Securitization of Credit: Inside the New Technology of Finance*, New York: John Wiley and Sons, Inc.

Rotberg, Eugene H. (1992), *Risk management in Financial Services*, France: OECD Publication.

Rousseas, Stephen (1985), "Financial Innovation and the Control of the Money Supply," in *Recent Economic Thoughts: Money and Macro Policy*, ed. Mark Jarsulic, Boston: Kluwer-Nijhoff Publishing.

Rugamn, Alan (1979), *International Diversification and Multinational Enterprise*. Lexington: Lexington Books.

———— (1981), *Inside the Multinationals.* London: Croom Helm.

———— (1983), *New Theories of the Multinational Enterprise*. New York: St. Martin Press.

Sabi, Manijeh (1988), "An Application of the Theory of Foreign Direct Investment to Multinational Banking in LDCs," *Journal of International Business Studies*, Fall: 433–447.

SAS Institute Inc. (1985), SAS User's Guide: Basics, Version 5 Edition. Cary, NC: SAS Institute Inc. 1290pp.

SAS Institute Inc. (1985), *SAS/STAT User's Guide*, Version 6, Fourth Edition, Volumes 1&2. Cary, NC: SAS Institute Inc. 1789pp.

Saunders, Anthony (1990), "Off-Balance-Sheet Activities and Banking," in *Off-Balance-Sheet Activities* by Ronen, Joshua; Anthony Saunders and Ashwinpaul C. Sondhi, editors; New York: Quorum Books : 1–4.

Schumpeter, Joseph. A. (1964), *Business Cycles: A Theoretical, Historical, and Statistical Analysis of the Capitalist Process*. New York: McGraw-Hill.

Shao, Lawrence Peter (1989), *Mortgage-Backed Securities, Duration and Implied Prepayments (Bond Risk)*. PhD, University of Tennessee.

Sharpe, William F. (1981), *Investments*, 2nd ed., Englewood Cliffs, N.J.: Prentice-Hall, Inc.

Shaw, Zoe (1992) "If it Moves, Trade It," *Risk* (January): 29+.

Shirreff, David (1990), "LDC Debt: Into the Next Dimension," *Risk* (March): 37–40.

Shirreff, David (1986), "Down With Innovations," *Euromoney* (August):23ff.

Shirreff, David (1985), "The Fearsome Growth of Swaps," *Euromoney* (October): 247–261.

Short, Brock K. (1979), "The Relation Between Commercial Banking Profit Rates and Banking Concentration in Canada, Western Europe and Japan," *Journal of Banking and Finance*, Vol.3 February.

Silber, William L. (1983), "The Process of Financial Innovation," *American Economic Review*, Papers, 73(2): 89–95

Silber, William L. (1981), "Innovation, Competition, and New Contract Design in Futures Markets," *Journal of Futures Markets* (Summer): 123–156.

Silber, William L. (1975), "Toward a Theory of Financial Innovation," in *Financial Innovation*, ed. William L. Silber, New York: Lexington Books/D.C. Heath: 53–85.

Silver, Daniel B. and Peter J. Axilrod (1989), "Pushing Technology to Its Limits: Securitizing C&I Loans," *The Bankers Magazine* (May/June): 16–21.

Smith, Roy C. *The Global Banker*, New York: Truman Talley Books, 1989.

Smith, Stephen Drew (1988), *Financial Innovation, Market Structure,and the End of the National Banking Era*, Ph.D. Washington University.

Smith, Clifford W., Charles W. Smithson, and Lee Macdonald Wakeman (1987) "Credit Risk and the Scope of Regulation of Swaps." *Proceedings of a Conference on Bank Structure and Competition.* Federal Reserve Bank of Chicago: 167–185.

Smith, Clifford W. Charles W. Smithson, and Lee Macdonald Wakeman (1986), "The Market for Interest Rate Swaps," University of Rochester, Working Paper Series No. MERC 86–04.

So, Jacky C. (1987), "Some Emprirical Evidence on the Outliers and the Non-Normal Distribution of Financial Ratios." *Journal of Business Finance and Accounting* (Winter): 483–496.

Soybel, Virginia E. (1992), "Municipal Financial Reporting and the General Obligation Bonds Market: New York City, 1961–1975." *Journal of Accounting and Public Policy* (Fall): 207–231.

Stevens, James (1992), *Applied Multivariate Statistics for the Social Sciences*, 2nd. Edition. NJ: Lawrence Erlbaum Associates. 629pp.

Stewart, John E. (1989), "Accounting Considerations," in *The Asset Securitization Handbook*, by Zweig, Phillip L., Editor, Illinois: Dow Jones-Irwin.

Swamy, P.A.V.B and P. Von Zur Muehlen (1987), "Further Thoughts on Testing for Causality with Econometric Models," *Special Studies Paper—Division of Research and Statistics*, Federal Reserve Board, Washington, D.C.,:1–54.

Terrel, Henry S. (1979), "U.S. Banks in Japan and Japanese Banks in the U.S.: An Empirical Comparison," *Federal Reserve Bank of San Francisco*, Summer: 18–30.

Tschoegl, Adrian E. (1981), *The Regulation of Foreign banks: Policy Formation in Countries outside the United States*. Saloman Brothers Center for the Study of Financial Institutions, Monograph No. 1981–2.

———, (1987), "International Retail Banking as a Strategy: An Assessment," *Journal of International Business Studies*, Summer: 67–88.

Tschoegl, Adrian E., and P.N. Subba Narasimha (1987), *The Expansion and Operations of Indian banks Abroad.* Societe Universitaire De Recherches Financieres (SUERF).

Tufano, Peter (1989a), *Three Essays on Financial Innovation*, Ph.D., Harvard University.

——— (1989b), "Financial Innovation and First-Mover Advantages," *Journal of Financial Economics*, 25, 213–240.

United States. Congress. House. Committee on Banking, Finance, and Urban Affairs. Subcommittee on Policy Research and Insurance (1991), *Asset Securitization and Secondary Markets: Hearing Before the Subcommittee on*

Policy Research and Insurance of the Committee on Banking, Finance, and Urban Affairs, House of Representatives, One Hundredth Second Congress, First Session (July 31).

Van Holland, Phyllis (1988) "Why Banks Fail," *Bank Administration*, (April): p. 37.

Van Horne, James C. (1985), "Of Financial Innovation and Excesses," *Journal of Finance* (July) :621–31.

Van Horne, James C. (1984) *Financial Market Rates and Flows*, 2nd ed., Englewood Cliffs, N.J.: Prentice-Hall, Inc.

Vang, David Olaf (1988), *The Role of Interest Rate Swaps in Financial Institutions*, Ph.D., Iowa State University.

Vogelstein, Fred (1995), "Credit Cards Fuel Asset-Backed Issues," *Wall Street Journal* (October 30): C1+.

Vojta, George J. (1973), *Bank Capital Adequacy*, Citibank, New York.

Waldman, Michael (1992), "Beyond Duration: Risk Dimension of Mortgage securities." *Journal of Fixed Income* (December): 5–15.

Wall, Larry D. and David R. Peterson (1995), "Bank Holding Company Capital Targets in the Early 1990s: The Regulators Versus the Markets." *Journal of Banking and Finance*, (June): 563–574.

Wall, Larry D. and John J. Pringle (1987), "Alternative Explanations of the Interest Rate Swaps," *Proceedings of a Conference on Bank Structure and Competition*. Federal Reserve Bank of Chicago: 186–205.

Wall Street Journal (1995), "Japanese Panel To Consider Approval of Market For Asset-Backed Securities," (Aug. 25): A5F.

Wall Street Journal (1994), "Mortgage Derivatives Claim Victims Big and Small", C1 (April 20).

Wall Street Journal (1994), "Firms Seek Quick Derivatives Education," C1 (April 19).

Walter, Ingo, and H. Peter Gray (1983), "Protectionism and International Banking," Presented at the International Conference on Multinational Banking in the World Economy, Tel Aviv.

The Washington Post (1994), "The $10 Trillion Toss: Derivatives Deals are Complex, Fast Growing, and Some Fear, Dangerous," (April 24, H1).

The Washington Post (1994), "Steadiness is the Best Strategy," (April 24, H1).

The Washington Post (1994), "Mutual Funds Dodge Derivative Bullet: Complex Investments Baffle Some Managers," (April 24, H9).

The Washington Post (1994), "Crossbreeding Comes to the CD: Banks Offer Hybrid Certificates of Deposit That Push Limits of Banking Rules," (February 26, C1,2).

West, R. (1970), "An Alternative Approach to Predicting Corporate Bond Ratings." *Journal of Accounting Research* (1970): 15–21.

Westergaard, Richard (1995), "Securitizing Small-Business Loans (Speech Adaptation)," *Bank Management* (Sept/Oct.): 52–4+.

Whalen, Gary (1991), "A Proportional Hazards Model of Bank Failure: An Examination of Its Usefulness as an Early Warning Tool," *Economic Review Federal Reserve Bank of Cleveland* (1st. Quarter): 21–32.

Whalen, Gary and James B. Thomson (1988), "Using Financial Data to Identify Changes in Bank Conditions," *Economic Review, Federal Reserve bank of Cleveland*, 2nd. Quarter: 17–25.

Wilson, Kevin (1996), Personal Interview (February 19), Board of Governors of the Federal Reserve System. Washington D.C.

Winchell, William and Michael Levine (1992) "Understanding Inverse Floater Pricing," in, *The Handbook of Mortgage-Backed Securities*, Fabozzi, Frank J., Editor 3rd. Edition. Chicago, IL: Probus Publishing Company, pp 519–532.

Wirtz, Philip W. (1992), *Exploratory and Multivariate Data Analysis: Management Science 276 Transparency Set*, the George Washington University (Summer).

Woodward, Steven, Joel G. Siegel, and Anique A.Qureshi (1996), "FASB 119 & derivative financial instruments : Disclosure & fair value." *National Public Accountant* (Jan): 18–21+.

World of Banking (1996), "Emerging Markets Increasingly Use Securitization," Spring: 40.

World of Banking (1996), "New Supervisory Framework For Derivatives Activities Of Banks And Securities Firms." Spring: 32–33.

Yannopoulos, George (1983), "The Growth of Transnational Banking," In *The Growth of International Business*, pp. 236–57, edited by Mark Casson. London: George Allen and Unwin.

Zanakis, Stelios and Gary A. Walter (1994) "Discriminant Characteristics of US Banks Acquired With or Without Federal Assistance." *European Journal of Operational Research* (Sept): 440–465.

Zigas, David (1987), "Asset-Backed Securities are Coming Into Their Own," *American Banker* (February 18): 56.

Zweig, Phillip L., editor (1989) *The Asset Securitization Handbook*, Dow Jones-Irwin, p. v.

Index